Heaven

and the

Afterlife

Books by
James L. Garlow
FROM BETHANY HOUSE PUBLISHERS

Heaven and the Afterlife (with Keith Wall)

Encountering Heaven and the Afterlife (with Keith Wall)

James L. Garlow *with* Keith Wall

Heaven

and the

Afterlife

BETHANY HOUSE PUBLISHERS
Minneapolis, Minnesota

Published by Bethany House Publishers
11400 Hampshire Avenue South
Bloomington, Minnesota 55438

Bethany House Publishers is a division of
Baker Publishing Group, Grand Rapids, Michigan.

Printed in the United States of America

In keeping with biblical principles of creation stewardship, Baker Publishing Group advocates the responsible use of our natural resources. As a member of the Green Press Initiative, our company uses recycled paper when possible. The text paper of this book is comprised of 30% postconsumer waste.

Library of Congress Cataloging-in-Publication Data

Garlow, James L.
    Heaven and the afterlife: what happens the second we die? if heaven is a real place, who will live there? if hell exists, where is it located? what do near-death experiences mean? and more– / James L. Garlow with Keith Wall.
       p. cm.
    Includes bibliographical references.
    Summary: "A comprehensive and straightforward exploration of beliefs about heaven, hell, and what happens when people die, written from a Christian perspective"–Provided by publisher.
    ISBN 978-0-7642-0576-7 (pbk. : alk. paper) 1. Future life–Christianity. I. Wall, Keith A. II. Title.
    BT903.G37   2009
    236'.2–dc22

2009014976

DEDICATED TO ALL WHO BLESSED
AND CONTINUE TO BLESS MY WIFE, CAROL,
DURING HER STRUGGLE TO OVERCOME CANCER:

Dr. Afshin Bahador, MD

(His wife)
Dr. Shadi Omidi, MD

Dr. Francisco Contreras, MD

(His nephew)
Daniel Ernesto Kennedy (Contreras), MC

Dr. Andrew Hampshire, MD

Dr. Timothy Yeh, OMD

The people who prayed and are praying:
The Skyline Pastors Prayer Partners
The Skyline Intercession and Prayer Team
The Skyline Church family, in general

— *and* —

The thousands of friends who are praying for her.
And finally, to my profoundly courageous wife, Carol.

TO ALL OF YOU LISTED ABOVE,
I LOVINGLY DEDICATE THIS BOOK.
JIM GARLOW

In loving memory of Louis McBurney,
faithful friend, gracious guide, encourager extraordinaire,
connoisseur of nonconformity.
If it's possible to improve upon perfection,
heaven just got a little better and a little brighter with your arrival.
KEITH WALL

Acknowledgments

B ooks are almost always a collaborative effort. This one is no exception. I am deeply indebted to an incredible team who helped so very much.

I am so grateful for Tracy Burger, my administrative assistant, who from her first day on the job—due to my wife's unexpected battle with cancer—had to assume an exorbitantly heavy load. Her thoroughness, heart of service, and uncomplaining and joyous spirit are important components in how this book came to be. Thank you, Tracy.

A special thanks to Priscilla Hammond, who with such a gracious spirit helped in so many ways, too numerous to mention. In addition, a heartfelt thank-you to Ray Christenson, whose graphs and charts are used throughout this book.

Special thanks to April Williams, who has worked with me on so many projects, along with Bill Coe and Kate Murray, who were willing to open up their calendars on very short notice to research and write with great skill. And they did so with joy and delight. It is always special to work with persons with exuberant attitudes. In addition, thank you to Adam Palmer for some hastily requested research and writing. Thank you, April, Bill, Kate, and Adam.

I am deeply indebted to Craig Bubeck, with whom I have worked on numerous projects. Craig's definitive writing, objective sense of expression, skilled wordsmithing, theological insights, persistence, and profound patience are "all over" this project. May we get to work together again! Thank you, Craig.

Words cannot express my appreciation to my co-laborer Keith Wall, who was patient with me beyond words as I faced one distraction, detour, and delay after another as this book was coming together. Keith's research is thorough and systematic; his writing is paced and engaging. If you enjoy this book, the major factor will be Keith's superb contribution throughout. In all candor, without Keith this book would not have the flow, the appeal, the grace, or the charm. The really "good" writing came from him. Thank you, Keith.

I thank God for Kyle Duncan, of Bethany House, who is the consummate gentleman, with the highest integrity. Kyle knows—as any editor or publisher must—when to extend grace and when to be insistent on deadlines. Kyle is the "dream editor/publisher" for any author. This is not my first project with Kyle; I hope it is not my last. This book required not only someone to think of it—that was Kyle—but someone to shepherd it—that was Kyle again—to its bumpy but glorious completion. Thank you, Kyle.

I am thankful for the people of Skyline Church who were gracious to listen to a sermon series—not once but twice—on the topic of this book, and who heard incalculable sermon illustrations that eventually became part of the book. They endured much in the writing and completion of this project. In addition, I am so grateful for their prayers that this book would, in fact, finally be written. Thank you, church.

The board of Skyline Church has always attempted to "fan the flame" of any gifting they have seen in me. I am grateful for their consistent encouragement during this elongated experience. Thank you, church board.

I am so blessed to be able to serve with the most wonderful group of pastors at Skyline Church, who never once complained when they heard me groan in my attempts to meet various writing deadlines. They always encouraged. They were my cheerleaders. Thank you, pastoral staff.

I owe a debt of thanks to family members—my wife, children, grandchildren, mother, brother, sister, in-laws, extended family—that tolerated my "hiding away" in an attempt to finish what became a rather lengthy journey. Thank you, family.

I praise God that in his infinite wisdom he came up with a place called *heaven*. Thank you, God.

I am thankful for the sacrificial death of Jesus that provides me—in fact, all of us—the way to this glorious place. Thank you, Jesus.

A most grateful,

Jim Garlow

San Diego, CA
April 2009

A thousand thank-yous to Alan Wartes for his insights, research, and editorial expertise–a truly skilled and steadfast partner in this project. Jenny Mertes and Karen Linamen also made valuable contributions to the manuscript, talented word wizards both. Christopher Soderstrom of Bethany House employed a deft hand and cool head under less-than-ideal circumstances.

We owe a debt of gratitude to those who shared their stories–those who appear in the final manuscript and those who don't. The openness of everyone who talked about their experiences is genuinely appreciated.

Many thanks to my family–Robin, Juliana, and Logan–for patience and perserverance above and beyond the call of duty.

–*Keith Wall*

Contents

PART ONE

Through Death's Door

I

The Undiscovered Country

— ✳ —

*The Veil Between Life and the Afterlife Is
Thinner Than We Think*

It is impossible that anything so natural, so necessary, and so
universal as death should ever have been designed by Providence
as an evil to mankind.

JONATHAN SWIFT

It is fitting that we begin with a true story involving three main
characters: an elderly man nearing death, a kindhearted woman in
robust health, and a deceased boy very much alive.

Five months earlier, physicians had diagnosed sixty-five-year-old
Vernon Samuels with terminal lung cancer. They could do nothing but
admit him to Rocky Mountain Hospice, in Colorado Springs, to live
out his days with as much dignity and comfort as possible. Sadly, what
relief palliative medicines could provide, human contact wouldn't. For

decades, Vernon had been known to one and all as a cranky killjoy—a miserable person who made everybody around him miserable too.

And so almost no one came to visit him, despite the dwindling of his days on earth. Only the most intrepid family members straggled in from time to time, and they didn't stay long. Even the nurses braced themselves for barrages of criticism when they entered his room.

Vernon had just one regular visitor: Dee Ring Martz. A social worker with a cheerful disposition—in other words, Vernon's exact counterbalance—Dee stopped in daily to check on him. Undeterred by his toxic attitude, she would linger by his bedside and chat, assessing his moods and seeking ways to bring solace. Asked how he was doing, Vernon would scowl and complain about the asinine shows on TV, or the ruckus made by the kids who visited across the hall, or the nurses being incapable of doing anything right.

It came as a shock, then, when Dee arrived one Tuesday afternoon and found the withered, pajama-clad man sitting up in bed and smiling— you could almost say *beaming*. The room, usually stuffy and dark, was bright; the curtains were uncharacteristically pulled open.

"Hello, Dee!" Vernon called out. "Don't you look lovely today! And I want to tell you how much I've appreciated our daily visits."

Dee's first thought, naturally, was that the doctors had upped his medication. But they hadn't.

"Vernon, you're in high spirits today," she replied. "In fact, you seem happier than I've ever seen you."

"And with good reason," he said. "Joey came to see me. My son, Joey!"

Dee had talked with the occasional visiting relative, and there had never been a son—she was sure of it. She asked him to tell her more.

Joey, it turned out, was Vernon's long-dead child who'd drowned at age five. Vernon had always blamed himself for his beloved boy's tragic death and had vowed never to get close to anyone again. His grouchy disposition was an all-too-effective defense mechanism to keep others at arm's length.

"I'm telling you, Dee, Joey came into my room, just as clearly and visibly as you just walked in," the man went on, words tumbling from his mouth. "He told me my time on earth is short and that I should be nice to people."

Dee smiled at how seriously he took his son's admonition.

"Joey said something else," Vernon continued. "He's coming to get me at noon on Friday. That's when I'll die, and Joey will be here to escort me to heaven. He said he was *chosen* to be my guide. Isn't it wonderful?"

As much as Dee had been around dying people, she was no stranger to spiritual encounters: children who saw angels, semiconscious people who reported heavenly visions, those who in their final moments called out, "It's so beautiful!" Still, she wondered about the specific timetable.

The next time she ran into the doctors overseeing Vernon's medical care, she told them of his experience and asked about his life expectancy.

"He's terminal, all right," one said. "But I'd give him three or four months. He's not so bad off that he'd die on Friday."

The other concurred: "You better be ready to tell him something on Friday when he expects to be in heaven but discovers he's still here."

Friday came, and Dee showed up at 11:30. She and Vernon chatted as usual, Vernon offering more compliments and encouragement. As the minutes ticked by, Dee didn't dare check her watch, knowing what he would think. She began rehearsing words of consolation.

Soon enough, the grandfather clock out in the hallway began tolling the noon hour. *Gong, gong, gong.* . . .

As if on cue, when the twelfth gong sounded, Vernon sat up, spread his arms wide, and shouted, "Joey!"

In that exact instant, the room filled with a palpable energy, as with the ionized air after a lightning strike. Dee felt the hairs on her arms stand up.

A split second later, Vernon slumped back on his pillows, his head lolled to one side, and the last gush of air escaped his lips. "Vernon? Vernon!" Dee shouted. No response. She pressed the emergency call button, and nurses scurried in. Checking his pulse, one announced, "He's gone."

Dee thought to herself, *Yes, he's gone—gone on to a better place with the son he longed to see again.*[1]

———

We usually don't dwell on thoughts of the afterlife. Life here and now is challenging enough, with obligations to cover and deadlines to meet and kids who need to be at soccer practice on time. Most of us don't want to think about death when there's so much to be enjoyed in life—and who can blame us?

But sometimes inklings of the afterlife intrude on our predictable orderliness. Maybe it's when you attend the funeral of your favorite aunt. Or when your mother calls and says, with perceptible desperation, "Dad's had a heart attack." Or when a close friend reveals that she has a life-threatening illness. Or when, on an otherwise typical rush-hour drive, you have a near collision that surely would've killed you.

> Most of us, when we hear the word *afterlife*, immediately assume this means heaven and hell.

It doesn't always come with grim circumstances, however. Perhaps you watch the sun rising over the ocean and can't help but ponder what heaven must be like. Or a radio show features someone who had a near-death experience, and the story stirs your heart and fires your imagination. Or you catch a magical glimpse into the wondrous innocence of your giggling child, and you hope beyond hope that you will spend eternity together, exploring, playing, laughing.

Most of us, when we hear the word *afterlife*, immediately assume this means heaven and hell. Those are the dominant features of the life beyond this one. But if you're like me, you acknowledge that there is a spiritual world buzzing all around us, every moment of every day, though we usually aren't aware of it and don't regularly take the time to notice it.

We're pretty sure spiritual beings, like angels, participate in our lives, but we don't know exactly how. Even though we've heard our parents say, "There's no such thing as ghosts," we wonder if there might be something more to it. We read reports about people "crossing over" through near-death experiences, and we think of gleaning insight about what awaits us. Deep down, we want to know:

- What happens when we die? What will transpire at the moment we expire—when we pass from life into death?
- What is heaven like? Certainly, it's more than the halos, harps, and hallelujah choruses portrayed in Sunday school versions.
- What about hell—must be more to it than fire, brimstone, and pitchfork-wielding creatures, right?
- What are angels and demons? What do they do for us or want from us?
- Could ghosts be real, and could people really see them?
- Is it possible to talk with dead people?
- So many people believe in reincarnation—is there anything to it?

These are some of the questions and ideas we'll explore in *Heaven and the Afterlife*. With one eye on the Scriptures, the other on credible accounts and research clues, let's pull back the veil and consider what we see.

The truth is, for a very long time people have been searching for the answers. With remarkably few exceptions, from the moment civilization began humans have upheld some kind of hereafter. For millennia, beliefs about the "geography" of the afterlife—and the road map we must follow to get there—have varied widely, but few cultures have doubted there *is* such a place or that human consciousness survives to see it. Funerals always have been rites of passage from this life to the next, ranging in form from a simple burial or cremation to immensely complex procedures lasting days or weeks.

Ancient Egyptians, for instance, took weeks to mummify their dead, carefully keeping the body and all its organs intact so that the soul would continue to have a place to live. After embalming was complete, they wrapped the body in strips of linen that bound charms, amulets, and talismans to the deceased.[2] Clearly, like the vast majority of those who have ever lived, they didn't subscribe to a lights-out philosophy of death.

For all our skeptical denial and rational thinking, beneath the modernistic veneers we've been no less preoccupied with the afterlife.

- A 2005 Harris poll revealed that 82 percent of Americans believe in God, 70 percent in life after death, and six out of ten in the existence of heaven and hell.[3]

- Medical studies say that 11 to 30 percent of all who survive a cardiac arrest report some kind of near-death experience (NDE) in which their conscious mind appeared to be independent of their physical body.[4]

- One out of three respondents to a 2007 *Associated Press/Ipsos* poll said they believed in ghosts. Nearly one in four claimed to have had a *personal* encounter with one.[5]

Even allowing for a broad margin of error, numbers like these are hard to ignore. Though we don't talk much about the matter, it seems real-life ghost stories are happening all the time. In your lifetime, the odds of encountering an apparition (one in four) apparently are better than rolling a six on your first try.

What's going on here? Have we forgotten the legacy of pioneering philosophers like René Descartes and Sir Francis Bacon, who helped us escape the "ignorance" and "superstition" of the Dark Ages? After enjoying the tangible fruits of the scientific revolution for centuries, do we still doubt that material reality is the *only* reality?

Seemingly, yes. And the reason may be that it's easy to demand verifiable "proof" of the afterlife—until you've had *your* turn to see an apparition or witness the appearance of a dead loved one or have your own near-death experience. In other words, brainy lab-coat logic might get revisited when it appears to contradict compelling, firsthand experience. People might not know how or why something "weird" happened to them, but those who've been there largely are adamant that something really did happen nonetheless.

Consider as a representative example the story of Brenda, who has degrees in both mathematics and physics and runs her own land surveying business. Well-trained in the scientific method of inquiry, Brenda makes her living by putting faith in hard, cold, precisely measurable facts.

> Several years ago my kids and I moved into an old house in a small Colorado mountain town—a storybook Victorian-style home with lots of character. One night, not long thereafter, my teenage son came running into my bedroom, obviously terrified. From his room downstairs he had watched the bathroom door across the hall open all the way and then shut nearly to the point of latching—not once, but fifteen times in a row. Then he felt a "presence" enter his room and heard an audible sound like someone exhaling deeply.
>
> I didn't know what to think. His fear was real, so I couldn't imagine he had made it up. Still, I thought there must be a logical explanation. At about the same time we began having electrical problems in the part of the house near his room. The lights were unreliable. They would go off and on at odd times, and the switches didn't always work right.
>
> Then, not long after my son's encounter, I was standing near the kitchen where my kids were hanging out with a couple of friends. From the corner of my eye I clearly saw a tall male figure walk across the living room floor and disappear into the hallway toward my son's room. It wasn't just a vague impression. I had no doubt a real person had walked by.
>
> My first thought was that my son's friend had slipped past me unnoticed. But when I looked, all the kids were there in the kitchen. No one else was in the house. It spooked me enough that we left and stayed at a friend's house that night.

Most of us similarly "don't know what to think" when we hear a story like this. Are there other possible explanations for what Brenda and her son saw besides a ghostly visitation from the afterlife? Sure, and a dedicated skeptic could come up with a dozen. But several years later, Brenda remains convinced there was more to the experience than drafty windows, creaky floorboards, or unexpected hallucinations. "I know what I saw," she says. "It was very real."

Whether or not we like it, testimony from credible sources just won't go away. On the contrary, in recent decades there has been an explosion of firsthand accounts that not only suggest an afterlife is real but also imply that the border between here and there is not the impassible iron curtain we perhaps have imagined it to be. Advances in emergency medical technology, for instance, have dramatically increased our chances of surviving a life-threatening illness or injury. And, thanks to the work of researchers (e.g., Elizabeth Kübler-Ross, Ray Moody, and Melvin Morse), more survivors are willing to talk about what they encountered at death's door. The result is a growing body of anecdotal evidence piling up in unavoidable heaps.

Once more, here's the point: Humans have a persistent belief in an afterlife, and a surprising number of us have had some encounter that keeps the fires of curiosity burning. Shakespeare's Hamlet said the "dread of something after death, the undiscovered country from whose bourn no traveler returns, puzzles the will." Are we forever stuck there, stymied in the dark, without a way to know more? Are we afraid of what we might find if we take a closer look?

Of course, some might say certain matters are tainted by association with "evil spirits" and should be avoided. They have a point; as we will see, there are hostile entities in the spirit world whose nature it is to make trouble. Certain kinds of recreational spiritual "dabbling" are like throwing open our doors and inviting that trouble into our lives. Caution is a good policy.

On the other hand, there is strong evidence that conscious contact with spiritual beings can be a helpful, healing experience. Could it be that informed knowledge is a better defense than ignorance when we're faced with realities we don't fully understand? After all, Jesus didn't teach the disciples to run from evil spirits but showed them how to take care of the problem. Is it possible that stubborn skepticism at one end of the spectrum, and blinding fearfulness at the other, actually cost us more in the long run than open-minded investigation?

I think the answer is yes, for at least three reasons.

IGNORANCE PROMOTES FEAR

Norman Cousins said, "Death is not the enemy, living in constant fear of it is."[6] As children we learn that the best way to deal with fear of the dark is to turn on a light—in this case, the light of knowledge—and see what's really there.

> Norman Cousins said, "Death is not the enemy, living in constant fear of it is."

IGNORANCE PROLONGS GRIEF AFTER A LOSS

Ray Moody wrote,

> A number of studies . . . have established that a high percentage of bereaved persons have visions of the deceased. For instance, as many as 75 percent of parents who lose a child to death will have some kind of apparition of that child within a year of the loss. This experience is a relief for most of the parents and will greatly reduce their grief.[7]

Moody concluded that such visions are comforting because they provide us with another reason to trust that our loved ones are not "gone" but still survive—and thrive—in an afterlife. The more we know about these stories, the less likely we are to be wracked by prolonged, excessive grief when we lose someone we love.

IGNORANCE LEAVES US UNPREPARED FOR OUR OWN DEATH

In *On Death and Dying*, Elizabeth Kübler-Ross introduced a significant idea: Leaving this world with dignity is not so easy to do, and there are difficult stages in the process that all of us go through.

It might be helpful if more people would talk about death and dying as an intrinsic part of life, just as they do not hesitate to mention when someone is expecting a new baby.[8]

That is to say, the more we know about all aspects of the afterlife, the easier it will be to make the trip when our turn arrives.

Belief in the afterlife is a cornerstone of Christian faith. Jesus told us, "God so loved the world that he gave his one and only Son, that whoever believes in him shall not perish but have eternal life."[9] We accept that Christ has conquered death—not just for himself but for anyone who repents and believes. It's normal to want to know more; however, when it comes to probing the mysteries of death and dying—and beyond—Christians are often just as afraid as anyone else. *Why should we be?* Fear is a well-known enemy to faith and freedom. Are there reasons to be prudent? Yes. Paranoid? I think not.

Freedom from fear generally is the fruit of knowledge, though this isn't always easy to come by. At times, the material in this book may make you uncomfortable. It may make you incredulous. It may even make you mad. All I ask is that you keep an open mind as you listen to the following stories and ideas. Let's go forward in the spirit of discovery, protected by God's perfect love that "drives out fear."[10]

2

There . . . and
Back Again

———— ✳ ————

*The Near–Death Experience:
A Miracle of Modern Medicine*

We sometimes congratulate ourselves at the moment of waking
from a troubled dream; it may be so the moment after death.

NATHANIEL HAWTHORNE

Imagine that you got up this morning knowing today is your day to
kick the bucket, pass away, check out, cash it in . . . *die*. There's no
point arguing over whether or not it's fair, or whether the timing could
be better, or any of a hundred other objections people typically raise
when confronting their mortality. As of now, you're simply out of time.
Nothing you can do about it.

Facing this imminent appointment, wouldn't it be nice to have some
idea of what to expect from the experience? Will it be painful? Comforting? Frightening? Exhilarating? Exhausting? Hot? Cold? Will you
wink out forever like a done-for light bulb? Or do you have a spirit that

will leave your skin and carry on? Given the magnitude of the journey you're about to take, wouldn't you like to have a reasonably accurate map of the terrain "over there"?

> Will you wink out forever like a done-for light bulb? Or do you have a spirit that will leave your skin and carry on?

These days you can find a travel guide for even the most obscure earthly destination. No one goes on vacation without reading up on what sights to see, what local foods to eat (or avoid), and how to speak a few words of the language so as not to wind up in jail or a hospital. It's the prudent thing to do.

Why, then, do most of us approach this ultimate, inexorable adventure so thoroughly unprepared and ill-informed? Frankly, the reason is that we're just plain afraid of what we'll find. We've decided that instead of turning on the light, the best way to deal with unknown things going bump in the night is to keep our eyes glued shut and pray they'll go away. For lack of a clear alternative, a lot of people imagine dying to be like a bad horror movie in which Good Guy (you) gets tossed out of an airplane over moonless, vampire-infested Transylvania. It's not much fun to sit around and contemplate such an ending—so we don't.

Here's the million-dollar question: *Must* it be this way? Is our best metaphor for death really the black hole, a singularity in space with gravity so intense that nothing—not even light—ever bounces back with hints about what goes on in there? Is it actually true that "death devours all lovely things"?[1]

Increasingly, it appears the answer is a resounding *No way!*

It turns out there are clues lying around for anyone willing to take a look—convincing ones that may astonish and inspire. Even so, if you want to convince a jury of *skeptics* that we can know what happens after death, you need more than mere inference. You need hard-core evidence, which even dedicated investigators admit is in short supply. There is a burden of proof surrounding the subject that—so far—is difficult to satisfy.

This problem confronts us when we strain to see beyond the frontiers of material (observation) science. It's fuzzy, awkward territory where reason and intuition, knowledge and faith must work together if we hope to replace blind dogma—either naturalistic or religious—with resonant and relevant discovery. A willingness to consider clues and anecdotal evidence may be the nonnegotiable price of admission if we want answers to "What's it like to die?" That said, we're still not interested in any old scrap of speculation. We've set out to do the best we can with what we have, to honestly look at *what* we know and *how* we know it.

Which brings us to the intriguing subject of this chapter: what we might learn about the moment of death from eyewitness testimony.

That's right. It turns out lots of people—millions, in fact—have had a close encounter with death and lived to share about their experience with the rest of us. These days we call it a "near-death experience," or NDE, which sounds impressively contemporary. But judging from literature and other accounts, such stories have been around for ages. For instance, people taking care of the seriously ill or injured have long reported hearing them speak of seeing dead loved ones or about "angels of light" come to escort them to the other side. When it was more common for people to die at home, in the company of friends and family, these deathbed "visions" almost certainly were more regularly shared.

But when we started doing most of our dying in isolated hospital wards, surrounded by medical professionals whose training disallowed any notion of nonphysical reality, people became understandably reluctant to talk about having had a spectacular metaphysical episode. You can't really blame them; when they've just survived a narrow brush with death, why risk a trip to the psychiatric ward as well? As NDE researcher Melvin Morse wrote:

> Although George Gallup has estimated that 5 percent of the general population has had a near-death experience, people were afraid to talk about them for fear of being ridiculed. Far too often

they themselves doubted the validity of what had happened to them.[2]

Five percent is a lot—roughly fifteen million Americans, at today's population levels. How have we managed to ignore so common an experience for so long?

This began to change, though, in the early 1970s. Led by Raymond Moody, author of the landmark bestseller *Life After Life*, a few specialists started paying attention to the occasional bedside NDE and started to be increasingly intrigued by the remarkable consistency in what they were hearing. Ignoring the prevailing medical wisdom and conducting the first systematic, scientific studies of the phenomenon, they discovered that while no two NDEs are precisely alike, there are startlingly significant similarities.

Now their file cabinets are bursting with documented cases that range from accounts of patients being temporarily "outside" their bodies to astonishing, multifaceted adventures that defy explanation. There were—and are—no accepted medical theories that provide a basis for human consciousness surviving, fully aware, after ER monitors indicate that the brain has completely ceased to function.

By listening to their patients with an open mind and then publishing their findings, these researchers have forever altered our perception of death and dying. Nearly four decades after the discussion went public, people who have a near-death experience are no longer as afraid to speak up. Medical professionals, still skeptical as a whole, at least have lost much of their hostility toward the idea of conscious survival after clinical death. In fact, hardworking doctors and nurses unwittingly have done more to advance the study of NDEs than anyone.

> It is ironic that the same medical technology that contributed to the degrading and humiliating conditions of dying patients allowed us to successfully resuscitate people so that they could report their near-death experiences. . . . Modern intensive-care medicine and rapid-response medic teams have made the cheating of death routine.[3]

This has created an amazing opportunity for us to pull back a veil we'd thought was impenetrable and get a peek at what perhaps is beyond. Keeping in mind that stories—even believable, compelling ones—don't constitute proof, let's check out the composite scenario they suggest. Very few people report each and every one of the elements that follow, but all of them frequently appear in NDE accounts from a wide range of people from diverse backgrounds. Buckle up and hang on.

Your adventure begins on a hospital gurney; you're in substantial pain and distress, being rolled into an emergency room. As vital signs plummet, the ER staff responds with flurried, energetic activity to resuscitate your body. Clearly they believe they're losing you. The monitors agree: you are flatlining.

Suddenly you realize you no longer feel any pain and are now looking down on the frantic scene from above, as if bobbing like a balloon near the ceiling. You see your body lying on the table, but for a moment you don't recognize it as yourself. You observe the doctors' attempts to bring you back. You attempt to communicate with the others in the room, but they can't hear you. (And later you will describe the procedures in accurate detail, even though your brain has ceased to function normally—and even though your "waking" self has no such knowledge or experience.)

After a moment of confusion, you become aware of sensing new freedom, clarity, and well-being. You still possess a body, but it's very different from the one in the room beneath you. You feel *good*.

Before long you see an opening appear nearby; it's a dark tunnel, and at the other end is an attractive bright light. Entering the tunnel, you quickly feel as if you're moving at incredible speed toward the light, which grows more and more intense. The brightest light you've ever seen doesn't hurt your eyes. In its warmth, you feel indescribable peace, joy, love, and contentment.

You notice that others are with you, and you recognize them as deceased people you have known: grandmother, sibling, and/or friend, there to help guide you through your experience. Their presence brings exceeding comfort.

Then, a being who is surrounded by (or perhaps made of) even more radiant light approaches and asks something along the lines of "How did it go?" or "What did you learn?" The question prompts your life's events to flash before your eyes in lightning-fast, 3D Technicolor. You not only see it all happening again, you also feel (for instance) the effects of your actions on others.

Throughout the review, even when reliving uncomfortable moments and realizing mistakes, you feel nothing but unconditional love from the being of light. You comprehend that only two things really matter during life on earth: your relationship with God, and how well you demonstrate love. Everything else is meaningless. You feel such joy and peace that you don't ever want to return to your previous life.

But you suddenly become aware of a boundary before you, and you know if you cross it you'll have moved on forever. Someone tells you now is not your time, that you must go back. The instant you reluctantly agree, you are back inside your physical body.

After your recovery, you attempt to tell people what you experienced, with frustrating results. For starters, language is completely inadequate to describe and illustrate what you've seen and felt; you usually start by saying, "Words just don't cut it, but. . . ." Further, most people don't know how to respond, and it's easier for them to think you're crazy or hallucinating than to expand their views of spiritual reality.

In addition, you're no longer afraid of death like you were before. You're not exactly eager for it to happen, but you know now what to expect when it *is* your turn to go for good. You're less likely to get caught up in petty dramas and trivial pursuits. You place greater importance on loving others and living each moment for God.

––––––––––

It's not hard to see why an experience like this might change how you live your life. Again, while there are many variations in the exact chronology and details, one thing nearly all people who've had an NDE share is the insistence that everything they saw and felt was *real*–often even more so than anything they've experienced in the "real world."

(There also are less frequently reported accounts of *unpleasant* experiences near death; we'll examine these in chapter 4.)

But what does all this *mean* in the grand scheme? Because, once more, so many people from all over the world reporting a remarkably similar experience does not prove the existence of life after death. Many scientists and religious leaders are equally unimpressed. As the pioneering death-and-dying researcher Kübler-Ross wrote in her foreword to the first edition of Moody's *Life After Life*:

> Dr. Moody will have to be prepared for a lot of criticism, mainly from two arenas. . . . Some religious representatives of a denominational church have already expressed their criticism of studies like this. One priest referred to it as "selling cheap grace." . . . The second group are scientists and physicians who regard this kind of study as "unscientific."[4]

True enough. Near-death experience researchers do get charged with everything from peddling crackpot theory to being tools of the devil.

As for objections on scientific grounds, studies conducted to investigate possible medical triggers of the NDE so far have not produced a smoking gun to settle the issue. Although a thorough discussion of these alternatives is outside the scope of this book, a short list includes oxygen deprivation, hallucination caused by drugs used in emergency situations, or deficiencies of calcium, potassium, and/or other essential bio-chemicals during resuscitation. Many have suggested the experience is purely psychological—the mind's defensive apparatus for coping during the trauma of serious illness or injury.

Interestingly, some researchers have found no correlation at all between physical factors and the NDE occurrence.

Interestingly, some researchers have found no correlation at all between physical factors and the NDE occurrence. For instance, during a Dutch study involving 344 cardiac arrest patients, 18 percent reported some kind of NDE, "including specific elements such as out-of-body experience, pleasant feelings, and seeing a tunnel." Yet the team found no link to drugs used during treatment, to the duration of the arrest, or even to the patient's previously held beliefs about dying. Lead researcher Pim Van Lommel said, "If there was a physiological cause, all the patients should have had an NDE."[5]

Others, doubting whether the NDE can be used to examine the afterlife, object on the grounds that walking up to a door is not the same thing as going through it. The prominent Catholic theologian Hans Küng wrote:

> What then do these experiences of dying imply for life after death? To put it briefly, nothing! For I regard it as a duty of theological truthfulness to answer clearly that experiences of this kind prove nothing about a possible life after death: it is a question here of the last five minutes *before* death and not of an eternal life *after* death. These passing minutes do not settle the question of where the dying person goes: into nonbeing or into new being.[6]

Good point; and most NDE researchers agree wholeheartedly. No account has been given by someone who actually *died,* since death, by definition, is an irreversible condition. That's why it's called a *near-death* experience.

As we have seen, this discussion, at least for the time being, is dominated by clues, hints, and suggestions—not proof—about what happens when we die. It's like examining something with only the benefit of peripheral vision—an oft-frustrating exercise that may not yield the clearest possible picture, but neither is it necessarily false. In fact, the most compelling facet of NDE narratives may be an aspect that the rational brain cannot see fully, no matter how much light we shine on it: the ineffable, almost mystical effect it has on those who've been there, and even on those who happen to hear the experiences firsthand.

After many months of research and countless hours of listening to people tell their stories, Moody put it this way:

> I am left, not with conclusions or evidence or proofs, but with something much less definite—feelings, questions, analogies, puzzling facts to be explained. In fact, it might be more appropriate to ask, not what conclusions I have drawn on the basis of my study, but rather how the study has affected me personally. In response

I can only say: There is something very persuasive about seeing a person describe his experience which cannot easily be conveyed in writing. Their near-death experiences were very real events to these people, and through my association with them the experiences have become real events to me.[7]

Christians, of course, are accustomed to discerning the reality of an experience by its effect on people. Salvation is "proved" authentic every day by its self-evident power to produce real change in even the most incorrigible life: "Faith is being sure of what we hope for and certain of what we do not see."[8] Then comes modern medicine—coupled with an increasing cultural openness about these issues—to give faith in life after death a boost through the firsthand testimony of those who have "been there."

———

Our quest for real knowledge about the afterlife is like following a trail of bread crumbs through the forest. They are there, but we must have our eyes wide open. The clues we glean from NDE stories may not clear up all our queries. Actually, like all expeditions to unknown territory, they raise as many new questions as they answer. But so many fellow travelers—millions of ordinary folks from every walk of life—have seen something promising that invites us to accept what people of faith have long believed: *Death is not an end but a doorway we walk through as automatically as we take our next breath.* The nonphysical part of us is not a mythical fantasy; it is our truest essence, created in God's image, the part of us that survives our travails in this life to begin a new journey in the next.

And who knows? These "crumbs" may well show us something we'd all like to see: a glimpse of heaven.

3

Hints at
the Hereafter

— ✳ —

*For Most People, "Near Death" Is a Doorway
to Indescribable Light and Love*

Take all the pleasures of all the spheres, and multiply each through
endless years—one minute of heaven is worth them all.

SIR THOMAS MOORE

Time for a field trip. Let's go *camping*.

Picture it: gathering the gear, stocking the cooler, loading up
the car, driving to the woods, setting up the tent, gazing at the zillions
of stars coming out above the pitch-black wilderness, crawling into your
sleeping bag, drifting off to the mysterious sounds of nature.

Sound like fun? Well, depends on who you are.

To many, such an impromptu trip would be a dream come true, a
nostalgic reprise of fond childhood memories or of outings with their
own kids. They'd relish the quiet, the nighttime darkness, the comforting solitude.

But to others, this scenario represents their worst nightmare. Sleep on the ground? Eat beans straight out of the can? Risk facing a bear? Step on a snake? Get munched by bugs? Forget it!

What makes the difference between these two extremes? What separates those eager for an outdoor adventure from those who'd rate the prospect somewhere between a tax audit and a broken leg? Personal experience? Perhaps. Yet these days a majority on either side of the coin have never set foot in the wild or knowingly been within miles of a free-ranging bear. What accounts for their point of view? The answer can be given in a single word: *Stories.*

Chances are, your particular feelings about camping depend on the outdoors-related stories you've heard all your life—firsthand or through the media. Does the prospect of a weekend in the woods elicit romantic images of a thrilled Tom Sawyer on the Mississippi? Or of a lonely Tom Hanks hopelessly marooned on a deserted island?

Stories make the difference. By telling stories we gather up the threads of human existence and weave them together, seeking to create coherence out of what seems convoluted. Stories are how *meaning and belief* emerge from the confusing and sometimes contradictory tangles of everyday experience. Listen to master storyteller Robert McKee:

> The world now consumes films, novels, theater, and television in such quantities and with such ravenous hunger that the story arts have become humanity's prime source of inspiration, as it seeks to order chaos and gain insight into life. Our appetite for story is a reflection of the profound human need to grasp the patterns of living, not merely as an intellectual exercise, but within a very personal, emotional experience. . . . Why is so much of our life spent inside stories? Because as critic Kenneth Burke tells us, stories are equipment for living.[1]

Stories help us know how to live. For our purposes, let's carry that idea a step further: *Stories are equipment for dying as well.*

The tales we tell and take in about death—and beyond—form a blueprint for what we inevitably will believe about what happens when we die. Those who study the issue largely concur: "Because we learn about dying only indirectly by experiencing the death of others, it is reasonable to hypothesize that our attitudes about death and dying could be influenced by mass mediated messages."[2]

If McKee is right that the commercial "story arts" have become our prime source of insight into these mysteries, it's not hard to see why so many—Christians included—are deeply afraid of looking too closely at death. For most novelists and scriptwriters, dying is the mother of all worst-case scenarios, to be avoided by any heroic means available, whatever the cost. Think back to all the dramatic deaths you've "witnessed" via media, including the nightly news. How many were portrayed as painful, tragic, and terrifying? Nearly all. But is the portrait of death these stories paint an accurate one? Do they tell the truth? *No.*

We can answer so confidently because, as powerful as they are, mass-marketed stories are not the only ones available to us. As we've discussed, our era is unique to all of human history in that medical advances have made cheating death almost routine. It's as if ER techniques and technologies have lengthened the cord that tethers us to this life—just enough to permit a clearer view of what lies ahead. More people than ever have a close encounter with death and, as the saying goes, live to tell the tale.

> For most novelists and scriptwriters, dying is the mother of all worst-case scenarios, to be avoided by any heroic means available, whatever the cost.

The following pages, continuing into the next chapter, provide a sampling of these astonishing first-person stories. We want to see how they differ from the common societal message about death. What clues do they carry about the existence of heaven, or of hell? What light do they shed on the age-old question: *Where do we go when we die?*

We've noted that while those who've had an NDE—knocked on death's door only to be sent back to the here and now—give accounts containing different elements and variations, most include at least a few common aspects. What do they see and feel on the other side? Here are three prevalent answers.

Unparalleled Peace

Imagine you've come to the hospital today for a minor laparoscopic procedure. Your doctor plans to work using a tiny camera inserted through a small abdominal incision. It's strictly routine, you're told.

But something goes wrong. The surgeon accidentally cuts deeper than he intends, puncturing an artery and damaging your intestines. You are thrust instantly into a life-threatening emergency.

Be honest—just *envisioning* yourself in this situation is enough to fill you with fear and dread, right? Your body tenses at the very thought of such pain and trauma. Yet here is how Laurelynn told her real-life story to highly respected NDE researcher Kenneth Ring. As the dramatic situation unfolded, she suddenly found herself floating above the scene—outside her body—watching detachedly.

> The surgical team was frantic. Red was everywhere, splattered on the gowns, splattered on the floor, and a bright pool of flowing red blood, in the now-wide-open abdominal cavity. I couldn't understand what was going on down there. I didn't even make the connection, at that moment, that the body being worked on was my own. It didn't matter anyway. I was in a state of freedom, having a great time. I just wanted to shout to the distressed people below, "Hey, I'm okay. It's great up here." But they were so intent, I felt like I didn't want to interrupt their efforts.
>
> I then traveled to another realm of total and absolute peace. There was no pain, but instead a sense of well-being, in a warm, dark, soft space. I was enveloped by total bliss in an atmosphere of unconditional love and acceptance. . . . The freedom of total peace was intensified beyond any ecstatic feeling ever felt here on earth.[3]

Peace, love, freedom, ecstasy, bliss—hardly the words that leap to mind when you imagine seeing your own blood splattered everywhere during a brush with death. But such language shows up repeatedly in firsthand NDE accounts. Pain and fear instantly disappear, replaced by wellness far greater than ever felt on earth. Laurelynn put it this way: "I find it very difficult to describe where I was, because the words we know here in this plane just aren't adequate."

Raymond Moody shares representative testimony from people he interviewed for *Life After Life*. Below, the first is from a woman resuscitated after a heart attack, the second from a man recalling what he felt when he received a would-be fatal wound in Vietnam.

> I began to experience the most wonderful feelings. I couldn't feel a thing in the world except peace, comfort, ease—just quietness. I felt that all my troubles were gone, and I thought to myself, *Well, how quiet and peaceful, and I don't hurt at all.*

> A great attitude of relief. There was no pain, and I've never felt so relaxed. I was at ease and it was all good.[4]

Sally, who clinically died during surgery to repair internal bleeding after giving birth, left her body and looked back at herself in the bed from above. "I felt so loved, calm, peaceful, happy," she reported later. "I can't find words to express what it was like."[5]

Chris was only ten when he clinically died from complications after a kidney transplant. Afterward he told his mom, "I have a wonderful secret to tell you, Mother. I've been climbing a staircase to heaven. It was such a good and peaceful feeling. I felt wonderful."[6]

―――――――

We could retell hundreds of these stories. What do they have in common with the sensationalized mass-media tales? Almost nothing at all. What can we conclude? Perhaps that, for many people at least, death is not the nightmare we've been led to fear. Maybe it's no more than an effortless step out of this world into the next—nearer to God's heavenly kingdom. Accordingly, is it really so surprising that our first sensation would be of indescribable peace and wellness? I think not.

"Death has been swallowed up in victory."
"Where, O death, is your victory?
Where, O death, is your sting?"[7]

UNEXPECTED REUNIONS

Elizabeth Kübler-Ross has said her patients most fear the prospect of dying alone. This is even more understandable when we consider how common it has become for people to approach life's end tucked away in bland, antiseptic hospital rooms with only complete strangers nearby. *Crossing the final threshold alone is not the same as being lonely when the moment comes.*

However, even when we face it without loving support from others, is death ever truly a solitary event? Not according to thousands of documented NDE stories. Those who have "died" and returned usually report being met and guided by people they know very well— even those already dead many years.

Donna clinically died on the operating table during emergency surgery to keep her gallbladder from rupturing. Her heart stopped; she had no blood pressure; when she suddenly felt herself float free of her body to a spot above the commotion, the distressed nurses said she was dead, but she felt "fine" and "free." As a team rushed through the door with electroshock equipment to try to restart her heart, Donna traveled through a tunnel away from the trauma:

> Suddenly I was in a place filled up with love, and a beautiful bright white light. The place seemed holy. Plants and flowers, I could see beautiful scenes.
>
> As I walked through this meadow I saw people separated in little bunches. They waved to me, and came over and talked to me. One was my father who had died about two years before. He looked radiant. He looked happier than I had ever seen him before, and much younger. My grandmothers and grandfathers were there too. Everyone was happy to see me. But my father told me it was not my time and I would be going back.[8]

> Those who have "died" and returned usually report being met and guided by people they know very well—even those already dead many years.

Said a woman who'd hemorrhaged during childbirth and was near death:

> The doctor gave me up, and told my relatives that I was dying. . . .
> I realized that all these people were there, almost in multitudes it
> seems, hovering around the ceiling of the room. These were all
> people I had known in my past life, but who had passed on before.
> I recognized my grandmother and a girl I had known when I was
> in school, and many other relatives and friends. . . . I felt that they
> had come to protect or to guide me. It was almost as if I were
> coming home, and they were there to greet or to welcome me.
> All this time, I had the feeling of everything light and beautiful. It
> was a beautiful and glorious moment.[9]

Even skeptical Christians might be swayed by the words of Dwight
L. Moody, one of history's greatest evangelists. In 1899, Moody was
near death. At one point he lost consciousness, and the people gathered
around him thought he'd passed away, but his doctor succeeded in
reviving him. When Moody opened his eyes he exclaimed, "I went to
the gate of heaven. Why, it was so wonderful, and I saw the children! I
saw Irene and Dwight." He died a short time later, apparently in great
peace and anticipation, having already seen his deceased children waiting for him in heaven.[10]

———————

Many accounts suggest that it isn't necessary to undergo clinical
death and return from a dramatic NDE to have visions of departed
loved ones come to guide us to the other side. In her remarkable *Glimpses
of Heaven,* hospice nurse Trudy Harris shares many memories she collected over a thirty-five-year career of helping terminally ill people die
as gracefully as possible. As they draw nearer to the moment of death,
her patients frequently speak of seeing someone in the room who has
come to ease their passage.

Frank, suffering from inoperable lung cancer, told Harris during
a routine visit, "My son, John, is here with me now; he said it's time
for me to go. Can you see him? He's sitting over there in the chair; he

is beckoning me to go with him." John had died many years earlier in Vietnam.[11]

Sometimes the guide is not a previously deceased human but an angelic spirit. Harris tells this story about a conversation with Lenora, a middle-aged woman dying of a brain tumor:

> One day while I was visiting, she [Lenora] asked to speak to me alone and, much to everyone's surprise, she excused her entire family from the room. "This big angel comes and stands near my bed," she said to me very sternly. "Right there," she said, pointing to the corner of her bedroom. "Ms. Nurse, when I see that angel, do you really think I see that angel?"
>
> "Yes, you do," I said. . . . I explained to her that this is a very common experience for people getting ready to go to heaven.[12]

Once again, these stories suggest death is not a lonely game of solitaire. The implication is that loved ones or spirits wait on the other side to take your hand and welcome you into familiar, warm, comforting arms—or to send you gently back to finish your time on earth. Why should it be any other way for God's children? God has promised: "Never will I leave you. Never will I forsake you."[13] That's as reliable in death as in life.

Unearthly Light and Unconditional Love

Don Piper, author of *90 Minutes in Heaven*, was as close to truly dead as anyone ever comes without finishing the journey and ending up in the cemetery (or urn). After an eighteen-wheeler ran head on into his Ford Escort on a rain-slicked Texas highway, EMTs on the scene declared that he'd died on impact. Unable to extract him right away from the crushed vehicle, they covered it with a tarp. He had no measurable heartbeat for *an hour and a half*—a fact for which medical science has no ready explanation. It remains a mystery.

Piper didn't view the scene from outside his body. He didn't travel through a tunnel. He simply "woke up" in heaven—bathed in the most wonderful light he'd ever seen.

> I realized that everything around me glowed with a dazzling intensity. In trying to describe the scene, words are totally inadequate, because human words can't express the feelings of awe and wonder at what I beheld.
>
> Everything I saw glowed with intense brightness. . . . I wasn't blinded, but I was amazed [as] the luster and intensity continually increased. Strange as it seems, as brilliant as everything was, each time I stepped forward, the splendor increased. . . . The light engulfed me, and I had the sense of being ushered into the presence of God. Although our earthly eyes must gradually adjust to light or darkness, my heavenly eyes saw with absolute ease.[14]

The amount of time Piper remained unconscious and without vital signs is highly unusual, even among growing numbers of reported NDEs. However, his experience of an ineffable light was not. Many people who have died and returned use similar language endeavoring to describe an encounter with a source of light that does more than transmit love.

Many say it *is* love.

———

Here is the testimony of a teenage girl who came near to death while undergoing treatment for leukemia:

> All of a sudden I could feel myself being pulled upward. It was slow at first, then the pace became increasingly faster and faster. By this time I was in a black tunnel, but at the end of the tunnel was a light. As I got closer to it, it got brighter and brighter. It wasn't like any light I could describe to you. It was beautiful.
>
> When I was almost to the end, I slowed down and then I was there. This light was so bright, and it surrounded me and filled me with a total love and joy. I don't know how else to describe it to you. I felt intensely pure, calm, and reassured. I just wanted to stay there forever.[15]

Consider the account of Betty Eadie, author of *Embraced by the Light*, who clinically died from complications following surgery.

> As I got closer, the light became brilliant—brilliant beyond any description, far more brilliant than the sun—and I knew that no earthly eyes could look upon this light without being destroyed.

Eadie saw the figure of a man in the light and somehow *knew* she was in the presence of Jesus: "I felt as if I had stepped into his countenance, and I felt an utter explosion of love. It was the most unconditional love I have ever felt."[16]

Love and light are the essential fruits of a Christlike life. What else should we expect to see when the earthly veil is removed from our eyes and we no longer "see but a poor reflection as in a mirror"?[17]

Naturally, we would rather live, not die. We don't want to die alone or suffer terribly when our time comes. Even Jesus, facing death, prayed, "Take this cup from me."[18] But, again, wishing to avoid a lonely, painful death is quite different from the intense fear and foreboding many feel when they contemplate dying. The prospect is so terrifying that we rarely speak of it at all.

But now having heard a few accounts of what may await us, does it really stretch your imagination to see glimmers of heaven in them? Are these stories more than last-gasp hallucinations of oxygen-starved brains, as some scientists insist? More than trauma-induced dreams? More than wishful thinking?

As you ponder the evidence, remember this is by no means the first time Jesus has been described as being full of loving light:

> In him was life, and that life was the light of men. The light shines in the darkness, but the darkness has not understood it.[19]

Here's one thing we know for sure: The more you immerse yourself in the story of God's light in this life, the more likely you are to see it again on the other side.

4

A Taste
of Torment

———— ✳ ————

Not All Roads After Life Lead to the Light

Here sighs, plaints, and voices of the deepest woe resounded
through the starless sky. Strange languages, horrid cries, accents
of grief and wrath, voices deep and hoarse, with hands clenched
in despair, made a commotion which whirled forever through that
air of everlasting gloom.

DANTE ALIGHIERI, "INFERNO"

These days, the term *near-death experience* has become practically
synonymous with the word *light*. In the last chapter we saw why:
So many who survive a close encounter with death tell a remarkably
similar story, depicting the next world as being full of light, love, joy,
and peace. Dying, they say, is by far the easiest, most pleasant thing
they've ever done. Far from being dark, lonely, and frightening, the
over-there landscape is full of familiar faces and radiant spirits to guide
and welcome us when our time comes to move on.

Most books on the subject have titles like *Closer to the Light, The Light*

Beyond, and *Lessons from the Light.* Even Raymond Moody's classic that helped launch the NDE revolution, the one that forever changed how our society views death, is optimistically called *Life After Life.*

It's settled then, right? So much compelling eyewitness testimony all but establishes that death is a joyous reunion; a child's sweet coming home to a Father's feast of unconditional love and acceptance. We all can relax and look forward to the embrace of a warm welcome at life's end.

Well, not quite. As it happens, the stories we've examined, the ones eagerly gleaned for heavenly glimpses, aren't the only ones being told by those who come close to dying. There is another, much less common version—and it's far less comforting. Some people reluctantly report an exact opposite experience to what we've considered so far, in surroundings that seem an "anti-heaven" in every way: dark, oppressive, extremely frightening. In short, they believe they've been to the brink of *hell:* a place like Jesus described where God's enemies would be thrown, where "their worm does not die, and the fire is not quenched."[1]

Before we get complacent and start thinking a soft, cushy afterlife is a done deal for everyone, we'd be wise to take a closer look at what these sobering stories have to teach us. Understandably, if you visit hell while near death, you might be hesitant to admit it, to share as readily as someone else who got to walk with angels in fields of heavenly flowers. What might that say about how you've lived so far? As cardiologist and NDE researcher Maurice Rawlings says, it's like getting an F on your report card—not something to brag about. What's more, many who have had a "taste of torment" found the experience so horrifying that they didn't want to speak of it once back on solid ground.

"I'M IN HELL"

In *Beyond Death's Door,* Rawlings shares how his view of the afterlife forever changed on the day one of his heart patients "died" in his office. During a routine stress test on a treadmill, the man's heart stopped and he collapsed. Immediately, Rawlings and his staff began emergency resuscitation measures.

> The patient began "coming to." But whenever I would reach for instruments or otherwise interrupt my compression of his chest, the patient would again lose consciousness, roll his eyes upward, arch his back in mild convulsion, stop breathing, and die once more.
>
> Each time he regained heartbeat and respiration, the patient screamed, "I am in hell!" He was terrified and pleaded with me to help him.[2]

The man experienced clinical death—cessation of heartbeat and breathing—four times. Each time he was revived, he was anguished: "Don't stop! Don't you understand? I'm in hell! Each time you quit I go back to hell. . . . How do I stay out of hell?"

An unbeliever at the time, Rawlings replied, "I'm busy. Don't bother me about your hell until I finish getting this pacemaker into place." But he soon saw that his patient was immersed in extreme panic. Despite his own doubts about God and the reality of an afterlife, Rawlings told the man he should ask for God's forgiveness and turn over his life. They prayed together—the dying man and the agnostic—on the clinic floor. Soon, the man's condition stabilized, and he was transported to the hospital.

> Now I was convinced there was something about this life after death business after all. All of my concepts needed revision. I needed to find out more. . . .
>
> A couple of days later, I approached my patient with pad and pencil in hand for an interview. At his bedside I asked him to recall what he actually saw in hell. . . . What did hell look like?
>
> He said, "What hell? I don't recall any hell!" Apparently, the experiences were so frightening, so horrible, so painful that his conscious mind could not cope with them; and they were subsequently suppressed far into his subconscious.[3]

Rawlings surmises that this provides an example of why NDE literature contains relatively few hellish accounts—most people don't even want to remember the horrors they've seen, much less examine and discuss them. (This story, however, has a hopeful postscript: Rawlings reports the man is "now a strong Christian." Rawlings himself became a believer as a result of his patient's brush with hell.)

Fortunately, a courageous few who've been to hell and back have come forward to share what happened, most for the purpose of helping others avoid the fate to which they themselves came so close. In chapter 2, we drew a sort of composite *positive*-NDE sketch with elements that commonly appear in documented accounts. Though the reservoir of documented *negative* stories is much smaller, let's once again stitch them together and see what they could tell us about the reality and nature of hell. Once again, few people report an NDE identical to this one, but all the elements appear in multiple accounts.

As you read the following, don't do so from a safe, self-assured distance. Imagine yourself in this scenario with as much realism as you can muster.

> You're on a hospital gurney, suffering in agony from a life-threatening illness or injury. Your body is in severe crisis, and despite their best efforts the ER staff is unable to stabilize your vital signs. Your heart stops beating; your blood pressure falls to nothing; your measurable brain activity ceases.
>
> You suddenly realize you no longer feel any pain and are watching the frantic resuscitation attempts from outside your body. You observe the pandemonium with detached interest but experience no fear or regret.
>
> After a moment you feel yourself sinking toward the floor; a dark tunnel has appeared, and you're being pulled into it. Involuntarily, you enter and move downward at incredible speed. As you go, the walls seem to close in tight around you. The atmosphere begins to grow disturbingly hot and stifling.
>
> The first thing you notice after emerging at the other end is impenetrable darkness—deeper and blacker than anything you've ever seen on earth—seeming to radiate evil hostility toward you. The heat is now truly unbearable, leading you to wonder how

anyone could possibly survive it. There's a sulfuric scent in your nostrils. Your thirst is beyond description.

Something in the darkness touches you or pulls at you. You can't see what it is; discerning vague movement, you feel the most intense terror imaginable. Despair and hopelessness close around your heart and mind like a vise.

You start to notice an orange glow, and a horrifying scene unfolds: a lake of fire that contains countless people, all screaming and thrashing about in agony. They plead for relief, but there is none. You know there never will be, and it fills you with anguished dread. Evil creatures are in the fire as well; they seem to delight in inflicting terror and torment on the souls imprisoned there.

In a flash of horror, you realize the fate you're witnessing is exactly what *you* deserve. The life you lived on earth has led you inevitably here.

Despite your sense of unworthiness, you cry out, "God, help me!"

Instantly, across the vast darkness, a light appears, as if from a great distance. As it approaches, you feel overwhelmed by unconditional love and forgiveness. The light lifts you away from the fire, out of the devastating blackness.

You accept and are taken into the light itself, where you experience many of the elements common to a "positive NDE." Afterward, you return to your body.

It is impossible to fathom a more horrifying fate. If you truly have succeeded in putting yourself in the shoes of someone who's been to the edge of hell, then you understand why D. L. Moody is quoted as saying, "When we preach on hell, we might at least do it with tears in our eyes."

Here again are the common elements present in hellish NDEs:

- Darkness
- Heat
- Terror and despair
- Souls in torment
- Evil, menacing creatures

- A way out of darkness and into the light for now, or so it appears.

As we'll see in the following stories, people usually are irrevocably changed by this experience. They are gripped by a determination to make the most of their second chance at life and to warn others in jeopardy of a tortured eternity. Most of all, they return to life convinced of one thing: *Hell is real.*

"The Sewer of the Universe"

Howard Storm was a survival-of-the-fittest kind of guy. He believed he'd been born into a dog-eat-dog world, so he "might as well be a winner instead of a loser." An artist and university professor, he sought greatness and immortality in his own creations, which would hang in museums and be adored forever.

> Why would I need to believe in a higher power? Who would put the needs of others ahead of their own needs? You have to watch your back always. Life is every man for himself. The one who dies with the most toys wins. Compassion is for the weak. If you don't take care of yourself, nobody else will. I thought I was the biggest, baddest bear in the woods. Wasn't I good enough?[4]

Storm would get an answer to that question sooner than he thought. During a trip to Paris with his wife, Beverly, he was overcome by intense pain in his abdomen; the cause was a tear in the lining of his stomach. He was rushed to the hospital in agony . . . only to languish there, waiting for a surgeon to arrive. (At the time, Parisian hospitals typically were understaffed on weekends.)

After many hours of suffering with no relief, Howard Storm died, or so it seemed. He found himself standing up in the room, looking back at his body in the bed. Despite his bewilderment, he felt more alive and more real than ever before. He tried to communicate with his wife, who sat slumped in exhaustion beside him. But no matter how loudly he screamed, she could not hear him.

Then he heard voices calling his name in the hallway outside the room: "Come out here. Let's go, hurry up. We've been waiting for you a long time."

Confused and uneasy, at first he was reluctant to go. But when the voices promised to help him, he stepped into the hallway. There he saw several people motioning for him to follow; they were fuzzy and indistinct, as if he were looking through a dense fog. The longer he walked with them, the more belligerent and abusive they became, telling him to "quit moaning and hurry up."

Finally they reached their apparent destination. Storm recalls:

When I looked around I was horrified to discover that we were in complete darkness.

The hopelessness of my situation overwhelmed me. . . . I could feel their breath on me as they shouted and snarled insults. Then they began to push and shove me about. I began to fight back. A wild frenzy of taunting, screaming, and hitting ensued. As I swung and kicked at them, they bit and tore back at me. All the while it was obvious that they were having great fun. . . . I was aware there were dozens or hundreds of them. . . . They were playing with me, just as a cat plays with a mouse. Every new assault brought howls of cacophonous laughter. They began to tear off pieces of my flesh. To my horror, I realized that I was being taken apart and eaten alive, methodically, slowly, so that their entertainment would last as long as possible.[5]

As he lay on the ground, Storm heard a voice that sounded like his own, but what it said didn't come from his thoughts: *Pray to God*. At first he argued that prayer is stupid and pointless; nevertheless, by the third time the voice said, "Pray to God!" he was ready to try. He managed to string together bits and pieces of barely remembered Scriptures and prayers he'd heard, finishing with "Jesus loves me." As the words escaped his lips, he knew he wanted them to be true—*really* true—more than he'd ever wanted anything.

Far off in the darkness, I saw a pinpoint of light like the faintest star in the sky. . . . The star was rapidly getting brighter and brighter. . . . I couldn't take my eyes off it; the light was more intense and more beautiful than anything I had ever seen. It was brighter than the sun, brighter than a flash of lightning.[6]

As the light approached, Storm realized it was not some*thing* but rather some*one*. Jesus picked him up off the ground and healed his wounds. Thus began the story's part 2: Jesus lifted him out and showed him the other possible end to life, a heavenly vision of inconceivable love and light. It was up to Howard Storm to decide which he would inherit.

When he returned to his body, he became a passionate believer and dedicated pastor. In the conclusion of his book, he writes:

> Why didn't I say "Yes" to God sooner? Why did I wait so long? How much of my life have I wasted with my eyes closed to the truth? If you make one step toward God, God will take a giant step to you.[7]

"The Place Where Hope Came to Die"

Angie Fenimore had struggled her whole life with what she called "the cycle," recurring periods of deep depression. Sexually abused as a child, she'd never escaped the toxic combination of shame and rage in her heart. She attended church off and on but didn't find lasting comfort there. After years of struggle and failure, she became convinced her husband and small children would be better off without her.

She took an overdose of medication. She killed herself. Free from her body, she was suddenly in darkness that "wasn't just blackness, it was an endless void, an absence of light." But that wasn't all.

> I landed on the edge of a shadowy plane, suspended in the darkness, extending to the limits of my sight. Its floor was firm but shrouded in black mist, swirling around my feet, that also formed the thick, waist-high barrier that held me prisoner. The place was charged with a crackling energy that sparked me into hyper-alertness. . . . The fog-like mist had mass—it seemed to be formed of molecules of intense darkness. . . . It had life, this darkness, some kind of intelligence that was purely negative, even evil. It sucked at me, pulling me to react and then swallowing my reaction into fear and

dread. In my life I had suffered pain and despair so great that I could barely function, but the twisting anguish of this disconnection was beyond my capacity to conceive.[8]

As she looked around, Fenimore became aware of many others "standing or squatting or wandering about on the plane. Some were mumbling to themselves . . . completely self-absorbed, every one of them too caught up in his or her own misery to engage in any mental or emotional exchange . . . they were incapacitated by the darkness."[9]

Then, like Howard Storm, just as she was about to abandon hope, a voice sounded in the dark:

> . . . a booming wave of sound . . . that encompassed such ferocious anger that with one word it could destroy the universe, and that also encompassed such potent and unwavering love that, like the sun, it could coax life from the earth.[10]

The voice came from a point of light that appeared outside the veil of mist surrounding her. The light grew "far more brilliant than the sun," and she knew she was in the presence of God.

"Is this really what you want?" God asked.

Then they were joined by another, one she knew to be God's Son, Jesus.

> He spoke to me through the veil of darkness, "Don't you understand? I have done this for you." As I was flooded with His love and with the actual pain that He bore for me, my spiritual eyes were opened. In that moment I began to see just exactly what the Savior had done, how He had sacrificed for me. . . . My trust had been violated so many times in my life that I had very little to spare. And so I had clung to my pain so tightly that I was willing to end my life rather than unburden myself and act on the chance that a Savior existed. . . . He had been there for me all through my life, but I had not trusted Him.[11]

Immensely sorrowful over the pain she'd caused her family, Angie Fenimore realized she was being given a second chance to live wisely. With a fierce determination not to waste the opportunity, she was returned to her body. Although she still needed to overcome old attitudes and patterns of behavior, she was no longer alone and at the mercy of the darkness.

"THE STENCH WAS TERRIBLE"

Ronnie Reagan (no relation to the former president) was a drug addict and a convicted criminal. His marriage was a wreck; his children were afraid of him. In the documentary *To Hell and Back*, Reagan said after all the pain and hardship he'd endured, he thought there was nothing left that could frighten him. All that changed one evening after a senseless brawl outside a neighborhood market left him bleeding to death.

Inside the speeding ambulance, the attending paramedic leaned close to his ear and said, "Sir, you need Jesus Christ."

Reagan responded to the suggestion as he always had—with angry curses. Undeterred, the medic repeated himself. "You need Jesus." Reagan recalls:

> As he was talking to me, it appeared like the ambulance literally exploded in flames. I thought it had actually blown up. It filled with smoke and immediately I was moving through that smoke as if through a tunnel. After some period of time, coming out of the smoke and out of the darkness I began to hear the voices of a multitude of people screaming and groaning and crying. But as I looked down the sensation was of looking down on a volcanic opening and seeing fire and smoke and people inside this burning place. They were burning but weren't being consumed.[12]

He instantly recognized some people he'd known who had already died. "The most painful part of it was the loneliness. And the depression was so heavy that there was no hope, there was no escape."

Then he awoke in the hospital. He could still feel hell's heat and smell its stench but had no clue what to do next. After his recovery, he tried to get drunk and stoned as usual but couldn't. Nothing worked to make him forget what he'd experienced. Finally, in desperation, after his wife became a Christian a few weeks later, Reagan followed her to church. The minister rose and said, "Behold the Lamb of God that takes away the sins of the world."[13] What happened next surprised even Reagan:

> I turned to leave, but instead I started down the aisle toward the front of that building. I didn't know the sinner's prayer. . . . But my prayer was this: *"God, if you exist, and Jesus, if you are God's lamb, please, please kill me or cure me. I don't want to live anymore, I'm not a husband, I'm not a father, I'm no good."* And at that instant, it was like the darkness and the blackness left my life. Then the tears began to flow and for the first time since I was nine years old, the tears did run. The guilt left my life, the violence, anger and the hatred left my life. And Jesus Christ became Lord and Savior of my life that morning.[14]

Reagan no longer hears the tortured cries or smells the smoke, but he knows his life was spared so he can tell his story and warn others about the terrible torment he witnessed—about the *reality* of hell.

———

Some stories inspire in us the hope of heaven; others warn of hell's horrors. Does either qualify as admissible evidence in the court of scientific inquiry into the afterlife? No. Do they settle the theological questions (e.g., "Who goes where?") once and for all? Not that either. They certainly are suggestive, and in many respects they support biblical teaching. Still, in the mysteries that remain, there is ample room for differing interpretations.

In the previous two chapters, I wrote about the persuasiveness of elements that appear again and again in NDE accounts, full of light or full of darkness. You may have noticed there is one more commonality present in these stories, one not yet called to your attention. Of all the clues surfacing in NDE testimony, this is the most important to our understanding of what to expect when we die.

What's this common thread?

God's presence.

If you go toward the light at death—his love is there, enfolding you in a soothing blanket of acceptance and welcome.

Go into the darkness and return—God is still there, lovingly holding open the door to forgiveness and redemption.

Knowing what you know now, why cut it close? Why leave life's really important choices to the last minute? Why bother living through the hell on earth of separation from God when the kingdom of heaven is fully available?

As Howard Storm learned, it's as easy as saying and believing that "Jesus loves me. . . ."

Knowing what you know now, why cut it close? Why leave life's really important choices to the last minute?

PART TWO

What Lies
Between Worlds

5

Things That Go
Bump in the Night

—— ✳ ——

Yes, Virginia, There Really Could Be a Ghost in the Attic

Penetrating so many secrets, we cease to believe in the unknowable.
But there it sits, nevertheless, calmly licking its chops.

H. L. MENCKEN

When David retired, he bought land in a remote corner of Colorado—nine thousand feet above sea level, fifteen miles from the nearest town, light-years beyond the stress and strain of urban life. From the front porch of his home—a rustic log cabin he built himself—he looked out over a forested valley rimmed in all directions by majestic mountains. Deer often grazed just outside his windows.

To David, it was the closest thing to paradise this side of heaven . . . and the last place on earth he expected to encounter a ghost. "I moved there to get away from people and enjoy a little peace and quiet," he said. "My nearest neighbors were two miles away. The nearest *living* ones, anyway."

On one side, his property abutted a national forest. He spent many hours there, walking the game trails and jeep roads crisscrossing the woods. An avid outdoorsman, he was at home in the wilderness—cautious, but not easily frightened. Even on the darkest night, he didn't hesitate to walk anywhere.

"But one spot was different," David recalled. "There's an old, overgrown logging road that hasn't been used in decades. From the top of a ridgeline, it drops into a narrow ravine, crosses a dry creek bed, and then climbs out the other side. The first time I walked there, it was after nightfall. The moon was bright, and I could see just fine. Yet when I descended toward the creek, suddenly the hairs on the back of my neck stood up. I had the overwhelming sensation I wasn't alone."

The feeling was so strong that he turned around and took a different route. By the time he returned home, he was convinced he'd imagined the whole thing. He laughed at his foolishness—and forgot all about it. Until a month later. Out again after dark, David came to the same road.

"It was the shortest way home, so without any thought I started down that path," he said. "Then, sure enough, at the exact same spot, I felt my skin start to crawl. Even then, I refused to believe there was anything to it. I gave myself quite a pep talk. 'Come on, you big sissy. When did you get afraid of the dark?' But this time there was more. I not only sensed someone was there, I had the feeling this 'someone' was really *angry*."

David didn't believe in ghosts or boogeymen—in fact, he scoffed at those who did. He believed God gave us five perfectly good senses for telling the difference between fantasy and reality. What happened next changed his mind.

> He believed God gave us five perfectly good senses for telling the difference between fantasy and reality. What happened next changed his mind.

"I was determined not to let my imagination get the best of me again," he said. "I decided to let my spine tingle if it wanted to and kept on walking."

When he reached the bottom of the ravine, David looked to his right. There he saw the figure of a man standing in the creek bed, looking up intently toward the ridgeline. His face was a mask of anxious concentration. He wore plain clothing—dusty pants and shirt—and a floppy cowboy hat.

"It's like he was there and not there, kind of luminous and see-through," he recounted. "Then he looked at me, and I knew he felt threatened by my presence. He turned and walked away from me—and just disappeared into the dark. I wasn't going to wait around for him to come back, I can tell you that. I got out of there."

David freely admits his experience doesn't prove the reality of ghosts. But the encounter was so convincing he decided to do a little digging to find out more about the area's history. He discovered his property was less than a mile from one of Colorado's forgotten so-called "ghost towns"—a late-1800s mining camp called Iris. In its heyday, Iris was home to five thousand prospectors, merchants, hoteliers, dreamers, gamblers, and other fortune-seekers. The surrounding hills and ravines were a patchwork of homesteads and claims, now abandoned and reclaimed by the forest. Many of the roads David hiked were originally built to carry fresh-cut timber to the town's sawmill.

By the turn of the century, the gold and silver were gone—and so was Iris. All that remains today are a half-dozen dilapidated log cabins and scattered piles of rusty tin cans and broken glass. Oh, and one more thing: There is a weed-choked cemetery on a rise overlooking the old town.

David mused, "Maybe the man I saw died out there defending his stake in the gold rush. Maybe he's still at it a century later, like one of those Japanese pilots who didn't know the war was over decades after getting shot down on a deserted island in the Pacific. All I know is what happened to me felt very, very real."

No Such Thing as Ghosts—Right?

It turns out that there are hundreds, perhaps thousands, of accounts similar to David's reported each year. Lots of sane, rational, otherwise highly skeptical people insist they've seen a ghost. What are we to make of this? As we saw in chapter 1, popular surveys indicate similar experiences are remarkably common—nearly one in four people claim to have had a personal encounter with a ghost or other apparition. Bookstore shelves are crammed with collections of well-documented tales about "hauntings" worldwide: spooks that scare the heebie-jeebies out of the living by gliding uninvited through the halls of damp castles . . . rattling windows, slamming doors, banging pipes everywhere from stately mansions to forgotten farmhouses . . . refusing to leave a tragedy-stricken hotel room decades after check-out time . . . or filling a room with an unexplainable scent—cigar smoke or lilacs or rotting meat.

Creepy stories are nothing new. Ghosts and demons have populated our imaginations from the dawn of storytelling. The Sumerian *Epic of Gilgamesh*, widely believed to be the earliest ghost story on record, was preserved for centuries on twelve clay tablets in the ruins of ancient Nineveh, with the earliest known versions dating back to around 2100 BC. Gilgamesh begs "the gods" for one last meeting with his fallen friend Enkidu, who reports on the horrors of the underworld. Enkidu says that the spirits of the "unloved dead" are present in the world and eat "the leftovers from the pot, the scraps of bread thrown into the gutter, things not even a dead dog would eat."[1]

Millennia later, William Shakespeare terrified Elizabethan audiences with the ghost of King Hamlet. The apparition appeared to his son at midnight, announcing that his death was no accident: He had been murdered by his own brother, Claudius, who'd poured poison in his ear. This knowledge propels young Hamlet into the classic story about the cost of vengeance.

Then there was "Old Jeffrey," a poltergeist said to have caused commotion during the year 1717 in Britain's Epworth Rectory. Over a period of weeks the "ghost" disturbed the peace with frightening "groans, squeaks, tingling and strange knockings in diverse places." A number of people heard sounds like breaking bottles and saw door handles rise and fall of their own accord. No rational explanation was ever found, though some have suspected a prank played by local parishioners. The story is famous in ghost lore, because at the time the rectory was home to Samuel and Susanna Wesley, among whose children was a young boy named John—who would go on to become a great evangelist and the founder of Wesleyan Methodism.[2]

Even Jesus' followers were prone to blame ghosts when they witnessed things their minds told them couldn't be real. One stormy night, they found themselves in a boat on a wind-tossed lake. Jesus had said to go without him.

> During the fourth watch of the night Jesus went out to them, walking on the lake. When the disciples saw him . . . they were terrified. "It's a ghost," they said, and cried out in fear.[3]

Let's face it—for as long as humans live in this world, we will continue to experience eerie things we interpret as visitations from the other side. So we might as well roll up our sleeves and tackle obvious questions: What's really behind all the goose bumps? All the sleepless nights? What *are* ghosts, anyway?

As you might have guessed, there isn't a single, definitive answer. Let's look at four possibilities.

(1) NOTHING BUT NONSENSE

In modern societies this likely would be the most common reply. "Nothing but nonsense" certainly is the most rational response to the notion of haunted houses, candles mysteriously igniting, and garbled voices recorded in empty rooms. When children cry out from their beds claiming to have seen a ghost, most parents offer comfort by invoking the materialist mantra: Anything you can't see, smell, taste, touch, hear, capture, measure, reproduce, dissect, and display in a museum simply does not exist. Now, go to sleep, dear.

"There is no such thing as a ghost."

"Your eyes were playing tricks on you."

"No more pizza before bedtime."

"It was only your nightgown hanging on the peg."

"It's all in your imagination."

We've heard the argument *ad infinitum*—from parents, teachers, ministers, and playground peers. The professor Geddes MacGregor summed this up in *Images of Afterlife:* "There can be no disembodied life. For mind, whatever it is, to exist there must be not only matter but life; that is, as we cannot have life without embodiment, we cannot have mind without life."[4]

To materialists, ghosts can't exist because material manifestation is the supreme, compulsory condition of being considered "real." Despite countless firsthand stories throughout history to the contrary, they dismiss as absurd the very idea of disembodied spirits that move, speak, and act without the physical apparatus to do so. Why, it's an affront to reason and logic.

"Ghosts?" they say, like Ebenezer Scrooge. "Bah!"

(2) A Glitch in the Matrix

The Matrix film trilogy is based on the premise that everything humans perceive as objective reality actually is an interactive neural computer program. People live out their lives blissfully unaware that the whole world is a grand illusion designed to hide the truth—that they're slaves to rogue machines, artificial intelligence gone bad. Within the matrix, "anomalies" in the code usually are "paranormal" experiences. So-called psychic phenomena often are really just programming relics that make perfect sense when the mechanisms of "reality" are truly grasped.

Many scientists studying the nature of consciousness think something similar is going on in our perception of the real world. Ghost sightings and other extrasensory encounters, they say, are not supernatural but are glitches in the mind's ultra-natural biological machinery. Accordingly, our lack of knowledge—a curable condition (with enough additional research)—is what makes us susceptible to all manner of superstitious speculation.

Melvin Morse introduces this in *Where God Lives*:

In 1997, neuroscientists from the University of California at San Diego bravely proclaimed that they had found an area of the human brain that "may be hardwired to hear the voice of heaven." In specially designed research, they found that certain parts of the brain—the right temporal lobe, to be exact—were attuned to ideas about the supreme being and mystical experiences. . . . This region is instrumental in facilitating mind-body healing. It is responsible for visions as well as psychic powers and vivid spiritual experiences.[5]

Here's the crux of the argument: If you have a ghostly "vision," you needn't look further than your own head for an explanation. Such an experience may suggest nothing at all about the existence of parallel spiritual realms, or whether you have a soul that survives beyond death. It might merely be the ordinary way the brain relates to its environment.

My analysis of more than ten thousand ghost stories convinces me that they represent complex interactions between the individual and universal memory. We tap into this universal memory in the same way that a radio receives radio waves. And just as the air around us is filled with radio and cell phone waves, it is also filled with thought and memory from people and events, both past and present. When tapping into this memory field, the right temporal lobe acts as a receiver because it is at times calibrated to receive memory that exists in the memory bank.[6]

The key idea is that human thoughts and emotions create an energy "imprint" that's preserved in the very fabric of the universe. All that has ever occurred is still present around us—in storage, so to speak. We don't have access to this information normally because our brains are concerned with more mundane tasks, like ferrying the kids and paying the bills. But that doesn't mean we *can't* see it. What Morse and others suggest is that some of us *do*; we all appear to be equipped with a receiver capable of translating this programming code into visible and audible forms. For whatever reasons, from time to time the receiver switches on. Being ignorant of how this mechanism works, we typically label the experience "paranormal" and pull the covers over our head.

If that thinking is correct, then ghosts are no more real than images on the cinema screen. They reveal more about the mind's impressive technology as a mental projector than about wispy visitors from the afterlife. Like moviegoers, we're sometimes drawn convincingly into the illusion and lose ourselves in the drama. But when the lights come on, nothing of any substance remains.

(3) DEAD PEOPLE—SOMETIMES CALLED "DISEMBODIED SPIRITS"

Among possible explanations, the materialistic and mechanistic ones definitely are the new kids on the block. For most of history, few people would have hesitated to answer—fearfully whispering, maybe, so as not to attract otherworldly attention—that ghosts are "the restless dead."

Many diverse cultures have believed that successfully leaving this life and crossing over to the next at death is not as straightforward or automatic as it may seem. Spirits can become trapped on the earthly plane, held back by unfinished business, powerful attachments to people or objects, or a thirst for vengeance. Some believe victims of untimely or violent death are easily confused and may not even know they're dead. Not all are malevolent or threatening, though—just in need of directions. (There are many reports of spirits apparently hanging around to offer comfort to loved ones left behind. More about that in chapter 6.)

For this reason, complicated rituals and taboos concerning proper treatment of the dead can be found all over the globe. According to adherents, it's incumbent upon the living to make sure the departed have a safe trip—meaning that they actually reach their destination. They eagerly perform this service to avoid the terrible consequences of offending the spirit or of letting a lost soul stick around. As paranormal historian Brian Righi writes:

> Intricate burials, festivals honoring the dead, and prayers for the departed served one basic purpose—to keep the dead in their graves. Man, both modern and ancient, has tempered his curiosity about the spirit world with a good dose of fear, which in turn has led to some rather colorful ways of dealing with returning ghosts.[7]

Here's a handful of examples:

- Ancient Greeks wouldn't have dreamed of burying a dead body without equipping the soul for the arduous journey ahead. Money was placed in the corpse's mouth as payment for "Charon, the Ferryman, to take it across the River Styx." Greek sailors at sea carried money with them at all times in the hope that if they drowned, the reward would entice whoever found their body to bury it properly.

- Romans assumed their dead relatives remained an important, albeit invisible, part of this world. They stocked ancestral tombs with food and drink and even invited the departed spirits, called *Lares*, into their homes to act as guardians.

- Pacific Islanders held vigil over the dead for at least seven days to be sure the devil didn't come and steal the body. They provided food and shelter in case the spirit grew hungry or tired of wandering.

- In most Spanish-speaking countries, the first day of November is *el Dia de los Muertos*—the Day of the Dead. People offer food and treats to dead relatives and attend prayer vigils, cleaning and decorating their graves.

- People in the British Isles believed someone who died violently or unexpectedly might return seeking retribution. To thwart them, the body was to be buried at a remote crossroads (to confuse the spirit about the way back) with a stake through the heart (to prevent it from getting up and causing mischief).

- The prospect of ghosts spooked the Danes so much that "before burial, the big toes of the corpse were tied together to hobble the spirit, pennies were placed on the eyes to blind it, and scissors were left on the stomach, opened in the form of a cross, to prevent evil."[8]

Clearly, "visitations" have been around a long time. With few exceptions, *our* ancestors blamed *their* dead ancestors when things went bump in the night.

(4) Evil Spirits—Often Called "Demons"

A great many of the hauntings reported in paranormal literature involve ghosts that are not overtly threatening. In fact, many appear oblivious to their earthly surroundings, as if it's just as uncommon for a ghost to "see" the living as for the living to see a ghost. That doesn't mean the experience isn't frightening, only that the apparitions show no apparent malice toward others present. They simply appear, and that's enough to send us scurrying to turn on all the lights.

But there is a subset of stories for which this isn't true. These encounters are characterized not by glimpses of figures in outdated clothes but by a terrifying experience of focused, purposeful, violent *evil*. In such cases, witnesses often become the target of physical and psychological attacks.

> If suggesting that ghosts are disembodied *human* spirits can get you laughed at, then pointing the finger at *Satan's* minions can land you under heavy psychiatric care.

Ironically, materialist dogma—enjoining a nearly fanatical skepticism of all things unseen—objects forcefully to the possible existence of demons and their manifestation on earth. If suggesting that ghosts are disembodied *human* spirits can get you laughed at, then pointing the finger at *Satan's* minions can land you under heavy psychiatric care. Claiming demons are in your attic isn't widely accepted as a sign of mental health.

Before his own personal encounters with evil spirits, psychiatrist M. Scott Peck (*The Road Less Traveled*) certainly would have agreed with this diagnosis—describing himself as "99+ percent sure the devil did not exist." But in his *Glimpses of the Devil*, Peck tells the story of two patients under his care–both of whom he concluded were "possessed" by evil spirits. At substantial risk to his professional reputation, he agreed to participate in classic rites of exorcism for the women–one successful, one not. The most formidable obstacle to overcome was his rational resistance to the idea that such spirits even existed. What he saw and heard during direct confrontations with Satan was enough to do the trick:

> I had been converted . . . to a belief–a certainty–that the devil does exist and probably demons (under the control of the devil) as well. By the devil, I mean a spirit that is powerful (it may be many places at the same time and manifest itself in a variety of distinctly paranormal ways), thoroughly malevolent (its only motivation seemed to be the destruction of human beings or the entire human race), deceitful and vain, capable of taking up a kind of residence within the mind, brain, soul, or body of susceptible and willing human beings.[9]

That's as definitive a statement as you're likely to get from a trained scientist and medical doctor, and the Bible agrees with his "conversion." Jesus often confronted and drove out evil spirits that had invaded human beings. In one case, a man who spent his days wandering among tombs, crying out and cutting himself, saw Jesus coming from a distance and ran to meet him.

> He shouted at the top of his voice, "What do you want with me, Jesus, Son of the Most High God? Swear to God that you won't torture me!" For Jesus had said to him, "Come out of this man, you evil spirit!"
> Then Jesus asked him, "What is your name?"
> "My name is Legion," he replied, "for we are many."

The demons begged Jesus to send them into a nearby herd of pigs. He did; the herd ran off a cliff and drowned.[10]

To those who are the least bit spiritually oriented, that demons exist is indisputable. Their purpose is to harass, harm, and deceive. But is it reasonable to assume they're behind *all* ghostly phenomena? Authors of *The Kingdon of the Occult* say the answer is yes.

Poltergeists (demons masquerading as humans) are usually imaginative in creating their manifestations: they slam doors, walk up steps, throw objects around the room, moan, cry, touch people, and materialize as dark clouds, red eyes, figures, or colorful moving orbs of light. . . . In some cases, foul smells or ice-cold temperatures manifest along with other phenomena.

The world persists in its definitions, but the biblical revelation stands: poltergeists are *demons,* not lost human souls caught between this world and the next. They are not ghosts a la Patrick Swayze in the romantic tearjerker *Ghost.* Demons enjoy playing games with human beings, and they have had centuries to perfect their technique.[11]

It is unlikely anyone will ever prove beyond doubt that all ghosts are really demons in disguise. But, if nothing else, it certainly is the most prudent possible answer to our question. As C. S. Lewis once wrote, "There is no neutral ground in the universe: every square inch, every split second is claimed by God and counterclaimed by Satan."[12]

In other words, better safe than sorry.

Though I've had many other spiritual encounters, I am among the ranks that have never seen what I would call a *ghost.* That doesn't mean I'm not open to the possibility. As a grad student in the late '70s, I toured England, retracing the steps of John Wesley, born in 1703. I visited the hamlet of Epworth to see the house where Samuel and Susanna Wesley raised nineteen children.

Arriving on a cold, rainy day, I discovered I was the only visitor to the sprawling two-story house. Tired from long hours of air travel, followed by more via train and taxi, I finally viewed the place I'd read so much about and, completing my tour, prepared to leave.

Aware of my exhaustion, the curator said, "Guests are allowed to rent rooms in the house. Since no one else is staying here tonight, you can have your pick."

I thought how wonderful it would be to stay in the world's best-known rectory. Then I recalled all the stories—confirmed by the curator—involving "Old Jeffrey," who allegedly had roamed the corridors. Letters from family members specifically referred to the resident apparition and his shenanigans.

Suddenly I envisioned myself all alone in this drafty, creaky house on a cold, rainy night—and the thought of scurrying back to London sounded very appealing. I might as well admit it: I was too chicken to stay.

But perhaps you're among the 25 percent who say they've seen a ghost. I imagine the first words out of your mouth—after you regained the ability to speak—were, "What *was* that?" It's a curiosity many of us share.

While we still draw breath as living humans, we don't stand a ghost of a chance (forgive the pun) of knowing for sure what ghosts are. While many will theorize and speculate and pontificate, this will remain an intriguing mystery.

Here's the wisest course of action: Wrap yourself every day in the safety of God's love and protection. Again, as Paul wrote:

> I am convinced that neither death nor life, neither angels nor demons, neither the present nor the future, nor any powers, neither height nor depth, nor anything else in all creation, will be able to separate us from the love of God that is in Christ Jesus our Lord.[13]

There's no brighter night-light than that, no matter what's in the shadows.

6

Grace-Filled Guests

— ✳ —

A Visitation From a Deceased Loved One
Is a Gift to Be Accepted Gratefully

Miracles do not happen in contradiction to nature, but only in
contradiction to that which is known to us of nature.

AUGUSTINE

Nearly seventy years after his comic-book debut, Casper the
Friendly Ghost is still a popular character. He has starred in
theatrical shorts, Saturday morning cartoons, even a feature-length
film. Casper's always the same. He's a ghost, but not a typical one.
He's about as spooky as the Pillsbury Doughboy.

Unlike his three spectral uncles—Fatso, Stinky, and Stretch—who delight
in terrifying every mortal in sight, all Casper wants is to be someone's
friend. But that's easier said than done when you're a ghost. One look at
Casper and people's hair stands on end; then they run for their lives.

The character has enjoyed endurance in part because the premise is so ironic. Even people who completely disbelieve in ghosts are just as sure there's no such thing as a *friendly* ghost. The kinds of scary stories we've examined certainly contribute to that belief. But what if it's wrong?

- What if many people have had a pleasant encounter with the "friendly ghost" of someone who is deceased?
- What if that someone is a person they knew well and loved in life?
- What if nearly everyone who's had the experience describes it as comforting and healing after a painful loss?
- What if prominent grief counselors and hospice caregivers have said that after-death encounters like these are remarkably common?

There's no need to speculate, because all of the above is true. This isn't to say there is scientific proof of after-death communication. As we've already seen, that goal may always remain just over the horizon. It simply means convincing, firsthand testimony continues to accumulate about spontaneous communication with the spirit of a deceased loved one.

Notice that key descriptive word: *spontaneous*. We're not talking about people who seek out communication with the dead through psychics, mediums, or other means (we'll start addressing this in chapter 7). These encounters come unbidden to people of all ages, sometimes within moments of the death of their loved one, sometimes months or even years later. There is no obvious trigger other than an ongoing state of grief over their loss.

Evelyn's father, a retired English teacher and high school principal, died of a heart attack at eighty-nine, and despite his advanced age, losing him was a heavy emotional blow. Several months later, Evelyn still felt depressed and empty. Then something happened to break the logjam of sorrow.

It was the first time my mother and siblings had all come to my house after Daddy died. We were missing him but not talking about it much. After all, he'd raised us to face adversity with a stiff upper lip. It was a beautiful spring day, but it might as well have been overcast and rainy, considering our mood.

One of Daddy's favorite things was to gather around the piano together and sing our way through a couple of hymnals. This was somewhat stressful for me, since I don't play the piano very well, and he had a knack for picking the most difficult hymns. But that was easily overcome by his pure delight, his lovely tenor voice, and the way we bonded through the music. Eventually, other people would drift in and join us.

I'm not sure how it happened without him there to get us started, but that day we all wound up around the piano. It was as if singing his favorite hymns was a safe way to let our feelings out.

> I stopped in my tracks when I saw Daddy sitting there in his old rocking chair. He looked younger and healthier than he was before he died.

After a while, I slipped away from the group for a moment (my sister was playing the piano) and went into the living room. I stopped in my tracks when I saw Daddy sitting there in his old rocking chair. He looked younger and healthier than he was before he died. He had a glow about him that's hard to describe. The look on his face was one of deep satisfaction, as though he was enjoying the music as much as ever, with no sense of regret that he wasn't still with us. He said, "It's so good that you are still singing."

All I could manage to say was, "Daddy!" He smiled, and I *knew* he was happy and well wherever he was now. Then suddenly, he was gone. But the room was filled with deep peace and love that I have trouble expressing. Although I missed him, I can't say that I grieved for him after that. I knew he was still, for lack of a better word, *alive* and that we'd be together again.

After her father's death, Evelyn thought she'd never see him again on earth. But when she did, the experience filled her with new hope that *death is not an end but merely a transition to a new state of life.* Until then she'd struggled with the fear that her daddy was lost forever and that with him had gone the love they'd shared. Within seconds that fear was dispelled and her healing began in earnest.

———

Psychotherapist Dianne Arcangel is former director of Houston's Elizabeth Kübler-Ross Center and chaplain for The Hospice at the Texas Medical Center. Over the years she's heard hundreds of stories like Evelyn's from people grieving over a painful loss. She calls these *afterlife encounters* and says they can consist of anything from a strong impression of a loved-one's presence to detailed conversations with visible, even tangible, apparitions. Sometimes they come as meaningful dreams, symbols, sounds, or smells, and frequently the experience is shared by more than one person, which tends to lend credibility.

Many of Arcangel's grieving clients turned to her after such an event and asked, "Am I going crazy? Should I be afraid of this?"

After scouring the existing literature for answers—and coming up empty-handed—Arcangel launched a five-year international study called "The Afterlife Encounter Survey." Her purpose wasn't to prove continuation of life after death; she set out to determine the prevalence of after-death communication and its effect on those who experience it. Does it bring comfort or more pain? Does it facilitate closure or prolong grief? Do we have anything to fear in this arena?

Arcangel published the results in *Afterlife Encounters: Ordinary People, Extraordinary Experiences.* Here she reports that 64 percent of the bereaved who responded had an afterlife experience following the death of a loved one. Furthermore, an astonishing 98 percent of those said the encounter had brought much comfort and helped them cope with their grief, even many years later.[1]

These numbers suggest the phenomenon is much more widespread than most would readily believe and almost universally beneficial to those who experience it. If so, why is it not taken more seriously? Given its potential therapeutic value, why haven't researchers done more to investigate it as a standard part of the grieving process?

Professor Louis LaGrand, with over thirty-five years' experience in hospice care, death education, and counseling, offers a possible answer:

People fear ridicule and rejection. Again, in our materialistic culture, what lies outside the naturalistically defined boundaries of reality is considered to be imaginary—or worse, delusional. Few want to compound the pain of their loss with the sting of scorn from others, especially friends and family. And few scientists wish to risk their reputation on research that their peers consider to be quackery.

> One of my fantasies is that someday we will be able to demystify the ADC [after-death communication] so that it is looked at by all as a normal part of human wholeness and not an aberration to be endlessly debated. . . . It's a shame [that] we still have people who have an ADC and they have to be very careful about sharing it with others. Why? Because they feel the stabbing nonverbal responses of rejection—sometimes even from counselors. So they learn not to talk openly about it. We lose much valuable data when this happens.[2]

With this in mind, let's look at some of the "data" that has not been lost but is preserved in the following stories. These fall into three broad categories.

SIGNS AND SYMBOLS

Not all afterlife encounters involve direct communication with visible ghosts. Sometimes contact is made through objects or occurrences that are more subtle but no less meaningful to those who experience them. For example, when Donna lost her husband of forty-five years to a heart attack, she was nearly overwhelmed by shock and sadness—until a bedside lamp eased her mind.

> My husband and I always slept with a touch light on the lowest setting because I did not like to sleep in the dark. Since his death, this light has come on by itself on many days, especially when I am having a very bad time. We have had this lamp for sixteen years and it has never come on by itself. I have tried to stamp on the floor near the lamp; I have banged the dresser where it sits and it will not come on unless it is touched. One day, I just could not bring myself to turn it off because I always believed it is my

husband turning it on. So I left the light on. That night when I went into my bedroom, the light was on the second level setting. When I left for work it had been on the first level.[3]

While many skeptics would dismiss her experience as coincidental or chalk it up to faulty wiring, Donna accepts it as comforting proof of there being more to reality than she had realized. For her it's a sign that her husband's soul—his essence—did not vanish just because his body died.

In another example, Loretta was devastated when she lost two grandsons in a tragic car accident. In the following months several encounters convinced her that the boys' spirits were still very much alive and well:

[When he was alive] Tommy used to hold the [house's] front door shut on the other side of my daughter's front door when I was trying to leave. Well, he did this several times even after his death, and as soon as I would say, "Tommy, stop it," the door would suddenly open by itself. On his birthday in May, he would have been sixteen, and he had been looking forward to getting his driver's license. I was over at my daughter's house [and] Tommy started a clock that hadn't been wound since the boys died six months earlier. It continued to run for three hours. It helped both of us so much.[4]

Numerous variations exist in such stories: a music box played unexpectedly even though it hadn't been wound in years; a young woman's car started by itself while she visited her father's gravesite; meaningful objects were inexplicably moved or rearranged; flowers bloomed out of season.

Here's the important part: No matter how small or trivial such signs appear to casual observers, they regularly have profound significance—and bring much-needed comfort—to those on the receiving end.

DREAMS

When Mary's granddaughter, Amanda, died during the summer, the family knew Christmas would be especially hard that year.

In my box of decorations I found a single jingle bell tied to a red ribbon for wearing around my neck. I slipped it over my head remembering that Amanda had made it several years before. I wore it all day. . . . Early the next morning, I had a beautiful dream of Amanda. I do believe I had a visitation as I remember all of it in great detail.

She was standing in our bedroom smiling at me. She was beautiful! . . . She stood very straight, almost regally, with a faint glow around her. I finally said, "Amanda, is that you?" She replied in a voice I well remember, "Yes, Grandma, it's me!" And to my great disappointment, I awakened.

When we were on our way to church that Christmas Eve, I told Jim and Jane [Amanda's parents] about my beautiful dream. "Oh yes," I said, "I remember something else. Amanda's hair was braided—I could see it on one side." I had never seen her hair braided and thought that was unusual, but Jane replied softly, "Mother, we braided her hair in the hospital because it was so long and in the way. She died with a braid down her back." So I am quite certain that I did, indeed, have a visit from Amanda.[5]

Mary's story provides an example of what researchers call an *evidential encounter*—one that includes information previously unknown to the mourner. In a few cases, details from the deceased even have been instrumental in identifying the person guilty of their murder. While most instances are less dramatic, they're no less intriguing. Consider Jerri's story: When she was a young girl her grandmother died of a heart attack shortly before Christmas.

We were all so sad that we hardly had any Christmas at all. But that night, Grandma came to me in a dream and told me to go get my present from her. She said she'd wrapped it and hidden it away. The next morning, when I told my mom and grandpa, Mom said, "It was just a dream." My grandpa teased me . . . laughing about it, but it *seemed* so real to me. I looked and looked everywhere but I couldn't find any present, so I knew Mom was right—it was just a dream.

I was looking out my window that night, and I could've sworn I saw my grandma shining through the top of the trees, coming from the moonlight. That may sound weird, but then I heard her say, "Go get your present before something happens to it. It's a watch. Look in the bottom of my big sewing box in the back of the closet. . . . You'll see it—it's wrapped in a red and green box."[6]

The next morning Jerri again told her family what had happened. This time her grandfather said, "Let's go see!" They followed Grandma's instructions and found the gift—a wristwatch—wrapped in green and red paper, exactly where Jerri had been told it would be. A young girl received a final present that brought her immense joy; the experience was a reassuring gift to the whole family as well and helped ease their grief.

According to LaGrand, such dreams are among the most common vehicles or modalities for after-death communication. "Many, many more dreams than we realized—both symbolic and those that can be literally interpreted—do occur and bring peace and strength to continue on."[7]

Elizabeth Kübler-Ross agrees:

> "When people dream of a loved one, they often report feeling a sense of peace afterward, a reassurance beyond words."
>
> —ELIZABETH KÜBLER-ROSS

Our dreams show us that our loved one is not in essence the sick person to whom we tearfully said good-bye in the hospital. Neither is he or she the body we saw at the funeral home. . . . When people dream of a loved one, they often report feeling a sense of peace afterward, a reassurance beyond words.[8]

APPARITIONS

So far we've looked at instances of indirect communication through inanimate objects or via the highly subjective realm of dreams. But, like Evelyn, who saw her father in his old rocking chair, many people insist they've been visited by the ghost of a loved one while wide awake. Such encounters can involve one or more of the physical senses, even tactile contact. Consider Fred's experience, after the loss of his son.

Forty-five days after Eric's death in a car accident, I awoke at 6:45 A.M. along with my wife, Marilyn. . . . At 7:15 I got up off the bed—fully awake and up for one-half hour. My mind was clear. I was not crying and not under any stress. As I took my third step toward the bathroom, I felt a tremendous squeeze and hug on both sides of my body that stopped me in my tracks. Eric appeared right in front of my face, smiling, and the whole room was full of energy. It's like the molecules, atoms, and air are all moving at a tremendous speed. It was forceful, explosive, loving, highly energized—the most exhilarating experience I've ever had! I hugged Eric. . . . I kissed him on his right cheek and felt his beard/whiskers on my lips. . . . My mind was ecstatic, lucid, fully awake and aware of what was happening. I could see the tremendous love that Eric brought with him. I knew this was real, on purpose, planned by Eric as I could never have written or wished the events in this spontaneous experience.[9]

Like most people who have an afterlife encounter, Fred was comforted by what he believes was proof that his son was not dead and *gone* but had merely moved on to a "different plane or dimension"—and that he was happy there. The experience empowered him to cope with his grief and get on with his own life.

Sooner or later we all will lose someone we love. Grief is a universal human experience. Do afterlife encounters constitute proof that our spirits live on after death and sometimes offer comfort and healing to the living? No. The skeptics among us also will say, "What grief-stricken person, overwhelmed by emotion and perhaps sleep-deprived, wouldn't *want* to see their deceased family member or friend in a happy state? It's a matter of *projection* or *wish fulfillment*, a trick played by the mind." In some cases that's probably true. But can we so easily explain away the thousands of reported experiences that occur each year—often by people who were themselves skeptical at one point? I don't believe we can. Maybe it's enough to judge such encounters by the overwhelmingly positive effect they have on grieving people.

Joel Martin and Patricia Romanowski have spent years collecting stories of after-death communication. They believe such encounters are, by far, the most common—and most beneficial—of all so-called paranormal occurrences.

> Rather than turn away from these experiences in fear, doubt, or disbelief, we should learn to embrace and treasure them. While we do not always know the exact purpose of these trans-dimensional contacts, those who have experienced them gladly attest to the results. Even the most beautifully crafted words barely capture the joy, the comfort, the peace of mind one derives just from knowing that there is something beyond, that life does go on.[10]

LaGrand's interactions have led him to the same conclusion:

> In all the years I have been around people who have had an ADC, I have never heard of a single case in which the ADC resulted in spreading evil and discouragement. Instead, love wins out—there is no more powerful antidote for grief. A quiet reassurance begins to reign.[11]

Sometimes "ghostly encounters" aren't sinister or spooky—sometimes they represent *grace* in the form of a comforting visitation from beyond the grave to bring peace and relieve distress. As Jesus said to his followers when he appeared after his death and resurrection: "Don't be alarmed. . . . Peace be with you. . . . Why are you troubled, and why do doubts rise in your minds?"[12]

7

Calling
Long Distance

— ✳ —

Death May Be the Last Word in Life . . .
But Can Communication Continue?

What the eyes see and ears hear, the mind believes.

HARRY HOUDINI

At the end of 1847, an American blacksmith named John Fox needed a change of scenery. With his wife, Margaret, and two daughters, Maggie (15) and Kate (11), he moved to Hydesville, New York, a tiny hamlet in a rural area. While a place of their own was under construction, Fox rented a small house in the middle of town; owned by descendents of the village founder, Henry Hyde, it had been home to a steady stream of semi-transient renters for years.

Fox hoped the move would bring a new beginning. He got his wish but not in the way he imagined. Never in his wildest dreams could he have foreseen how life was about to change—for his family and for millions of others.

In the spring, the rental house was beset by inexplicable noises: "thumps on the ceiling, bumps on doors or walls, sometimes raps sharp enough to jar bedsteads and tables."[1] Curiously, the knocking happened only at night when the family was in bed in the single room they shared. Fox did his best to discover the cause, suspecting loose shingles or siding banging in the wind, an animal nesting in the attic, or perhaps a prank played by neighborhood kids. But despite his determined efforts he was unable to locate the source of the persistent clamor.

The story might have ended there—just an ordinary "haunting"— no different from countless other noisy mysteries that ever have been part of human experience. But on March 31, 1848, the episode took a dramatic turn. After several consecutive disquieting nights, Margaret decided the family had lost enough sleep. She put Maggie and Kate to bed early with strict instructions: If the noises return, pay no attention to them. Margaret herself would fatefully ignore that sage advice before the evening was done.

When the sounds did return, Kate playfully started to mimic them by snapping her fingers. This went on a few minutes until the roles suddenly reversed, and the mysterious raps began to follow *her* lead; knocks on the ceiling and walls repeated whatever patterns of sound she produced. Maggie quickly joined in, telling the unseen source to "do this just as I do." And it did, counting out knocks as if in direct response.

The girls became terrified by this development, huddling together on their bed. It was their mother who seized the initiative, telling the "spirit" to count to ten. It did. She asked the ages of her daughters. It replied with the right number of knocks. She recounted what happened next:

> I then asked if it was a human being that was making the noise . . . and if it was, to manifest it by the same noise. There was no noise. I then asked if it was a spirit . . . and if it was, to manifest it by two sounds. I heard two sounds as soon as the words were spoken. I then asked, if it was an injured spirit . . . to give me the sound, and I heard the rapping distinctly.[2]

Continuing along this line, Margaret discovered that the spirit had been killed near the house, that its murderer was still living, and that its remains were buried in the basement. (In subsequent weeks, the spirit would reveal that it had been a traveling peddler when alive. It spelled out its mortal name by rapping when someone called out letters of the alphabet. And it identified its killer, a former resident of the house named John Bell who still lived in Hydesville and who firmly denied any such crime.)

Finally, Margaret asked if the spirit would continue communicating in this way if she called her neighbors to witness it. *Yes,* said the knocks. Running to a friend's house nearby for backup, she unwittingly triggered an avalanche of fame and notoriety that would sweep over her family, especially the two girls.

Over the next few weeks, ever-growing crowds gathered to hear the knocks for themselves and to ask questions about the afterlife. By then it was apparent that the disturbances only occurred when Kate or Maggie were present. Of course, this led many observers to scoff and declare it an adolescent prank. Yet even the most skeptical could never uncover *how* the girls were producing the sounds—if they were. The house was turned upside down, the girls were searched and examined by doctors, but no clear-cut trickery ever was exposed.

News of the phenomenon traveled fast. People all over the country took philosophically opposing sides in the developing debate. Many hailed the Fox sisters' experiences as the long-sought proof of life after death; others ridiculed "believers" as the gullible victims of an obvious hoax; some denounced the entire business as the devil's dangerous work.

In any case, the genie was out of the bottle—modern spiritualism had arrived in the U.S. Hundreds of mediums sprang up, claiming similar abilities and using various techniques for communicating with the dead. Within a few years the Fox sisters themselves, for a fee, began giving public demonstrations of their percussive conversations with the dead. *Séance*—French for "session"—became a household word nearly overnight.

Christianity always had inspired people to put their hope in life after death. It's likewise something people have wanted to believe, especially if they've lost loved ones and longed for assurance that the departed is well cared for. But under this life's grinding pressures, belief in spiritual immortality often has required prodigious levels of courageous faith.

Now, in the form of two seemingly innocent girls, along came visible *proof.* At a time when astonishing scientific discoveries were transforming our view of the material world, Maggie and Kate Fox were at the leading edge of an ideological revolution about nonmaterial realms. The enticing message was clear: Not only do our loved ones survive death in a spiritual dimension, but they're also still present with us, ready (even eager) to go on communicating as before. All we need is a go-between, someone with a natural—many say God-given—spiritual sensitivity. In other words, we need a *medium.*

"WHY HAVE YOU DISTURBED ME?"

Of course, this wasn't a new idea at all, only a repackage. Necromancy—raising spirits of the dead to solicit a glimpse of the future or to keep in touch with a departed loved one—was a common (if not always acceptable) practice in many of the world's earlier cultures. Shamans or priests on every continent have claimed the ability to speak with the dead through a wide variety of methods.

Israel's King Saul himself sought an audience with the recently deceased prophet Samuel's spirit. Facing the formidable Philistine army, he was terrified and wanted Samuel's help, just like in the good old days. Having "expelled the mediums and spiritists from the land" (in accord with the Law), Saul, in disguise, approached a woman called the Witch of Endor. He asked her to awaken Samuel, and she complied.[3]

> When the woman saw Samuel, she cried out at the top of her voice and said to Saul, "Why have you deceived me? You are Saul!"
> The king said to her, "Don't be afraid. What do you see?"
> The woman said, "I see a spirit coming up out of the ground."
> "What does he look like?" he asked.
> "An old man wearing a robe is coming up," she said.

Then Saul knew it was Samuel, and he bowed down and prostrated himself with his face to the ground.

Samuel said to Saul, "Why have you disturbed me by bringing me up?"

"I am in great distress," Saul said. "The Philistines are fighting against me, and God has turned away from me. He no longer answers me, either by prophets or by dreams. So I have called on you to tell me what to do."[4]

Unswayed, Samuel told Saul both he and his sons would be killed in the ensuing battle, and that's exactly what happened.

This story offers valuable insight into *why* people throughout history have sought counsel and comfort from the dead. Who hasn't endured "great distress" from time to time, feeling that God has turned away and no longer answers? The temptation to reach actively through the veil of death during hard times and lean on someone you trusted in life can be appealing. What else explains the practice's persistence throughout the centuries?

> The temptation to reach actively through the veil of death during hard times and lean on someone you trusted in life can be appealing.

The Greeks, for instance, strove to solicit information from the dead. Every village had an "oracle," one or more who for a price would reveal a person's future. Ephyra, however, was different: the city stood over caves thought to be the entrance to Hades. There, it was believed, a supplicant could speak directly to the dead—if he were willing to undertake an ordeal (no doubt costly) that lasted up to twenty-nine days.

The seeker would enter a temple called a Necromanteion, which means "oracle of death." After offering the appropriate sacrifices, he was led to a dark subterranean room where he remained alone for many days, eating only foods associated with the dead: beans, pork, mussels, barley. (The diet also included narcotic substances.) At the appointed time, the priest returned to administer a ritual bath; then, thoroughly disoriented, he was taken to a chamber deep within the earth where he could finally speak with an "apparition" that mysteriously appeared from a cauldron suspended above the ground.

The message from beyond typically was a cryptic verse requiring a heavy dose of interpretation. After contact with the dead spirit, the living seeker was taken back to the surface and out into the blinding light of day–thankful to have survived a trip to the underworld.[5]

Few people now would go to such lengths (though attempting to connect with the dead is more popular than ever). Many present-day "oracles" have online sites, toll-free numbers, and TV shows. Since the Fox sisters of the nineteenth century enlivened modern spiritualism, peering into the beyond has grown into a profitable industry. Psychics and seers have steadily proliferated–and so have their communication techniques. Let's look at five in use today.

CRYSTAL GAZING

Chances are, the first image that pops into your head when you hear the word *fortune-teller* is of a cloaked old woman in a darkened tent waving her hands over a crystal ball. Hollywood certainly has done its part to plant that picture. Yet crystal gazing–also known as *scrying*–has been used since antiquity to open a window between this world and the next. Any reflective surface will do: a pool of water, a cup of wine, a polished stone. In *Snow White*, the wicked queen scries when she asks, "Mirror, mirror, on the wall, who's the fairest of them all?"

The sitter–as the living person seeking contact is called–comes with questions of her own. If all goes according to plan, a spirit appears in the murky reflected patterns and answers through the medium.

TABLE TILTING

Much like spirit rapping, in table tilting, the dead make their presence known via tangible physical manifestation. Sitters–with or without a medium–place their hands on a tabletop and ask a question; the spirits respond by moving, rattling, or even levitating the table. It's easy to see how "feeling the spirits" with your own hands might have a powerful psychological effect. As historian Brian Righi explains:

> Table tilting became so popular in its heyday that doctors and scientists thought the craze dangerous to the public's mental health. In reaction, a committee was formed to study the fad. . . . After heated debate, the committee's findings concluded that table tilting was due to the unconscious muscular activity of the sitters and not to any real spiritual presence.[6]

Predictably, that verdict did little to dampen enthusiasm for the practice.

TALKING BOARDS

Known today as a Ouija board, some accounts claim this device dates back 3,200 years to its use in China. The design is simple: letters of the alphabet are printed on a flat, portable board, along with the ordinal numbers plus the words *yes* and *no*. Sitters place their fingers lightly around the edges of a disc—called a *planchette*—that can glide easily over the board's surface. They ask a question and then allow the planchette to move where it will, spelling or marking out a response, presumably under a spirit's influence.

Like so many techniques for contacting the dead, the talking board gained popularity in the mid-nineteenth century, during the early days of the spiritualist movement. Today, it can be purchased in most toy departments; the box of the Parker Brothers edition has read, *"It's all just a game—isn't it?"*

Scientists studying the phenomenon maintain that any "messages" thus received originate in subconscious human minds, not with a discarnate spirit. Interesting but harmless, they say. But others warn the device is no mere parlor plaything; Christians believe using a talking board invites demons to masquerade as benevolent spirits in order to mislead or gain influence. Many secular researchers—for example, the well-known paranormal investigators Ed and Lorraine Warren—have come to the same conclusion.

Ouija boards are just as dangerous as drugs. . . . Séances and Ouija boards and other occult paraphernalia are dangerous because "evil spirits" often disguise themselves as your loved ones—and take over your life.[7]

It isn't uncommon for a "conversation" with a spirit through a talking board to turn suddenly harsh, obscene, and abusive. Consider: *If it's a game, then with whom do we play, and for what purpose do they accept the invitation?*

AUTOMATIC WRITING

Using this technique, a medium enters a trance and allows the contacted spirit to control his hand to write a message. The medium often is unaware of what he writes until after "coming to" again. Sometimes, the handwriting or language style dramatically differs from the medium's own. In this way, he claims the ability to channel an eager-to-communicate spirit.

Again, scientists think the only opened "channel" lies between the mind's conscious and subconscious regions. Some psychologists even have begun using automatic writing as a therapeutic tool to help patients access painful feelings and memories they're otherwise unable to face. However, as with talking boards, many warn of the danger of inviting an unknown spirit to enter one's mind and manipulate one's body.

PSYCHIC READINGS

Many mediums claim the ability to directly sense the spirits of dead people and communicate with them—without rapping or writing or other methods. When a sitter seeks contact with a dead person, the medium doesn't summon the spirit but simply acts as a go-between should it show up on its own. The assumption is that the ghost is as zealous to converse as the sitter.

This is the technique used by most "psychics" today, including famous ones who work in front of a studio audience. They commonly appear to access information about the sitter that only the dead person could have known, leading observers to conclude they must be "for real."

Skeptics, on the other hand, charge that the "medium" frequently is a mere con artist using pre-gathered data by snooping and scrounging around in *this* world. Advances in technology—transmitting information via hidden microphones and cameras, Internet searches, and wireless communication devices—have made the task easier than ever.

It's more likely that most psychics are skilled at a process called *cold reading*. This requires knowledge of basic psychology, body language, and old-fashioned theatrics—but not genuine communication with the dead. By prodding the sitter with vague and suggestive questions, the medium fishes for clues that can lead her to seemingly remarkable "hits"—presumed info from the other side. Furthermore, ambiguity is no obstacle when the sitter desperately wants the medium to succeed. As Robert T. Carroll writes:

> Clients of mediums who claim to get messages from the dead are very highly motivated clients. Not only do they have an implicit desire for immortality, they have an explicit desire to contact a dear loved one who has died. The odds are in favor of the medium that the client will find meaning in many different sets of ambiguous words and phrases. If she connects just a couple of them, she may be satisfied that the medium has made a connection to a dead relative. If she doesn't find any meaning or significance in the string, the medium still wins. He can try another string. He can insist that there's meaning here but the client just isn't trying hard enough to figure it out. He can suggest that some uninvited spirit guests are confusing the issue. It's a win-win situation for the medium because the burden is not on him but on the client to find the meaning and significance of the words.[8]

Of course, that some or even most psychics employ cold reading to fool the sitter does not necessarily mean all do. Gary Schwartz, professor of psychology and neurology at the University of Arizona, decided to put his reputation on the line attempting to settle the question once and for all. Properly designed experiments, he reasoned, could remove cold reading and previously gleaned info from the medium's toolbox. He wanted to know: If a psychic were prevented from seeing or even speaking to the sitter but still gave an accurate reading, could that prove the existence of afterlife communication?

To summarize, over the course of many carefully controlled sittings with well-known mediums, Schwartz calculated they retrieved accurate information 80 to 90 percent of the time, on average. These results were far better than we could expect from random chance or guessing.

> We delight in having professional magicians fool us. They have mastered the tricks for deceiving our senses—tricks developed over many, many years. How could I truly be sure I was not being fooled by these mediums in a similar way . . . ?
>
> Other scientists would demand incontrovertible proof before even beginning to accept what we thought we had witnessed. As a scientist myself, I had a nagging certainty I could not yet answer all the challenges that might be thrown at me. . . .
>
> Yet for the time being, I could hardly help but feel elated. In this territory so unknown to us, we had planned and carried out a significant experiment with fairly elaborate safeguards. The results were decidedly impressive, certainly enough to give us confidence and the strong desire to continue.[9]

As Schwartz predicted, most observers complained that the research raised far more questions than it answered. Still, it managed to keep the issue alive when it might just as easily have killed psychic interest on the spot.

Practitioners of modern spiritualism in all its forms have been hounded every step of the way by allegations of deception and chicanery. Escape artist Harry Houdini spent much of his career using what he knew about theatrical illusion to expose the fraudulent. "It takes a flimflammer to catch a flimflammer," he said.

In 1888, Maggie Fox stunned the world by admitting that she and Kate had perpetrated a fraud: They'd hatched the prank as children to frighten their mother. Then events took on a life of their own, and they didn't know how to stop—and perhaps didn't want to, especially once it became clear they had stumbled on a lucrative way to make a living at a time when most women had few such opportunities. How? By cracking the knuckles in their toes, Kate said. Maggie even went on tour to demonstrate the technique. It was proclaimed in the skeptical press and scientific communities as a death blow to spiritualism.

But—as has been the case throughout the long history of necromancy—there was more strangeness to come. Two years later, the sisters recanted and again took up the work of helping people communicate with dead loved ones. Supporters claimed they'd previously been threatened or even paid to denounce the movement. Many of the "psychic" phenomena attributed to them remain hard to explain even considering their short-lived confession. In any case, they never again achieved similar popularity and died impoverished within ten years.

Where Do We Go From Here?

Is it *possible* to communicate with the dead? The honest reply is "Probably, though who knows for sure?" Despite centuries of investigation and debate, a definitive, intellectually satisfying answer seems elusive. But assuming for a moment that the answer is yes—which the story of Saul and Samuel suggests—a more important question arises: Is seeking out such communication *advisable*? On that point it's far easier to reach a reasonable conclusion: No.

The mere possibility—convincingly raised by many researchers and firsthand witnesses—that necromancy amounts to an open invitation for evil spirits to make themselves at home in our lives is grounds enough to steer clear. God warned the Israelites to have nothing to do with one who "practices divination or sorcery, interprets omens, engages in witchcraft, or casts

> God warned the Israelites to have nothing to do with one who "practices divination or sorcery, interprets omens, engages in witchcraft, or casts spells, or who is a medium or spiritist or who consults the dead."

spells, or who is a medium or spiritist or who consults the dead."[10] Zero wiggle room!

Another reason to shy away might be found by asking, Why bother?

> When men tell you to consult mediums and spiritists, who whisper and mutter, should not a people inquire of their God? Why consult the dead on behalf of the living? To the law and to the testimony! If they do not speak according to this word, they have no light of dawn.[11]

In other words, what can a medium, speaking for a dead person, possibly tell you that you can't hear in Scripture and in prayer? With God there is no potential for fraud, deception, contamination, or disaster.

When it comes to communication with the dead, while many mysteries remain unsolved, one thing is clear: God has already granted you access to the wise guidance and comforting counsel you might want from a lost loved one. It is there for the asking—in your relationship with *him*.

8

Angels
Among Us

———— ✳ ————

God's Messengers Provide Protection and Provision

Philosophers have argued for centuries about how many angels can dance on the head of a pin, but materialists have always known it depends on whether they are jitterbugging or dancing cheek to cheek.

TOM ROBBINS

Ever been rescued by an angel? I have . . . in a manner of speaking.

I grew up three miles from a town—Ames, Kansas—with a population that numbered less than a hundred. One mile south of our farm was a dirt-road intersection graced by a small church, Morgan Chapel Wesleyan Methodist. That is where I experienced all my early spiritual training. One of the biggest events was the annual Christmas program, where you could count on nearly all town residents attending, far more than our average attendance of sixty-five.

To give a more professional ambiance, from a number nine wire strung across the front of the church hung curtains that opened and closed for various acts. When I was five, I had the opening recitation; something simple like "We welcome you to our Christmas pageant" with three rhyming lines to follow.

As the show was to begin, and the small varnished sanctuary filled with excited anticipation, the curtains parted three feet wide, just enough room for me to appear but not enough to reveal the nativity scene on the darkened stage. I stepped forward through the gap, as obediently as David going to face Goliath, though with far less confidence. After clearing my throat, I began to recite my carefully memorized lines. I got through the first two with hardly a wobble.

But suddenly I felt as if I were standing before a hundred *thousand* gawking onlookers. As my mind raced, my mouth froze. I stood motionless. The audience stirred nervously, as did my brain. When no words came, I cried. And cried some more. Then I cried louder.

When it became apparent that my distress would continue unabated, an "angel" suddenly appeared. My mother, standing out of view backstage, dressed as an angel for her appearance in the nativity scene, came to rescue her troubled child. She dashed toward the curtain opening, swooping in from her assigned position, and scooping me up with a long circular motion of her right arm. In an instant, the whimpering lad was cradled in an angel's arms. The winged white messenger then pirouetted with a ballerina's grace back to her original mark. The figure of deliverance and the relieved young thespian clung to each other as the curtains fully parted and the show commenced.

> I have no doubt that honest-to-goodness, God-sent angels do indeed exist and participate in our lives, probably far more than we realize.

The crowd was awed by the intervention. Some became convinced that the weepy opener and the angelic appearance were part of the plan. Many said it was the best beginning of a Christmas program they'd ever seen.

That, I must confess, is the closest I'm aware of having come to an "angelic visitation." But I have no doubt that honest-to-goodness, God-sent angels do indeed exist and participate in our lives, probably far more than we realize. Dozens of absolutely convinced people have told me of their encounters. Many more such accounts are recorded by credible books, magazines, and Web sites.

What do you envision when you think of an *angel*? A white-robed being with halo and harp, standing knee-deep in clouds? An effervescent and glittering figure of the Victorian variety, perched atop an opulent Christmas tree? Or perhaps you see the twentieth-century George Bailey's bumbling but loveable angel, Clarence (*It's a Wonderful Life*). Or maybe the more contemporary imagery from *City of Angels*: dark, long-coated beings straddling skyscrapers . . . ever watching, influencing, occasionally falling from grace and even in love. Hollywood strikes again! Let's try to form a more accurate perception of who angels are and what they do.

BACKGROUND ON HEAVENLY BEINGS

The term itself comes from the Greek *angelos*, which means "messenger." In ancient times, when travel was slow and communication limited, personally delivered messages were coveted and critical; battles could be won or lost due to a courier's expedience or delay. It's not surprising that Greek mythology has a winged messenger as one of its gods: Hermes also was known as Mercury in later Roman times. Other cultures and religions included the idea of messenger gods; Hebrew literature, regarding the people of Israel, also is full of stories about angelic messengers with names like Michael, Gabriel, and Raphael.

As for the New Testament, you've probably heard of Gabriel, who told Mary she would be the mother of Jesus. Through the ages, many angels described in Hebrew and Christian writings are depicted artistically as winged, superhuman beings, from the stoic, iconic, gold-haloed medieval figures to the cute little winged cherubs of the Renaissance.

Mormonism's roots trace to the story of an angel's alleged message to their nineteenth-century founder; a statue of this angel, named Moroni, adorns most Mormon temples.

Interestingly, having moved beyond passé modernist culture's rigid naturalistic doctrines, popular (postmodern) Western culture once again is embracing the supernatural and these beings in particular. Books like Doreen Virtue's *How to Hear Your Angels* encourage people to contact "angels" and harness their powers for assistance in life's journey.[1]

ANGELIC APPEARANCES IN SCRIPTURE

The Bible has much to say about angels, in more than three hundred references—about a hundred in the Old Testament and over two hundred in the New. Although no single passage gives us a complete picture, we can piece together snippets and glean much about the nature of angels from Scripture.

Could they be metaphorical figures, inserted to illustrate abstract ideas about truth or moral behavior? *The Bible portrays angels as literal, personal entities who play a role in historical events and individual lives.* They appear both in dreams and visions as well as to fully conscious people; the result of the encounters is always dramatic and life-changing, regardless of the manifestation. The life of Jesus especially points to literal angels: herein they tell others about Jesus, they help Jesus, and Jesus himself talks matter-of-factly about them.[2] They don't reproduce sexually, and they don't die;[3] they are immortal.

The book of Daniel is a combination of history and prophecy, written several centuries before Jesus' birth. Daniel was a young Jewish captive in the land of Babylon (modern-day Iraq). At one point, Daniel found himself in a tight spot and prayed to God for help. Some twenty-one days later, an angel showed up, and Daniel's astonishment is clear from his description:

> His body was like chrysolite,[4] his face like lightning, his eyes like flaming torches, his arms and legs like the gleam of burnished bronze, and his voice like the sound of a multitude.[5]

Here we learn that angels are powerful, knowledgeable, and helpful; breathtaking in appearance, not always fully visible. They can communicate with people. Some have names and rank—*Michael*, the *arch*angel. As the word implies, Daniel's angel was sent to deliver a message. But he couldn't be everywhere at once or do everything at once.

Then there's Revelation, which is filled with angelic descriptions. In about AD 95, John, one of Jesus' closest followers, received a glimpse of heaven, and what he saw (among many other details) were angels—*lots* of angels: "Then I looked and heard the voice of many angels, numbering thousands upon thousands, and ten thousand times ten thousand."[6] A literal interpretation would yield a hundred million angels. If we take this as figurative language, it affirms that heaven has *throngs* of angels.

Elsewhere John, awed by an angel's presence, fell down to worship but the angel stopped him: "Do not do it! I am a fellow servant with you and with your brothers. . . . Worship God!"[7] Unlike the mythological Hermes, angels are *not* divine; as impressive as they may appear, they serve God, just as mortals do.

In Luke 16, a foundational passage to what we know about heaven, we see the role played by angels even in our getting there: "The time came when the beggar died and the angels carried him to Abraham's side."[8] In Hebrews, a sort of theological treatise, the author speaks of angels via rhetorical question: "Are not all angels *ministering spirits* sent to serve those who will inherit salvation?"[9] So what exactly does this mean—how do angels minister?

NATURE OF ANGELS

The ambiguous word *spirit*, along with descriptions in the passages above, might cause us to wonder about the difference between angels and humans, with whom angels share some traits.

First, angels also are creatures, meaning God-*created* (they're not divine).

Second, they likewise have *personality*—intellect (thought), emotion (feeling), and will (choice).

Third, they *exist in time and space*. They function within time and space, although they have much more freedom than we do. In Psalm 148, a song of praise, the writer says the angels should praise God because God created them.[10] Another song of praise says humans were made "a little lower than the heavenly beings." (Even so, God "crowned [us] with glory and honor."[11])

Like us, angels are personal creatures: responsible, accountable, and dependent upon God. Again, as theologian C. Fred Dickason puts it, a person is not just a "human being" but a being that has the qualities of personality (intellect, emotion, and will).[12]

Though existing in time and space, angels seem able to appear and disappear

> Like us, angels are personal creatures: responsible, accountable, and dependent upon God.

suddenly or get from one place to another very quickly.[13] Biblically, they often appear in some kind of glorified humanlike form—with unusual brightness resembling fire, lightning, polished metal or precious stones, and/or blindingly white linen.[14] Other angels, not resembling humans at all, are likened to unusual beasts.[15] In the sixth century BC, the prophet Ezekiel had an astounding heavenly vision;[16] interestingly, the creatures John and Ezekiel saw had wings but didn't use them to fly.

There's no question angels are superhuman. Daniel's angel was stronger, smarter, and faster than any human; he could fight heavenly battles, see into the future, and, even though it took time, go between Persia to Babylon without breaking a sweat. But they aren't all-powerful or all-knowing,[17] and they cannot be everywhere at once.[18] Only God has these qualities.

OCCUPATION OF ANGELS

God created angels to help carry out his work, much of which occurs in heaven. There are mysterious things we don't know about and/or can't see—for instance, Ezekiel's cherubim and Isaiah's seraphim. Apparent guardians of the holy places, they're like priests—heavenly priests whose role and mission it is to glorify God. But while we don't know everything angels do, the Scriptures present them as being variously occupied worshiping God, carrying out his judgment, and ministering to humans by bringing messages and protection.[19]

Due to the biblical depiction of these beings as protectors, many have speculated as to whether there are "individualized," one-on-one angels. The early church seemed to think so, and this tradition is especially strong in Catholicism.[20] It's not such a farfetched idea, and there are a few allusions that some believe support the existence of guardian angels.[21] Protecting and caring certainly are among the angelic character traits; they often arrive to comfort God's people at their lowest point,[22] as with Jesus himself on a few occasions.[23]

THE ANGELIC ARMY

How do angels carry out all this strengthening, encouraging, guarding, and protecting? They are numerous, and they are highly organized; they have positions and ranks, as in the military. Jesus used Roman terminology, *legion,* to indicate the profuse array of angels, and he explained to the disciples and the crowd who wished to take him by force that it wasn't necessary to resist. After all, if he desired, God would supply backup with twelve legions of angels.[24] A Roman legion was comprised of six thousand soldiers, plus their slaves, so Jesus could have had the help of at least seventy-two thousand angels, though the point was not the literal number but the overwhelming available force.

As for angelic ranks, Paul tells us the names of some divisions: *rulers, authorities, powers, thrones,* and *dominions.* Regarding everything that has been created in heaven and on earth, some things are visible, while some, like thrones, powers, rulers, and authorities, are not.[25] God uses his people, the church, to reveal wisdom "to the rulers and authorities in the heavenly realms."[26] Peter links these invisible divisions with angels when he says Jesus is in heaven "at God's right hand—with angels, authorities and powers in submission to him."[27]

There are two known angelic offices as well: angel and archangel. *Arche* is Greek for "ruler"; the archangel is the head angel, or at least head of one rank. Michael, an archangel,[28] also is called a prince.[29] This office is mentioned only twice, and only once in connection with Michael or any other name.[30]

Some speculate that the six-winged seraphim hovering above God's throne may have the highest office of all.[31] Others say the cherubim are the highest ranking, present in Ezekiel's account of beast-like creatures with multiple wings and intersecting wheels.[32] Theologians through the ages have puzzled over angelic ranks and offices. A sixth-century mystic, Dionysius, proffered his ideas in *The Celestial Hierarchy*, placing seraphim and cherubim on top. He took his ideas from the Bible but added a lot of hocus-pocus.[33] Thomas Aquinas, one of history's most brilliant theologians, added to this work; earlier, Augustine had found the topic interesting but was reluctant to comment, pleading ignorance.[34] More recently, Billy Graham's organizational chart conversely placed angels and archangels on top, above the seraphim and cherubim.[35]

No matter what, we know these all are part of a larger group called the "heavenly hosts." This includes God himself, the angels, archangels, cherubim, seraphim, and the thrones, powers, authorities, dominions, and rulers that are God's army, the "extension of His power and providence."[36]

As the military terminology suggests, there also are enemies. The Bible refers to a rebellion in heaven led by one very high-ranking angel;[37] other angels joined him and were banished.[38] It also depicts an unseen spiritual battle between angelic and demonic powers. (We'll delve more deeply into this dark realm in chapters 9–10.[39])

ACTIVE AND AMONG US

Let's bring all this back down to earth: Is there reason to believe angels still interact with us? The Bible indicates there is. Recall the reference to "ministering spirits sent to serve *those who will inherit salvation.*"[40] Why wouldn't angels, as immortal creatures serving God, continue working to help his people?

Gary Kinnaman, who was senior pastor at Word of Grace Church in Mesa, Arizona, for several decades, shares stories of encounters gathered during a study he undertook for his doctoral work.[41] While Kinnaman cautions that this study was not scientific, he found commonality and credibility in the experiences described by people who didn't know each other. He confirms that angel visitations are rare, and for those few who have seen or sensed an angelic presence, it's usually a brief, unexpected, once-in-a-lifetime event.

As for *appearance,* among the similarities found in the descriptions is that angels are very tall—"as high as the ceiling," as one man put it.[42] In form they appear sufficiently humanlike, enough to be recognizable—as to Daniel—but their faces are such that they can't be distinguished as male or female.[43] Long hair is a frequent feature; often so is a robe-like garment, with a sash or belt. They are bright, glowing, and transparent. Respondents rarely reported wings.[44]

Regarding *actions,* often the angel imparted some kind of message, though not always with audible speech, somehow "communicating" so that the person would be as sure of the words as if they were spoken aloud. Usually the angel didn't appear to look directly at the person or solicit attention; the descriptions almost sound as if the viewer was being permitted to glimpse an angel going about mysterious business. Often, whatever that business might be was indiscernible at the time, though the person speculated about it thereafter.

Again, nearly everyone who reported such an encounter felt it to be life-altering. Some would discern the significance years later, after reflecting on events or changes in their outlook that had occurred since the visitation. For example, some became Christians as a result of their angelic encounter; for some, the process took years or even decades.[45]

ENTERTAINING ANGELS UNAWARE

What about angels appearing in human form? It happened to Abraham and Lot, but that was a long time ago—what about now? Once again Hebrews advises: "Do not forget to entertain strangers, for by so doing some people have entertained angels without knowing it."[46] It should still be possible for us to encounter angels who have assumed human form.

While there are many anecdotal stories to support this, though, how could anyone know for sure? Nearly all who report such an experience say something like, "I think it must have been an angel." Usually it's later, when they've had time to puzzle over the unlikely "coincidence" that a stranger "appeared" to help them at a desperate time. Maybe their old clunker broke down on a remote road. Or they were camped beside a cliff where a landslide was about to occur. Or were being stalked by hoodlums. Help shows up just in the nick of time and then—poof!—the disappearance is as sudden as the arrival. Not into thin air—but into the nearby woods . . . around a corner . . . or when heads were turned.[47]

This is common with missionaries. Ruth Graham told of growing up as the daughter of missionaries in China; her family experienced such providential encounters.[48] In addition to much anecdotal evidence, there is biblical implication that angels would be watching out for missionaries especially.[49] Angels do not preach, teach, or counsel; humans do those jobs. As we've seen, angels assist those who do God's work on earth.[50]

Kinnaman reports that on occasion parishioners have reported seeing an angel standing near him while he stood preaching.[51] I had such an experience when a woman who attends my church shared what she witnessed during a service; she was visibly impacted.

> My husband and I sensed an unusual presence last Sunday morning. I noticed some movement around you as you began to preach, but I dismissed it. A few minutes later I felt a cool breeze, then experienced a weight so heavy I could barely sit upright. I asked God what he was trying to tell me or show me. Then I saw a quick flash of light that moved behind your left shoulder. Every so often the light would reappear. It moved with great speed, darting back and forth behind you. Then as I looked across the platform, I saw it was filled with angels moving about. My hearing became so acute that I could hear you speaking even though the sound the angels were making was almost deafening. Not in a bad way—not like loud music you hear in someone's car at a stoplight but thunderous noise of angels in motion.

When you hear someone tell a story like that, are you skeptical? If so, know that I am too. While open to unexplainable and bona fide miraculous happenings, I have a natural bent toward skepticism. But be assured that if this woman, and her husband—a respected police detective—did not have credibility with me, I would not report the encounter. (Besides, if we truly believe God's messengers are active and involved in our world, why should we be surprised when we hear of such experiences from reliable sources?)

Another account comes from my friend Gary, an electrical engineer and business owner. Heading home after an extended road trip, towing a house trailer, Gary crossed the Cascade Mountains in darkest night, heading east into the high plains of Washington State. He struggled to stay awake by talking on the CB radio to his sister, who was driving behind him. In the first car were Gary, Gary's father, and Gary's two daughters. In the second car, besides Gary's sister, were his mother and his wife. Everyone but the drivers were asleep.

Dreaming that the car towing the trailer was veering off the road, Gary's father suddenly reached across and yanked the steering wheel, semiconsciously attempting to avoid an accident. At sixty-five miles per hour, pulling a heavy load, there was no way to correct the abrupt swerve in time. The car and trailer hurtled off the road, overturned, and came to rest right-side-up, flattened like an accordion, in the bottom of a ditch. The trailer had practically disintegrated—pieces of it were strewn across two hundred yards of roadway.

Gary's sister, observing the entire incident, had stopped some distance back. Afraid at what they might find if they ran down to the wreck, the three women, now wide awake, stood by their vehicle, repeating in stunned disbelief, "Oh no. Oh no. Oh *no*—"

Inside the smashed, rolled-over car, now half its original height, the four passengers struggled to get out through the one working door. Miraculously, no one was hurt. They were dirty, frightened, and stunned into near silence, but hardly a scratch could be found on any of them.

Back up on the highway there was complete quiet. No other traffic, no one around—not for miles and miles. No sound at all . . . except for a voice coming out of the darkness. A very tall man in a long black coat appeared, approached the mother and sister, put his arms around them both, and said, "Don't worry. Everyone is okay. They will be fine. No one is hurt." And then, just as suddenly, he disappeared back into the darkness.

Overcoming their shock, the women ran to the ditch, helping the struggling victims—now looking like coal miners with dirt-smeared faces—back onto the road and quickly verifying the truth of the stranger's statements. Everyone was indeed unharmed.

Minutes later, after the babble of voices recounting details had finally subsided, Gary's mother asked, "Where is the man who told us you were okay?"

"What man?" Gary and his father asked.

In the 2:00 AM stillness, in the middle of nowhere, in the midst of a near tragedy, the question repeated through the ages by God's children again was asked: *"Who was he?"*

To them there's no doubt about the answer: They'd encountered an angel.

ANGELS AT DEATH'S DOOR

Deathbed stories are replete with angel sightings, reports of which frequently are less about details of tall beings and more about brief comments of "I see an angel," accompanied by peacefulness on the face of the dying individual. Billy Graham, who has presided at the death-beds of many people, both believers and nonbelievers, says the first is a "glorious" experience, while the latter can be "terrible."[52] At his own grandmother's death, just moments before she died, the room filled with light; she sat up and said, "I see Jesus . . . I see the angels!"[53]

One of Kinnaman's survey respondents, a young father, recalls the birth—and death—of his prematurely born daughter. Every day she survived was a miracle. After one week, he began to hold out some hope that she would live.

When he came to the hospital, he was stunned to see her incubator flanked by two very tall, luminous visitors. He ecstatically related this to his wife, assured now that their baby had angels to safeguard her tenuous existence. But the tiny girl died the next day, and for weeks he felt betrayed—until he and his wife noticed Graham on television talking about angels. The bereaved father was comforted that his child had been escorted to heaven, just like Lazarus.[54]

We all will face physical death sooner or later. When that day comes for me, I want to be able to affirm this text: "I am sending an angel ahead of you to guard you along the way and to bring you to the place I have prepared."[55] Understanding the angelic role in life's great crossover extracts some of death's sting *and* gives confidence as we live here on earth.

When this life is over, we do not go alone. For the people who reported end-of-life sightings, there was comfort. It should be the same for us who may not be at death's door but know we someday will be. It is good to understand—as best we can on this side—the reality of angelic protection by God's provision.

9

More Than a Pitchfork and a Pointy Tail

—— ✳ ——

The Great Adversary, Satan, Prowls Like a Hungry Lion

I often laugh at Satan, and there is nothing that makes him so angry as when I attack him to his face, and tell him that through God I am more than a match for him.

MARTIN LUTHER

If you're a fan of *The Twilight Zone*, you might recall the 1960 episode "The Howling Man." David Ellington, an American, is on a walking trip through central Europe after World War I. Caught in a fierce storm, he chances upon an imposing medieval castle where he meets a reclusive brotherhood of monks.

At first they turn Ellington away. But after he passes out, they reluctantly take him in. As he's reviving, he hears someone or something howling. The brothers insist they hear nothing.

Later that night, the American discovers a man locked inside a cell. An ancient wooden staff holds the door closed. The prisoner claims he's held captive by the "insane" head monk, Brother Jerome, and pleads for his release. His kind face and gentle voice convince Ellington to help.

Ellington confronts Jerome, who says the prisoner is Satan himself, "the Father of Lies," held captive by the Staff of Truth, the one barrier he cannot pass. This incredible claim convinces the visitor Jerome is indeed crazy. As soon as he gets the chance, he returns to the cell and opens it. Big mistake—the former captive instantly transforms into a hideous creature that vanishes in smoke.

The stunned American is mortified upon realizing what he has done. Jerome responds sympathetically, "I'm sorry for you, my son. All your life you will remember this night and whom you have turned loose upon the world."

"I didn't believe you," Ellington replies. "I saw him and didn't recognize him."

"That is man's weakness—and Satan's strength," Jerome muses solemnly.

Shortly after Satan's release, World War II breaks out. Ellington devotes his life to recapturing the devil and finally succeeds. As he makes arrangements to ship him back to the brotherhood, he tells his housekeeper to ignore the howling. But as soon as he leaves, she lifts the bar on the door, and it swings open.

The episode ends with Rod Sterling's ominous warning, "Ancient folk saying: 'You can catch the devil, but you can't hold him long.' Ask Brother Jerome. Ask David Ellington. They know, and they'll go on knowing to the end of their days and beyond."[1]

It's a cautionary tale, an allegory for those who acknowledge the devil's power but don't always recognize him for what he is.

AKA SATAN

Stephen King, who's made a career of scaring the wits out of people, once said, "The beauty of religious mania is that it has the power to explain everything. Once God (or Satan) is accepted as the first cause of everything which happens in the mortal world, nothing is left to chance. . . . Logic can be happily tossed out the window."[2]

Lucifer, Abbadon, Asmodai, Antichrist, the Beast, Beelzebub (Lord of the Flies), Belial, Iblis, Lord of the Underworld, Mephistopheles, Old Scratch, Old Nick, Old Hob, Prince of Darkness, the Serpent . . . the being most commonly known in Western culture as either Satan or the devil has a long alias string that stretches through human history. And that's not including his many incarnations in Eastern religions.

Does a belief in Satan really mean logic has been "happily tossed out the window"? How relevant is the slithering, seductive serpent of Genesis today? Most modern skeptics argue he is at most a metaphor—a boogeyman of a bygone era who has no place in our rationalistic times.

Yet Satan remains a constant character. You might say he's a regular guest on every available medium, from classic literature to television, pop music to film.

Consider some of our heritage. The medieval German legend of Faust tells of a man who makes a pact with the devil in exchange for knowledge. In the

> *Does* a belief in Satan really mean logic has been "happily tossed out the window"?

seventeeth-century epic poem *Paradise Lost,* John Milton brilliantly portrays Satan as a protagonist reminiscent of Greek heroes. In the first scene the fallen angel proclaims defiantly to his just-banished followers, "Better to reign in hell, than serve in heav'n."

Two American legends featuring Satan in a prominent role are Washington Irving's *The Devil and Tom Walker* (1824) and Stephen Vincent Benét's *The Devil and Daniel Webster* (1937). Other incarnations include the Charlie Daniels Band's "The Devil Went Down to Georgia"; *The Simpsons* episode "The Devil and Homer Simpson"; and Tenacious D's rock opera, *The Pick of Destiny*.

The devil has starred in numerous contemporary movies as well. *Constantine* (2005) presents earth as a neutral war setting in God and Satan's wager over who will win the most souls. In *The Passion of the Christ* (2004), Satan carries a demon baby during Christ's flogging, perversely mocking Madonna and Child. You'll find thousands of such satanic "appearances" with a quick Google search.

Western ideas about Satan are mostly exaggerated, cartoonish, and inaccurate—based on medieval art and human imagination rather than on what the Bible says. Thus we have lighthearted stories, songs, films, illustrations, and games that glamorize the Prince of Darkness. He has become a stereotype that's more symbol than substance, even among many professing Christians. Indeed, Americans' belief in the devil fell from 68 percent to 59 percent between 2003 and 2008, approximately the same decline as beliefs in God, heaven, and hell.[3]

ORIGINS OF DARKNESS

Many argue that Satan is merely a concept adapted by Christians from ancient pagan religions with a dualistic approach to good and evil. There is, however, a distinct difference: Christianity asserts there is one God, the Supreme Creator, who is all-powerful, perfect, unchanging, just, loving, and completely good. Satan is an inferior, created being—not an opposing god.

> Though real, Satan is not an equal power but a created being who is part of the fallen creation and is utterly opposed to God.

In arguing against the reality of Satan, many have asked how a good and loving God could allow such an evil being to exist. Augustine of Hippo struggled with this very question, because while affirming the goodness of God's creation, he couldn't deny the existence of evil. Augustine came to understand evil as an *absence* (privation) of goodness; when angels or humanity turn away from God and choose sin, they turn from the source of goodness.[4] An analogy would be light and darkness, repeatedly used in Scripture to describe good and evil. Just as darkness is the absence of light (i.e., darkness is not a thing itself), so evil is the absence of, or lack of, good.

The Bible does not depict God and Satan as competing forces in a power struggle (like ontological dualism does). Though real, Satan is not an equal power but a created being who is part of the fallen creation and is utterly opposed to God. Jesus Christ, Light of the World, makes it clear that darkness can never overcome the light, in either the spiritual or physical realm.[5]

––––––––

Another argument seeking to discount Satan is that only ignorant people would believe in such "superstition." This implies that Jesus was primitive or that he presented his message to accommodate the world-view of his audience. However, calling a belief primitive or superstitious assumes it's outdated or in error. Countless careful students of the Bible are convinced Jesus spoke of timeless truths.

In the last one hundred years, there have been many attacks upon Scripture in academic circles. These don't alter the Bible's teachings; the eternal truths revealed in God's Word will not change.

THE STUFF OF LEGENDS

During the Middle Ages ordinary people didn't have access to God's Word as we do today. Monasteries, not universities, were the centers for learning. The monks and priests who served the local parishioners could not overcome the illiteracy and lack of education among their "flocks." The uneducated population (the majority of Europeans at the time) knew little about the Bible or church doctrine and quite often had little idea what Christianity is about.

Without solid biblical faith, people were easily convinced that folktales, legends, and sensational stories revealed the true nature of their world. They were fascinated by widespread beliefs about Satan, demons, angels, and other supernatural beings like fairies, trolls, werewolves, vampires, and witches. They didn't understand the difference between pagan myth and the tenets of authentic doctrine. They weren't able to examine Scripture and read for themselves the truth about Satan.

A FALLEN ANGEL

The biblical authors agree: There is a supernatural entity that constantly seeks to destroy God's creation, especially those persons who have chosen to love and serve their Creator. This demonic personality was present, for instance, when the first humans sinned against God, when Jesus went into the wilderness for forty days, and when Judas met with the chief priests to betray Jesus.[6]

In the Old Testament's earliest writings, this entity is called "the Satan" (which means "adversary"). *Satan* is not a name but a title that describes a particular set of characteristics, just as *the Christ* is a title that identifies Messiah or King. Satan is the embodiment of evil—the one *farthest* from God. As one progresses through Scripture, the title *Satan* becomes synonymous with an angel named *Lucifer,* which is Latin for "light-bearer" or "day star."[7]

We know from three different parts of the Bible that pride and jealousy led this highly ranked angel to forsake his special relationship to God in order to corrupt humanity.[8] We don't know exactly when, where, or why this happened; Scripture leaves these questions unanswered. There are, however, intriguing clues about Satan and the fallen angels.

> Now there was a day when the sons of God came to present themselves before the Lord, and Satan also came among them. And the Lord said to Satan, "From where do you come?"
>
> So Satan answered the Lord and said, "From going to and fro on the earth, and from walking back and forth on it."[9]

The "sons of God" have been interpreted as being part of a heavenly host. Notice that although Satan is with these "sons," his status in heaven is unclear. The author of Job seems indifferent to Satan's motivations.[10]

At the time Job is believed to have been written, the Hebrews did not yet identify Satan as a completely evil entity. His personality wasn't fully defined until the time of three important prophets: Isaiah (c. 740 BC), Ezekiel (c. 597 BC), and Zechariah (c. 519 BC). Today's reader benefits from the full biblical revelation and can easily see Satan's furious, hate-filled animosity toward humankind.

THE ANOINTED ANGEL

It happens every Halloween. If you live in a neighborhood, you get trick-or-treaters dressed as superheroes, princesses, witches . . . and devils. The latter are outfitted with horns, a pointy tail, a pitchfork, maybe even red skin. This is pop culture's most prevalent visual image. But the spiritual entity who became "the Satan" was created as a glorious heavenly being of indescribable beauty:

> This is what the Sovereign Lord says:
> "You were the model of perfection,
> full of wisdom and perfect in beauty.
> You were in Eden,
> the garden of God;
> every precious stone adorned you. . . .
> Your settings and mountings were made of gold;
> on the day you were created they were prepared.
> You were anointed as a guardian cherub,
> for so I ordained you.
> You were on the holy mount of God;
> you walked among the fiery stones.
> You were blameless in your ways
> from the day you were created
> till wickedness was found in you."[11]

This angel was not only magnificent but also very important. He walked on the holy mountain with God. The anointing upon him signifies he was special.

Isaiah describes this angel's beauty in terms of sounds: astonishing music flowed from him. Both Ezekiel and Isaiah say God blessed him with perfect beauty and gave him a place of honor. Like the archangel, he was created good and was bestowed with the ability to choose whether or not to love and serve God.

Several passages help explain the motives behind the disobedience. From Isaiah:

> How art thou fallen from heaven, O Lucifer, son of the morning!

How art thou cut down to the ground, which didst weaken the nations.

For thou hast said in thine heart, I will ascend into heaven,

I will exalt my throne above the stars of God: I will sit also upon the mount of the congregation, in the sides of the north:

I will ascend above the heights of the clouds; I will be like the most High.

Yet thou shalt be brought down to hell, to the sides of the pit.[12]

A similar description of this fall is found in Ezekiel:

In the abundance of your trade you were filled with violence, and you sinned; so I cast you as a profane thing from the mountain of God, and the guardian cherub drove you out from the midst of the stones of fire.

Your heart was proud because of your beauty; you corrupted your wisdom for the sake of your splendor. I cast you to the ground; I exposed you before kings, to feast their eyes on you.[13]

THE ORIGINAL TEMPTER

Both Genesis and Matthew highlight cunning and cleverness:[14]

The serpent was more subtle than any other wild creature that the Lord God had made.[15]

Behold, I send you out as sheep in the midst of wolves; so be wise as serpents and innocent as doves.[16]

In the New Testament, the relationship between Satan and the garden of Eden's serpent is revealed. John identifies Satan as "the dragon, that ancient serpent, who is the devil, or Satan."[17] And Paul warned the Corinthians to be watchful against the temptations of the same snake that tempted Eve:

I am afraid that as the serpent deceived Eve by his cunning, your thoughts will be led astray from a sincere and pure devotion to Christ.[18]

That this tempter was Satan makes these words from Genesis very provocative:

> God said to the serpent, "Because you have done this, cursed are you above all cattle, and above all wild animals; upon your belly you shall go, and dust you shall eat all the days of your life. I will put enmity between you and the woman, and between your seed and her seed; he shall bruise your head, and you shall bruise his heel."[19]

What does it mean when God refers to a future "enmity between you [Satan] and the woman [Eve]"? This refers to something greater than the two personalities. The next phrase, referring to "your seed and her seed," clarifies that Eve's descendants will hate Satan and his demons; this animosity, then, will always exist between Satan and people.

God's statement to Satan that "he shall bruise your head" is the first foretelling of the devil's ultimate destruction. The injury (the cross) Satan would inflict on Eve's descendent would be akin to a bruise on his heel, because the resurrection followed the crucifixion. In defeating death and darkness, the Christ would crush Satan completely.

OUR ADVERSARY

Zechariah joins Job in describing Satan as part of the heavenly court:

> Then he showed me Joshua the high priest standing before the angel of the Lord, and Satan standing at his right hand to accuse him. And the Lord said to Satan, "The Lord rebuke you, O Satan!"[20]

Note the adversarial role of Satan as accuser, and this reality is made much clearer in later biblical writings. Peter uses vivid imagery that leaves no doubt as to Satan's intent: "Your enemy the devil prowls around like a roaring lion looking for someone to devour."[21] To the church at Rome, Paul describes the relationship between God and those who love him as inseparable, despite the adversary's best efforts.

We are more than conquerors through him who loved us. For I

am sure that neither death, nor life, nor angels, nor principalities, nor things present, nor things to come, nor powers, nor height, nor depth, nor anything else in all creation, will be able to separate us from the love of God in Christ Jesus our Lord.[22]

Among the things that might try to part us from God's love, Paul includes "angels," "principalities," and "powers." He uses similar terms in another letter, this time to the church in Ephesus, when he reminds us we're not fighting against people . . .

. . . but against the principalities, against the powers, against the world rulers of this present darkness, against the spiritual hosts of wickedness in the heavenly places.[23]

Paul is speaking about personal spiritual forces that seek to destroy a person's relationship with God. These have turned away and strive to corrupt the goodness within his creation, and this message is consistent with the whole Bible's teachings: *Nothing* can stand between Christ and those who love him. However, there are powers that will try. I've heard it said that "when Satan tries to remind us of our past (failures and sins), we're to remind him of his future (ultimate destruction)."

Satan has indescribable animosity toward those who desire to follow Christ and live out his example. His plan is basic: he wants to tempt you into self-destructive choices and behavior. He and his demonic entities are actively trying to undermine (or prevent) your relationship with Jesus Christ. While God wants to enjoy fellowship with you now and forever, Satan is determined to keep you from this spectacular destiny.

Humans must choose between God and Satan. The nineteenth-century French poet Charles Baudelaire said it well: "There are in every [person], at every hour, two simultaneous claims, one towards God, the other towards Satan."[24]

In his renowned satire *The Screwtape Letters*, C. S. Lewis says,

There are two equal and opposite errors into which our race can fall about the devils. One is to disbelieve in their existence. The other is to believe, and to feel an excessive and unhealthy interest in them. They themselves are equally pleased by both errors.[25]

The evil one is no match for God. When you're following God and filled with his life, Satan is no match for you either.

10

Demons in
the Dark

— ✳ —

Emissaries of Evil Bring Chaos and Confusion

Demons do not exist any more than gods do, being only the
products of the psychic activity of man.

SIGMUND FREUD

Years ago I conversed with a friend who had been my undergraduate
classmate. We'd parted ways to pursue graduate degrees and now
had met again. During our visit, the topic of demons came up.

"You actually believe they're for real?" he said. "Everybody knows
that when the Bible speaks of demons it doesn't mean *literal* demons.
Ancient peoples were primitive in their understanding, and all those
stories refer to psychological aberrations. Two thousand years ago people
weren't as sophisticated as we are."

"What about Jesus?" I asked. "He seemed to believe in demons."

"Certainly Jesus knew better," he replied. "Jesus understood he was
dealing with people whose beliefs were primitive, so he talked about

demons in order to relate to their worldview. Obviously, Jesus would have known there is no such thing. Demons can't possibly exist."

While I disagree with my friend's interpretation, he did make an accurate observation: The way we see the world depends on our point of view . . . our worldview. For example, the Christian worldview is that God and creation are not the same. Trees, rocks, spiders, and eagles are not God, nor can they become God after several lifetimes or by spiritual achievement.

Many contemporary Westerners believe there is a spiritual realm in addition to the physical world, and in America the overwhelming majority believes there is a God. However, fewer people believe supernatural forces can enter material, earthly reality.

Scripture presents creation as a three-tiered universe: the unseen (spiritual) realm, the seen (material) world, and a third dimension that allows the seen and unseen to intersect. Paul Hiebert refers to this interactive realm as "the excluded middle," since it's been excluded from the thinking of many people.[1]

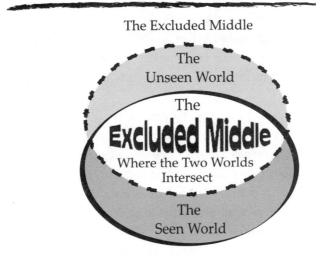

The Excluded Middle

The
Unseen World

The
Excluded Middle
Where the Two Worlds
Intersect

The
Seen World

If your worldview incorporates this excluded middle, you won't need to remove the supernatural from the biblical record. That's why there's a chapter on demons in this book about the afterlife—the topics

> **If Jesus encountered demons and evil spirits during his lifetime, his followers likewise may face them.**

of heaven and hell take us into unseen dimensions. These are not merely vacuous regions waiting for people; they have intended occupants and participants, whether angels or demons.

The Bible contains so many references to demons, demon possession (see below), demonization, unclean spirits, exorcisms, healing, and the casting out of evil spirits that even well-educated, sophisticated believers must allow for the possibility that the universe is more complex and mysterious than it may appear to our senses. If Jesus encountered demons and evil spirits during his lifetime, his followers likewise may face them.

WHO STILL BELIEVES?

Sometimes it seems *everybody* believes in angels. It's an extremely widespread conviction, generating a flood of related shows, books, magazines, films, and all manner of merchandise. The belief that benevolent supernatural beings watch over innocent earthly souls continues to gain followers—even in (and at least partially in response to) our naturalistic age.

Ask someone if she believes in demons, however, and she'll probably say *no*. The widespread popularity of angels doesn't extend downward, although most religions that include angels also depict their evil counterparts. Among Christians, few want to openly discuss demonic activity or accept that demons are as real as ever. Perhaps we don't want to sound naïve or backward; belief in dark spiritual forces may seem ignorant or paranoid.

Looking from the vantage point of the demonic world, it would be to their advantage if we denied their reality or wallowed in a lack of knowledge. Maybe the old saying is true: The greatest lie the devil ever told is that he doesn't exist. Those in doubt about demons should consider this historical account:

They [Jesus and his disciples] came to the other side of the sea. . . .
And when he had come out of the boat, there met him out of the
tombs a man with an unclean spirit, who lived among the tombs;
and no one could bind him any more, even with a chain; for he
had often been bound with fetters and chains, but the chains he
wrenched apart, and the fetters he broke in pieces; and no one had
the strength to subdue him. Night and day . . . he was always crying out, and bruising himself with stones. And when he saw Jesus
from afar, he ran and worshiped him; and crying out with a loud
voice, he said, "What have you to do with me, Jesus, Son of the
Most High God? I adjure you by God, do not torment me." For he
had said to him, "Come out of the man, you unclean spirit!" And
Jesus asked him, "What is your name?" He replied, "My name is
Legion; for we are many." And he begged him eagerly not to send
them out of the country. Now a great herd of swine was feeding
there . . . and they begged him, "Send us to the swine, let us enter
them." So he gave them leave. And the unclean spirits came out,
and entered the swine; and the herd . . . rushed down the steep
bank . . . and were drowned in the sea.[2]

POSSESSED OR AFFLICTED?

Over time the terms and phrases Scripture uses to describe human
encounters with supernatural evils have changed somewhat in meaning. For example, the term *possessed,* utilized several times in some
translations,[3] might be better stated today as *afflicted,* one of the many
ways some versions describe a person captive to a demonic force. For
example, "the people also gathered from the towns around Jerusalem,
bringing the sick and those *afflicted* with unclean spirits, and they were
all healed."[4]

Note that these people could distinguish sickness/disease from
demonic affliction. In a similar passage, we find another term:

[Jesus] came down with them and stood on a level place, with a
great crowd of his disciples and a great multitude of people . . .
who came to hear him and to be healed of their diseases; and those
who were *troubled* with unclean spirits were cured.[5]

Here again, those who presented themselves for healing recognized a difference.[6]

Affliction can be explained as a spectrum that ranges from demonic influence "on" a person to the extreme of a demon actually "in" a person's body. One way to understand this concept is to consider the way alcohol makes a person drunk. Using medical instruments to study its effects on the brain, we would find that the first sips cause changes and reactions. As more and more is consumed, the body's responses become more pronounced and noticeable (bloodshot eyes, slurred speech, loss of coordination). Our investigation would utilize a spectrum that measured *levels* of inebriation: sober . . . tipsy . . . drunk.

This type of model can describe the progression from demons *on* a person to a demon *in* a person (the final stage is the only time a person is truly possessed). This continuum is demonstrated as a gradual progression of influence, from low-grade affliction to eventual possession. (Complete bodily possession generally is rare, despite Hollywood's fascination with it.)

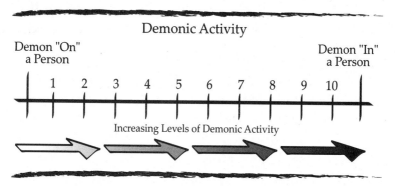

Demonic Activity

Demon "On" a Person

Demon "In" a Person

1 2 3 4 5 6 7 8 9 10

Increasing Levels of Demonic Activity

Demonic possession and various stages of demonization have been documented for thousands of years in cultures worldwide. The anthropologists, psychologists, sociologists, ministers and priests, and dedicated laypersons who have devoted their lives to studying such supernatural activity report an amazing consistency in the encountered cases. There are universal patterns, symptoms, behaviors, and rituals associated with affliction, and these phenomena are real.

WHAT IS A DEMON?

The Bible contains more details about the destruction and chaos around demonic affliction than about demons themselves. This isn't an oversight; the New Testament focus is on people being set free. In addition, the demonic world does not want to be understood—demons don't want to be revealed as a source of suffering and misery, preferring to see men and women directing their anger at one another or blaming God. On the other hand, it's erroneous to see demons in every circumstance or problem and behind every sin. Inexplicable behavior should not be prematurely labeled "demonic." Bible knowledge, spiritual discernment, and prayer are necessary tools to distinguish supernatural evil from natural misfortune or from the results of poor choices.

> Bible knowledge, spiritual discernment, and prayer are necessary tools to distinguish supernatural evil from natural misfortune or from the results of poor choices.

Jesus and his followers knew how to recognize what is truly demonic and how to set people free from demonic affliction. Demons don't have earthly bodies; they were often "in" the bodies of those Jesus healed. They seem to have a hierarchy that depends on their wickedness:

> When the unclean spirit has gone out of a man, he passes through waterless places seeking rest, but he finds none. Then he says, "I will return to my house from which I came." And when he comes he finds it empty, swept, and put in order. Then he goes and brings with him seven other spirits more evil than himself, and they enter and dwell there; and the last state of that man becomes worse than the first.[7]

The accounts of possession also reveal that demons can wield control in several ways: speaking, screaming, laughing, shaking, convulsing, seeing, and hearing. Most troublesome are the accounts of demons entering into a person and controlling thoughts, manipulating emotions, and creating visions and delusions.

Demonic affliction and possession also can distort a person's ability to make rational decisions:

> Then Satan entered into Judas called Iscariot . . . [who] went away and conferred with the chief priests and officers how he might betray him [Jesus] to them. And they were glad, and engaged to give him money. So he agreed, and sought an opportunity to betray him to them in the absence of the multitude.[8]

> During supper, when the devil had already put it into the heart of Judas Iscariot, Simon's son, to betray him, Jesus . . . rose from supper, laid aside his garments, and girded himself with a towel.[9]

It's not surprising that Satan, the very "source" of evil, had an active role in the betrayal of the man Judas knew to be Messiah. At the same time, *Christians do not need to fear demons—at all.* God has given us power over them; we must only understand what to do and how to do it.

DEMONS OF BIBLICAL PROPORTIONS

Although many ancient manuscripts contain elaborate myths about demonic forces, Christians uphold the Bible as the ultimate source for revealed truth.[10] Therein God doesn't reveal much about the origin or appearance of demons but emphasizes their weaknesses, trickery, and deceitfulness. Demons are dangerous only until they are confronted by the power of Jesus.

We know that demons can kill, are strong, and have what's been called a "Luciferian spirit"—that is, "It's all about me." Egregious self-absorption says, "I will, I want, I will get what I want, I will exalt myself."[11] We also know that numerous demons can afflict. As noted, when Jesus demanded a name from the spirit that possessed a man, it replied, "My name is Legion, for *we are many.*"

Although demons can be crafty and skillfully deceptive, it appears they have varied levels of intelligence. At times, they can be remarkably dumb. Once, a demon "shouted at the top of his voice, 'What do you want with me, Jesus, Son of the Most High God? Swear to God that you won't torture me!' For Jesus had said to him, 'Come out of this man, you evil spirit!'"[12]

This is amazing: The spirit acknowledged Jesus as God's Son, then it tried to get Jesus to "swear to God" he wouldn't act! The demon was invoking God's help against whatever Jesus might do to him, apparently thinking he could leverage one against the other.

———

In the early '80s, I visited a Houston church for a conference where the speaker was talking about demons. Suddenly, without warning, a man in the audience stood up, terror on his face. He left his chair, moved quickly to a column in the auditorium, positioned himself behind a supporting pole, and peered around it toward the stage, seeming to hope the speaker couldn't see him.

Making the scene comical was that the pole was a fraction of the man's body width—he couldn't hide behind it at all. Sadly, however, he demonstrated the characteristics of a demonically afflicted person. The speaker, not flustered in the least, easily took control. With the confidence of Jesus, he commanded the demons to come out of the man.

Stupidity or ignorance had led the demon to believe the man could hide behind the column. And, after the speaker had said, "I command you, by the authority of Jesus, to leave this man and to go to the dry places," someone asked, "Why did you send the demon there?" He said this phrase was from an exorcism in which demons shrieked, "Please don't send us to the dry places."

"As a result," he said, "we've been sending them there ever since."

How dumb is it for a demon to use the vocal chords of the afflicted person to name the very place he doesn't want to go! Later I realized that Scripture confirms what the demon said: "When an evil spirit comes out of a man, it goes through arid places seeking rest and does not find it."[13]

———

Although it's important to know some facts about demons, we don't need to dwell on them or focus on finding more details. History has shown repeatedly that any obsession with the demonic will always lead to tragedy.[14] One might even argue that, according to Genesis, the very first disobedient human choice was acting on something God had chosen to keep hidden.[15]

Many biblical narratives also reveal God's absolute authority over all creation. *There is not a balance of power or a struggle for control—God is in charge.* Demons fear the power of Jesus Christ, and even speaking his name can rebuke evil.

HOW SHOULD WE RESPOND?

Once again, Christians need not fear demons, "for he who is in you is greater than he who is in the world."[16] The Spirit of the living Christ lives in those who believe and trust in him; demons may not possess such a person.

> There was in their synagogue a man with an unclean spirit; and he cried out, "What have you to do with us, Jesus of Nazareth? Have you come to destroy us? I know who you are, the Holy One of God." But Jesus rebuked him, saying, "Be silent, and come out of him!" And the unclean spirit, convulsing him and crying with a loud voice, came out of him.[17]

The spirit could do nothing but obey Jesus' command. Invoking his name gives his disciples power over demons, so that even in the face of demonic activity believers can go forward without fear.

The first response in helping others suffering unusual havoc and chaos is to determine if the source of their problems is demonic. People can get into all kinds of trouble through sin, without any help from demons. One overarching biblical theme is that people have the choice to serve God or serve themselves. Mere belief in God is not the ticket to heaven: "Even the demons believe—and shudder."[18] Anyone can believe God exists but still maintain a life apart from him.

Sinful habits or lifestyles may open a person, unknowingly, to increasing

> Anyone can believe God exists but still maintain a life apart from him.

degrees of affliction. Immoral acts repetitiously committed over long periods can create opportunities for demonic forces to influence behavior and turn habits into bondage (a form of possession), weakening one's resistance to demonic influences.

So, demonic activity can occur in an individual's life through actions and attitudes contrary to God's clearly defined pattern for our lives. There is, however, another somewhat more complex way in which demonic activity can intrude. Though this isn't noted in Scripture, it's certainly not in conflict with Scripture; it comes from those who have studied and experienced the reality of demonic affliction.

Intrusive demonic activity unrelated to personal sinful practices seemingly can occur when a person has a highly traumatic experience, particularly one associated with extreme fear. An example might be an abusive parent's locking a small child in a dark closet. Years later, attempting to discern how his affliction began, the victim reflects on the terror with awareness that something tragic and significant happened in that moment.

How is this possible? Some think trauma of such intensity creates a fissure or weak spot—some type of break—in our natural "psychological armor." An unexpected tragedy or severe grief resulting from events beyond our control apparently can bring emotional and spiritual vulnerability to demonic intrusion.

This category is not the norm, however; *we* initiate most demonic activity. In addition to some obvious and common sinful practices, we can make ourselves more vulnerable by participating in biblically forbidden activities. Interest and participation in occult practices can be the door through which demons influence a person or become active in her life.

Scripture issues more than forty warnings about magic and witchcraft. Ouija boards, séances, fortune-telling, white magic, horoscopes, and tarot cards are just a few prohibited dark-arts tools. Many people report curiosity having turned into an obsession that has caused them damage and havoc.

Again, Jesus has taught his followers the disciplines needed to discern God's will: prayer, study of Scripture, baptism, tithing, Communion, worship, fasting, and service to one another. If a person appears to be demon-afflicted, and the practice of these disciplines makes no positive difference in her life, demonic activity is a real possibility. Signs may include bizarre behavior, prolonged depression, abnormal fears, even a persistent illness that cannot be diagnosed.

Simply recognizing evil influence is not sufficient for freedom. In most cases, a person suffers from demonization because of a spiritual blockage that has undermined her relationship with God. Bitterness, resentment, and unconfessed/unforgiven sin build a fortress behind which a demon has a legitimate claim—it's as if the spirit has the right to be there. Once a person experiences forgiveness, resentment and bitterness will leave; the fortress that protects the demon will be destroyed.

Mental and emotional blockages that protect evil spirits are not easily dislodged. Often there must be prayer for spiritual healing before deliverance can begin. Repentance and acceptance of God's forgiveness removes the barriers to physical healing and deliverance. It is during this process that the afflicted person may undergo physical displays or manifestations.

After reception of inner healing, physical healing and final deliverance can happen. Tools used during deliverance are prayer, the laying on of hands, the reading of Scripture, and the reverential use of Jesus Christ's name. This deeply personal and intimate process should not be opened to an audience beyond the participants. The dignity of the afflicted should be protected at all times.

A Deliverance Observed

Several decades ago I traveled to Southern California to attend a large church conference on the topic of demons, a subject on which I was quite naïve. On the second night, about two hundred people were praying near the front of the church, and many were praying out loud, so it got pretty noisy. Suddenly, over these sounds came an extremely loud voice, yelling one word. We were all startled to hear the F-word in a church.

Looking up, I noticed four or five men quietly surrounding another man—the source of the profanity—and gently leading him off the platform. Wanting to learn and to pray with them, I followed. We went to a confined room, where a man who seemed to have related and relevant experience immediately took leadership in praying for the man to be set free from a demonic presence.

What occurred over the next hour was one of the most amazing episodes of my life, my first and thus far only time to witness a fully possessed human being. This otherwise sophisticated gentleman would snap his teeth (trying to bite) and growl, his eyes glowing with hate. Then he would return to normal, and during those brief moments he would say, "Guys, I don't know what's happening. I'm not like this. This is not me. I'm not doing this." The fear in his eyes was exceeded only by his pleading: "Help me!" Suddenly he again would become demonically infused, growling and snapping.

The others didn't seem surprised—they'd dealt with this before. I hadn't and was stunned. I'd only read about such encounters. The men worked as a team, praying, alternately calling out for deliverance. However, no improvement occurred. The afflicted man continued to vacillate between ghoulish behavior and a kind of fearful innocence.

Finally, after nearly one hour, the demon cried out hauntingly, gutturally, *"Don't go get Becky!"* This made no sense to me, but the others instantly looked at each other, obviously knowing a Becky involved with the conference. One man went to get her. (Again, the stupidity of demons.)

Moments later Becky arrived. We'd been praying a long time; not having succeeded, we'd prayed louder. In the confines of a small, stuffy room, with several men praying in desperation and one demonized man terrorizing us all, we'd worked up quite a sweat. I remember being somewhat embarrassed that this well-dressed woman was entering what smelled like a postgame locker room.

Becky knew what was going on, took control of the situation with poise, and ordered the demonized man to sit down. He'd been leaning against the wall but now sat down facing her. She then ordered the demon not to speak or make itself evident in any way. She said to the man, "These men have prayed for you nearly an hour. The demon should have come out. The only thing that could allow it to stay in your life would be if it was hiding behind a fortress. And the likely fortress will be related to a lack of forgiveness. We are going to end this session. You are to go be alone with your Bible and with God. Ask God what areas in your life need forgiveness. Come back tomorrow morning at nine. They will meet you here and pray over you at that time."

Then she left. Her entire monologue had lasted less than two or three minutes. I thought, *So this is the "Becky" the demons fear?*

The next morning the afflicted man came on time to meet the team of men who'd prayed extensively the previous day. After just seconds of commanding the demon to come out, the man began to sense something had left him. He was joyful and certain that he'd been delivered.

Before long, the others went on their way. But I stopped him and asked if we could talk, as there was much I didn't understand. Graciously he consented, and we stood in the hallway as I asked questions: who was he, what was his job, where was he from, and above all, what exactly had happened, moment by moment, during his two-day ordeal?

He was a pastor in Canada, but was familiar with this area. As a child and youth he'd lived within a mile of this very Anaheim church building.

As a young teenager, with another boy his age, he had cornered his own younger sister in the garage, forced her into the backseat of a car, and assaulted her. Sometime later, he and his family moved away.

Decades passed. Now when he'd come back to the vicinity of the crime, a demonic presence consumed him and caused him to yell a horrible curse that described his own actions toward his sister.

Becky's words about forgiveness issues were true and twofold: He had never asked his sister for forgiveness, and he had involved a neighbor boy. The night before his deliverance, he had finally placed phone calls, seeking to make right what he had perpetrated many years before. His confession and repentance seemed to be the key to tearing down the fortress and breaking free from the demon.

I have since seen and sensed demonic affliction in many forms, but none compared with the intensity of this one. It became a model for me. Unforgiveness, resentment, and bitterness can give an excuse for demonic activity to remain in a life. With a cleansed heart, and with confession and forgiveness, a person can be set free from even the most insidious intrusion.

During his traveling ministry on earth, Jesus sent out seventy-two of his followers to tell others who he was. They returned with excitement and pride about what they'd accomplished, especially casting out demons. He said,

> I saw Satan fall like lightning from heaven. I have given you authority to trample on snakes and scorpions and to overcome all the power of the enemy; nothing will harm you. However, do not rejoice that the spirits submit to you, but rejoice that your names are written in heaven.[19]

In other words: "Don't get obsessed with your power over demons. That's truly not the big deal. Be excited that you have a relationship with *me*."

PART THREE

Crossing Over: The Upward Call

11

A Delightful Detour

——— ✳ ———

The First Heaven Is a Temporary Stopover
Before Permanent Paradise

We talk about heaven being so far away. It is within speaking distance to those who belong there. It is a prepared place for a prepared people.

D. L. MOODY

"If you build it, they will come."

Recognize that statement? If so, you've probably seen *Field of Dreams*, a film that manages to intertwine three universal interests: the pursuit of a dream, the nature of heavenly bliss, and the love of baseball (which may or may not be a love of yours). This whimsical movie requires us to suspend disbelief, what with the "voice" talking from a cornfield, old baseball players walking in and out of a centerfield "heaven," and time travel back to a Midwestern town in 1972.

The story centers on Ray Kinsella, who's struggling to scratch out a living on his farm. One day he hears a voice instructing him to build a baseball field in the middle of his cornfield. His long-suffering wife, Annie, encourages him to go for it despite her own misgivings. Townspeople suspect he's a few kernels short of a full cob. No matter— he heeds the mysterious voice's direction and pursues his dream, which catalyzes several paranormal events.

In the closing scene, Ray prepares to meet his long-dead father, John. They gather on the field Ray has carved out of his farmland. Ray stands along the chalk lines with Annie, their gaze turned toward home plate. There, standing with his back to them and pulling off his old-fashioned catcher's gear, is a young man dressed in the loosely fitting uniform he once wore as a minor leaguer.

Suddenly it dawns on Ray that he is witnessing a miracle. John Kinsella, his own father, has returned from "baseball heaven." John begins walking toward his son, looking around as if taking in the novelty of earth's air, the setting sun, and the smell of the grass.

Ray turns to Annie and says, "I only saw him years later, when he was worn down by life. What do I say to him?"

Father and son soon stand face-to-face.

"It's so beautiful here," says John. "For me, it's like a dream come true. Can I ask you something? Is this heaven?"

"It's Iowa," Ray answers.

"I could have sworn it was heaven."

"Is there a heaven?"

> Nearly all of us have an innate curiosity about where we'll end up.

"Oh, yeah—it's the place where dreams come true."

After a moment the two shake hands, but as the father walks away, Ray calls out, "Hey, Dad, want to play catch?"

"I'd like that," John replies.

They walk back onto the field together, Ray standing by the plate, John on the mound, and they begin tossing the ball. Just a little taste of heaven on earth.[1]

Movies like this, besides being fun escapist entertainment, may stir some questions after we shut off the DVD player and turn out the lights. What will my final destination look like? Will I recognize loved ones? What will I do there? Nearly all of us have an innate curiosity about where we'll end up.

Indeed, if you believe in life after death, you're in good company. Most religions uphold some form, whether that "life" is described as heaven, hell, reincarnation, soul sleep, limbo, or purgatory. Of the eight major religious groups, only two—atheists and certain Christian subsets—believe in annihilation, that after death we completely cease to exist.

Beliefs About What Happens After Death

Christian Protestant	
In Christ	To Heaven
Outside Christ	To Hell
Christian Catholic	
Sanctified	To Heaven
Partially Sanctified	To Purgatory
Unbaptized or In Sin	To Hell
Historical Catholic	
Death Before Christ	Limbo Until Resurrection
Infant Death	Limbo Permanently
Christian Subsets	
Outside Christ	Annihilation (Cease to Exist)
Conditional Immortality	Annihilation (Cease to Exist)
Christian Sect	
In Christ	Soul Sleep
Cultural Secularist	
All People	Heaven
Atheists	
All People	Annihilation (Cease to Exist)
Eastern / New Age	
All Believers	Reincarnation

Considering all the people claiming to believe in heaven, there's not a lot of solid instruction taking place regarding the destination most of us think we're heading toward. We can understand why there's not a lot of talk about hell—with its nightmarish imagery, we'd rather avoid the topic altogether. But what about heavenly wonders and glories? We should be wildly eager to learn as much as we can. Still, the information we get usually is sketchy and generalized. John Gilmore wrote that "silence on heaven by clergymen is puzzling. The pulpit is where one would expect to hear more about heaven. Yet . . . the matter is passed over briefly, if mentioned at all."[2]

Even in seminaries and classrooms, discussions of heaven are strangely absent. I've spent a lot of time in those classrooms, having earned six degrees in religious studies—an associate of arts in religion, a bachelor of arts in religion, a Master's in New Testament, a Master's of divinity, a Master's of theology in church history, and a doctorate of philosophy in historical theology. Throughout all those years I never took a single class on heaven. What's more, I don't recall a course on heaven even being offered. To make matters worse, I don't remember a single lecture on heaven or hell or even one vigorous discussion on the topic! As a result, when I became a college professor, I didn't lecture on the subject either. It wasn't until after pastoring for several decades that I finally began to study and preach on heaven.

> It seems to me that most of us know more about the vacation spot we'll be visiting next summer than we do about the place we're planning to spend eternity.

Believing in heaven is one thing, but what do we really *know*? It seems to me that most of us know more about the vacation spot we'll be visiting next summer than we do about the place we're planning to spend eternity.

Indeed, many of our perceptions of heaven come from the media. How can we form our opinions about something as important as "forever" from talk show hosts, celebrities on *Larry King Live*, fantasy books, or late-night guests? One man identified the concoction as "cosmic sausage." Our image of heaven, he wrote, is a combination of "childhood memories, tidbits from intellectual chopping blocks, and choice cuts from poetic doublespeak. Mixed in with the eclectic mass are down-home anecdote spices to add aroma and individual flavor."[3]

I enjoy baseball and have fond memories of growing up on a farm, even playing sports in the pasture (though not in a cornfield). Maybe there will be baseball and cornfields in heaven—but I know there will be far more than that. Surely far more than we can imagine.

So where *do* we turn for solid answers about heaven? It does make sense to take in the stories of people who have died and returned. As we've learned, those who have had near-death experiences and come back to share details about heaven provide helpful glimpses. I believe many of these reports are legitimate and credible. Yet they don't provide a complete picture, only disparate pieces we can attempt to put together. We need to turn to the most authoritative source of information if we want to get close to a true and accurate perspective.

OUR GUIDEBOOK TO THE GREAT BEYOND

It may not surprise you, this suggestion that we should go confidently to Scripture for insights into heaven, but you may be surprised at the reason. It's not just that the Bible is at the epicenter of theological belief for the faith with the greatest number of followers on earth. *We can go confidently to the Bible for answers about heaven because it's a completely trustworthy document.*

We know this because, while Scripture contains many spiritual claims that cannot be verified, it also contains countless statements that *can* be historically proven. When the provable statements are tested and prove to be accurate, we can know the "unprovable" statements have credibility.

This is not an unfamiliar concept. You and I make decisions all the time based on such reasoning. For example, if we've done business for years with someone who—every single time we've checked up on him—has showed himself trustworthy and honest, we know we can believe him when he tells us something that needs to be taken on faith, something that, for whatever reason, can't be double-checked.

Likewise, when it comes to Scripture's accuracy, the provable statements in its pages have been challenged repeatedly through the years and found to be historically, archeologically, and geographically correct. Using every accepted method of historical verification, the Bible has passed with flying colors. Is it any wonder, then, that we also can embrace unprovable claims and statements?

With this in mind, let's consider how Scripture answers two questions that, if we're honest, are foremost whenever we think of the afterlife:

Where will I go when I die?
What will I look like when I get there?

The Bible doesn't talk about just one heaven but three. Our first clue that there are multiple heavens could not be found any earlier. We see it from the start: God created the *heavens*—plural—and the earth.[4]

If you scanned this book's table of contents page, you may have been curious about two different chapters addressing two different heavens. Can that be right? Most of us have grown up hearing that when we die we go to heaven—that's it, end of story. But the Bible has much to say about what I'll call the *first heaven* and the *permanent heaven* (which we'll delve into at length in chapter 13).

It's clear that while the first heaven is temporary, the second heaven is permanent. Paul (in a letter to Christians in Corinth[5]) additionally makes reference to a third heaven, which we don't know much about.

Do these three heavens refer, as some have suggested, to layers of space in the universe? Some believe the first heaven is the space surrounding our stars and planets, the second heaven contains the galaxies beyond our own, and the third is where Christ-followers end up when they die.

Others believe the first heaven is the kingdom of heaven that is here now dwelling within us, while the second heaven is the one discussed in this chapter, meaning a temporary place believers go immediately after death until Christ returns, gathers his church (those who've died and those yet to die), and takes them to their permanent home in the third heaven described by Paul.

That viewpoint is certainly appealing. However, throughout *Heaven and the Afterlife* we're going to limit our discussion to what we know for sure by focusing on the two heavens directly pointed to in Scripture: a temporary heaven and a permanent heaven. If we were to number these, they'd be either numbers one and two or numbers two and three, depending upon your theological perspective. For our purposes, let's call them the first heaven and the permanent heaven; that seems to line up best with how the Bible refers to them.

FIRST HEAVEN: THE INITIAL STOP AFTER DEATH

What happens immediately after we die? Apparently, we leave our present earthly bodies and depart for someplace else, someplace better than where we are now, someplace where we're instantly in the presence of God. As Jesus was dying on the cross, he looked at the repentant thief next to him and said, "I tell you the truth, today you will be with me in paradise."[6] And when Paul wrote to the church in Philippi, he said, "I am torn between the two: I desire to depart [this life] and be with Christ, which is better by far; but it is more necessary for you that I remain in the body."[7]

One of the most fascinating passages regarding the first heaven is found in Luke's gospel, where Jesus tells a story about a beggar named Lazarus. About the time Lazarus died and went to heaven, a wealthy man also died, but he went to a very different place. While some would argue this is a parable and shouldn't be taken literally, it's the only occasion on which Jesus told a parable using an actual name, suggesting Lazarus may have been a real person. In any case, here's what Jesus had to say about the matter.

> In hell, where he [the wealthy man] was in torment, he looked up and saw Abraham far away, with Lazarus by his side. So he called

to him, "Father Abraham, have pity on me and send Lazarus to dip the tip of his finger in water and cool my tongue, because I am in agony with this fire."

But Abraham replied, "Son, remember that in your lifetime you received your good things, while Lazarus received bad things, but now he is comforted here and you are in agony. And besides all this, between us and you a great chasm has been fixed, so that those who want to go from here to you cannot, nor can anyone cross over from there to us."

He answered, "Then I beg you, father, send Lazarus to my father's house, for I have five brothers. Let him warn them, so that they will not also come to this place of torment."[8]

It seems the first heaven, to which we're transported immediately after death, is separated from hell by an impassible gulf. Furthermore, the people there are not only conscious and aware, but they also have memories of events and people from their years on earth.

HEAVENLY BODIES: FACT OR FICTION?

This raises another matter, having to do with our bodies. After all, how can we see without eyes? How can we talk without lips? Don't we leave these bodies behind when we die? Do we have any kind of body at all at that point, or are we disembodied spirits who can't kick the habit of using words and phrases that made sense back when we had forms that could hear and touch and thirst?

Actually, many verses suggest we will have some sort of physical body in this temporary (first) heaven. Randy Alcorn, author of an exhaustive work on heaven,[9] makes this case by noting the same account of Lazarus and the wealthy man, who certainly appear to have physical forms. Alcorn also references Christ's conversation with the thief on the cross, explaining that "today you will be with me in paradise" implies not only an immediate transition but a very personal one, pointing to a conscious, bodily existence on the other side.

Finally, Alcorn cites people coming and going from the first heaven *wearing bodies*. For example, when Enoch was caught up into heaven, he didn't leave anything behind[10]–can't we assume he took his body with him? When Moses and Elijah descended on the Mount of Transfiguration, they had bodies.[11] Did this apply only to them, or does it apply to the rest of us as well?

Whatever kind of body we'll have, one thing we know for sure: It's not the final, permanent, perfected, resurrected body we'll receive later when taken into the permanent heaven. I believe this is what Paul implies:

> We know that if the earthly tent we live in [our physical bodies] is destroyed, we have a building from God, an eternal house in heaven, not built by human hands. Meanwhile [after our earthly bodies are gone and before we get our eternal bodies] we groan, longing to be clothed with our heavenly dwelling.[12]

He apparently is giving us a glimpse into when, if not disembodied spirits, we're at least spirits clothed in something imperfect and temporary. This is the season between our individual death and Christ's triumphant return, when our spirit longs for perfection and completion, when we yearn to be clothed in permanent, resurrected bodies worthy of dwelling forever with Jesus in an eternal heaven.

Britain's N. T. Wright, one of the world's foremost Bible scholars, affirms that "Paul speaks of 'the redemption of our bodies' [Romans 8:23]. There is no room for doubt as to what he means; God's people are promised a new type of bodily existence, the fulfillment and redemption of our present bodily life."[13]

But when? When do we transition from the first to the permanent heaven, the point at which we finally get our redeemed and resurrected bodies? *When Christ returns to earth.* In this moment, Jesus will descend from the clouds, and those who believe on him—the living and the dead—will rise together to meet him.[14] For this grand event, if we are alive and well on earth, these bodies will be transformed into our new, permanent ones.[15] If we have already died (and have been waiting in the first heaven for this day) our bodies will be resurrected from the grave, clothed in glorified bodies, and transported to meet Jesus in the sky.

You might wonder: What if a person's earthly body is long gone? What if he died a very long time ago? Or drowned at sea? Or was cremated? *How* would he be raised from the grave?

Paul, asked this question, answered with an analogy from the harvest:

> When you sow, you do not plant the body that will be, but just a seed. . . . So will it be with the resurrection of the dead. The body that is sown is perishable, it is raised imperishable; it is sown in dishonor, it is raised in glory; it is sown in weakness, it is raised in power; it is sown a natural body, it is raised a spiritual body.[16]

In other words, our decomposing earthly bodies are like seeds planted in the ground, and even though they're "sown in dishonor," in time returning to the dirt, they will be gloriously raised. From the seed comes the flower. Our new bodies will be wonderful, and they will never die or fade away.

NEW AND IMPROVED?

Paul uses the illustration of Christ being the "firstfruits," which means exactly what it sounds like. The firstfruits of the harvest is important as a sign of what will come—it's a prototype of what will follow. Paul says, in essence, "If you want to know what resurrection will be like for you, look at Jesus."

Some have asked, since there are isolated cases in both Testaments of people being brought back from the dead before Jesus was resurrected, wouldn't they technically be the firstfruits? No. While some people did come back to life, they were brought back into their earthly bodies, which eventually had to experience death again. Without diminishing the miracle of these events, these people were divinely *resuscitated,* not raised as Jesus was into a new body and immortality. Complete *resurrection* means being raised and never dying again.

While we're on the subject of people who were raised from the dead, there is one most unusual verse in the Bible—so unusual (some would say disturbing) that it's rarely spoken of. Yet it's there, and it deserves to be examined.

According to Matthew, at the moment Jesus died, an earthquake rocked Jerusalem, and many tombs split open. People who'd been buried outside the city came back to life and began making their way back into town.[17] Maybe this sounds like a low-budget horror flick, but there it is, in Scripture. This story is so profound that it's easy to miss the point. What in the world happened? And more important: *why?*

I believe this was God's way of saying, "I'm showing you that what I say is true. It's too soon to bring *all* of you out of the grave, but I want you to know who I am, so I'm giving you a small sampling of what is yet to come. The power you see around you today—you will experience firsthand in your own life."

Jesus paved the way; you and I will one day follow in his steps. We will be like him. So what is his resurrected body *really* like? For starters, it's not limited by time and space. After all, on earth, following his resurrection, he entered a locked room without using doors or windows; he disappeared from the believers in Emmaus and reappeared elsewhere.[18]

Jesus' resurrected body *also* was tangible and physical in every sense. After his resurrection he could speak and be heard by human ears. He could be seen by human eyes. His body could be touched. Assuring his frightened disciples that it was actually him standing before them, he said, "Look at my hands and my feet. It is I myself! Touch me and see; a ghost does not have flesh and bones, as you see I have."[19] And there's something humorous about his asking, "Do you have anything here to eat?"[20] He enjoyed meals with his friends.

Jesus' body was still, well . . . *him.* Sure, it may have been transformed, changed, immortal—but Jesus was still Jesus. He looked like himself; he was recognized by Mary Magdalene and others. His transformed body still bore the scars from what had happened to him during his earthly life.

Fear of death is universal to every people, era, and culture; we often associate dying with pain and loss. The good news is that, beyond the veil, we don't have to be afraid. Immediately after death, you and I, conscious and alert, will be transported to a new place. We will be able to remember and reason. Whether we experience a season of being spirits without bodies or are given a "temporary body," we eventually will be clothed in transformed, resurrected, glorified bodies just like the one Jesus modeled for us after his resurrection.

But before you and I get to relax and enjoy the next hundred thousand millennia—and beyond—in the permanent heaven that's to be our home forever, one more event must occur. The very name—judgment day—strikes terror into the hearts of many. But have no fear: it's an awards banquet, really. And once you realize what it's about and truly grasp what's going to happen, you will never look at your life—or your death—the same way again.

12

A Rewarding
Experience

—— ✳ ——

God's Children Have Nothing to Fear of Judgment Day

God examines both rich and poor, not according to their lands
and houses, but according to the riches of their hearts.

AUGUSTINE

Susan edged as gracefully as she could across the threshold of the
CEO's office door. Ms. Anderson's e-mail had asked her to come
ASAP, but then she'd added a postscript with the reassuring words:
"Don't worry—it's good news." The leader of the entire worldwide
corporation had then punctuated that P.S. with a smiley face. That was
a good sign . . . right?

At the appointed time, Susan arrived to find John—Ms. Anderson's
admin—standing at the door, holding it open to usher Susan in, with
a broad smile that seemed to offer reassurance. Then why was she so
nervous?

"Welcome, Susan! Thank you for coming promptly." Ms. Anderson
glanced up, this time offering an actual smiley face. She motioned for

Susan to sit in the chair beside the desk as her eyes went back to her monitor. "Give me just a moment—I need to finish this."

Susan sank warily into the comfortable leather without a word—with hardly a breath. And she waited, as if perhaps Ms. Anderson might even forget she was there. For what seemed an eternity—a full thirty seconds—she glanced about the office, only her eyes moving. She scanned book titles from a shelf behind the massive oak desk. But she couldn't seem to distract herself from the nagging voice in the back of her mind, warning with despondency, *This can't truly be good. It feels like being called to the principal's office.*

"So, Susan," Ms. Anderson's voice halted the musings. "We need to talk."

Here it comes.

"I have great news for you," she said. "You've been doing superb work lately. How long has it been since you joined us?" Her expression still seemed warm and sincere.

"Um, six months, ma'am," Susan replied.

"Well, you've been achieving remarkably. And your manager has brought you specifically to my attention."

Just what I don't want.

"Susan, we want to reward you."

Susan responded quickly, almost interrupting. "Oh—you don't need to."

Ms. Anderson paused, still smiling, but cocked her head quizzically.

"I mean, that's not why I've been working hard," Susan said. "I didn't do it for a reward."

The boss nodded as her smile broadened. "I know, Susan."

"I know you know, ma'am," Susan responded. "So you really don't need to do anything more for me. I'm just happy to be a part of this company. That's honor enough."

There was an awkward pause for another few eternal seconds as the CEO continued to hold that smile, then said, "Susan, I know I don't have to." She glanced down at a folder. As she opened it, without looking up, she added—rather firmly—"But I *want* to. So let me tell you what I'm going to do for you. . . ."

Rewards Earned

What if I were to tell you that God the Father, CEO of the universe, for his own reasons wants to reward *you*? Many Scriptures tell us this is true. Realize that we're not talking about getting into heaven; that happens because of what Jesus has done. We don't and couldn't ever *earn* entrance into heaven.

So here you are, a part of God's people already, and you're thankful to be serving the kingdom. Your place is secure. Then you see this memo from God—his Word. And it tells you in no uncertain terms that you're going to meet him face-to-face and will discuss your evaluation. Intimidated?

> What if I were to tell you that God the Father, CEO of the universe, for his own reasons wants to reward *you*?

The good news is you're very close to the boss's son—Jesus. And he's made it clear to you what's important to his Father. Let's prepare for the job review and see what God himself says—the criteria by which you'll be weighed. It's no secret, and what's more, he wants you to succeed. He's rooting for you!

So here we are, right now, living this life. The question that should be driving us daily is *What are those things God wants me to invest in that will bring rewards in heaven?* The great news is he's given you all the directions you need.

Understanding the Judgments

Several years ago I attended a relative's funeral and afterward stood around talking with family members. We were commenting about the fact that this man had become a Christian so late in life—in his seventies. The frankness of his son's next comment surprised me. He said,

"I have no question about where he'll spend eternity. But I certainly doubt he'll get any rewards."

His bluntness aside, my cousin apparently understood the issues. Salvation comes about only by what Christ did on the cross. We cannot add to it; it's provided for us as we accept the forgiveness his death affords us. However, having been saved, there *are* actions that can result in heavenly rewards. One might think getting to heaven is all the reward we need. Possibly so. But God views it differently, and he openly discusses the rewards many will receive.

In all candor scholars and theologians do not agree on certain matters about judgment day, including how rewards or punishment will be handed out. Here are the key areas of dispute: Are there two judgments—one called "the great white throne judgment" (only for unbelievers) and the other called "the judgment seat of Christ" (for those "in Christ")? Or do these refer to one judgment for all people?[1] Why is the judgment seat referred to as the "bema seat"? Is the bema seat only for affirming and rewarding, or could it be for issuing punishment as well?

Paul said, "We must all appear before the judgment seat [Greek: *bema*] of Christ, that each one may receive what is due him for the things done while in the body, whether good or bad."[2] He shed more light on this in an earlier letter:

> If any man builds on this foundation using gold, silver, costly stones, wood, hay or straw, his work will be shown for what it is, because the Day will bring it to light. It will be revealed with fire, and the fire will test the quality of each man's work. If what he has built survives, he will receive his reward. If it is burned up, he will suffer loss; he himself will be saved, but only as one escaping through the flames.[3]

The word *bema* is used in contemporary Greek culture to refer to the stage area in a synagogue or church. This is the place occupied by a pastor and a choir in a Christian church. But in Bible times, the term referred to a "judgment seat"[4]; in simplest terms, it was a raised platform, occupied by a ruler, from which decisions, sentences, or punishments were announced. Influenced by Greek athletic contests, Paul used *bema* in a different fashion: he viewed it more like a judge's place at the end of an event, rewarding the athletes for their levels of accomplishment. Highlighting this theme, he wrote:

> Do you not know that in a race all the runners run, but only one gets the prize? Run in such a way as to get the prize.
> Everyone who competes in the games goes into strict training. They do it to get a crown that will not last; but we do it to get a crown that will last forever.[5]

Adopting *this* understanding of *bema,* as opposed to that of a Roman magistrate issuing judgments, leads many people to view the judgment seat of Christ as a place of reward. Considering the "reward" language in Paul's letters, we might conclude that this event sounds dramatically different from John's reference to the great white throne judgment[6] and allusions to the "lake of fire" (more on that in chapter 15).

All of this raises an obvious question: For *what* will we be rewarded? The Bible is straightforward on this topic, and the following is a partial list.[7]

INFLUENCING OTHERS FOR RIGHTEOUSNESS

The Old Testament uses poetic language to explain God's priorities: "Those who are wise will shine like the brightness of the heavens, and those who lead many to righteousness, like the stars for ever and ever."[8] God wants us to influence other people to righteousness—to have a right relationship with him.

And God promises to remember this work when evaluation time comes in the life hereafter: "God is not unjust; he will not forget your work and the love you have shown him as you have helped his people and continue to help them."[9]

When it comes to influencing others to righteousness, though, perhaps you're thinking, *Billy Graham—sure, he'll get a big reward. He preached to stadiums full of people. And those old-time missionaries, who used to pack all their belongings in pine coffins knowing they probably wouldn't go home alive. And the martyrs who died at the stake for believing in Jesus.*

Actually, though, the rewards will be distributed widely. This is because we participate in righteousness vicariously. Jesus himself plainly said as much:

> Anyone who receives a prophet because he is a prophet will receive a prophet's reward, and anyone who receives a righteous man because he is a righteous man will receive a righteous man's reward. And if anyone gives even a cup of cold water to one of these little ones because he is my disciple, I tell you the truth, he will certainly not lose his reward.[10]

Amazing! It's like a championship basketball team: you might be the one who swishes the winning shot at the buzzer or the one sitting on the end of the bench waving a towel and shouting encouragement. You're all going to get a ring.

> **If we have received a saint sent from God, we are going to participate in that saint's level of reward.**

If we have received a saint sent from God, we are going to participate in that saint's level of reward. So if your church received Billy Graham when he came to your community, you will receive the same reward as Billy for that. This is because of the honor shown to those who have been sent by God.

CARING FOR OTHERS

There's also the significance of hospitality to strangers—specifically, how we've cared for the downtrodden and the poor. Jesus told a parable about the King separating the sheep (those with faith in Christ) from the goats (those without). He spoke of the hungry, thirsty, naked, sick, and alienated. This reward goes to those who cared for these people, whom he describes as "the least of my brothers." Caring for the needy is the same as caring for Jesus himself.[11]

We want to hang out with the desirable people, don't we? But Jesus says,

> When you give a luncheon or dinner, do not invite your friends, your brothers or relatives, or your rich neighbors; if you do, they

may invite you back and so you will be repaid. But when you give a banquet, invite the poor, the crippled, the lame, the blind, and you will be blessed. Although they cannot repay you, you will be repaid at the resurrection of the righteous.[12]

We will be rewarded for how we treated outcasts, outsiders, and the oppressed.

RESPONDING TO THOSE WHO HATE US

Another way we'll receive rewards involves our response to suffering, mistreatment, and injustice. James says, "Blessed is the man who perseveres under trial, because when he has stood the test, he will receive the crown of life that God has promised to those who love him."[13] Our reaction to being treated poorly is factored into the equation of heavenly compensation.

On persecution, consider Jesus' Sermon on the Mount, in which he says,

> *Blessed* are you when people insult you, persecute you and falsely say all kinds of evil against you because of me. Rejoice and be glad, because great is your reward in heaven, for in the same way they persecuted the prophets who were before you.[14]

Some have sacrificed enormously for the faith. God says they're going to be rewarded for that—if not here, then in the life to come. The Bible is clear in its admonishment to "love your enemies."[15] There are eternal rewards for doing so.

USING OUR GIFTS

We'll also be held accountable—and receive rewards—for the appropriate use of our abilities, time, and resources. In one parable, a rich man entrusted his servants with different amounts of money, according to each man's ability. One invested his share, succeeded exponentially, and was rewarded greatly. Another doubled his share and was rewarded accordingly. The third just buried his portion in the ground and didn't do anything with it—didn't invest, didn't develop what he was given at all. The deeply displeased master took away his share and gave it to another.[16]

Jesus told this parable to illustrate that we should fully utilize the gifts and resources he has given us. We are responsible to develop these to their potential, and we can expect to receive rewards accordingly.

What *Are* These Rewards?

The Bible refers to our rewards as "crowns."[17] Literal crowns, or is this figurative language? I suspect they're not literal, though from our vantage point it's impossible to know for sure. One thing we *can* know: When we get them—whether literal or figurative—we'll be thrilled to receive them.

We know these crowns won't pass away but will last forever. Ever gone to a garage sale and seen a whole tableful of trophies selling for a nickel apiece? They once seemed important but are virtually worthless now. Conversely, eternal rewards will not diminish in value.

Many biblical passages talk about crowns, and there are at least five crown-types involved in heaven's reward system.

The Crown of Life

This is awarded to those who have endured suffering, those men and women who "gutted it out" through hardship and adversity. Jesus told the church in Smyrna: "Do not be afraid of what you are about to suffer. . . . Be faithful, even to the point of death, and I will give you the crown of life."[18] James also mentions this crown: "Blessed is the man who perseveres under trial, because when he has stood the test, he will receive the crown of life that God has promised to those who love him."[19]

The Crown of Glory

This is for church leaders who lead and guide with humility. Peter wrote,

> Be shepherds of God's flock that is under your care, serving as overseers—not because you must, but because you are willing, as God wants you to be; not greedy for money, but eager to serve; not lording it over those entrusted to you, but being examples to

the flock. And when the Chief Shepherd appears, you will receive the crown of glory that will never fade away.[20]

THE CROWN OF REJOICING

This is given to those who pour their lives into other people—uplifting, encouraging, serving, mentoring, and caring for others. That's a great name for it too. We'll see all those people we invested our lives in and joyfully dance on heaven's streets. As Paul says, "What is our hope, or joy, or crown of rejoicing? Is it not even you in the presence of our Lord Jesus Christ at His coming?"[21]

THE CROWN OF RIGHTEOUSNESS

This is given to those who crave intimacy with God. It's the special award for those who yearn for Jesus' coming: "There is in store for me the crown of righteousness, which the Lord, the righteous Judge, will award to me on that day—and not only to me, but also to all who have longed for his appearing."[22]

THE IMPERISHABLE CROWN

Using athletic competition to illustrate, again Paul explains,

Do you not know that those who run in a race all run, but one receives the prize? Run in such a way that you may obtain it. And everyone who competes for the prize is temperate in all things. Now they do it to obtain a perishable crown, but we for an imperishable crown.[23]

This crown is called imperishable to contrast it with the temporal awards Paul's contemporaries pursued. The olive wreath—the "crown" for competitors—was sure to wither away. The ever-enduring "endurance crown" is given for profound examples of self-denial and perseverance.

THE PURPOSE OF THE CROWNS

Suppose you end up with a few heavenly crowns—maybe even a whole cartload. What exactly will you do with them? We'll be given accolades for some reason, but what is it? John gives a clue:

The twenty-four elders fall down before him who sits on the throne, and worship him who lives for ever and ever. They lay their crowns before the throne and say:
"You are worthy, our Lord and God,
to receive glory and honor and power,
for you created all things,
and by your will they were created
and have their being."[24]

The crowns will be given us so that we can give them back to the Creator of all things. Scripture suggests we will be so awestruck by Almighty God—we will find him so awesomely all-consuming and entirely sufficient—that with rejoicing we will return rewards to him as an act of worship.

Are you one of those who dread the thought of judgment day, when the celestial CEO will deliver your performance review? The thought justifiably gives us pause—and motivates us to carefully consider our actions and attitudes. But God's children need not fear that day, for it will be a day of reward, not punishment. I appreciate the perspective of Frederick Buechner:

The New Testament proclaims that at some unforeseeable time in the future, God will bring down the final curtain on history, and there will come a day on which all our days and all the judgments upon us and all our judgments upon each other will themselves be judged. The judge will be Christ. In other words, the one who judges us most finally will be the one who loves us most fully.[25]

Jesus himself said, "I tell you the truth, whoever hears my word and believes him who sent me has eternal life and will not be condemned; he has crossed over from death to life."[26] The equation is simple, really: Influence others toward righteous living, care for the poor and oppressed, love your enemies, and use wisely your God-given gifts. Then anticipate a delightful reward.

13

Beyond Halos, Harps, and Hymns

———— ✳ ————

Permanent Heaven Is a Place
of Riches, Rest, and Rewards

The best is yet to be.

JOHN WESLEY

Suppose you go downtown tomorrow and select a busy corner to conduct a survey. With clipboard and pen, you'd say to passersby, "Excuse me, can you tell me the first things that pop into your head when you think of heaven?"

Assuming people actually stopped to answer, I imagine you'd discover recurring themes in their responses. In fact, you'd probably hear, over and over, the words *clouds, pearly gates, angels, harps, halos, streets of gold, St. Peter, white robes,* and *choirs.* Some may add idyllic images of rainbow-filled skies, majestic mountain peaks, and sunsets over oceans. Perhaps a few would speak of reunions with deceased family members, friends, and pets.

With these prevalent "heavenly" images floating through our minds, it's no wonder we don't get more excited about floating up to heaven. Talking with Christians and non-Christians over the years, I've discovered that most in *both* groups have a lackluster impression of heaven. I like how John Eldredge puts it:

> Nearly every Christian I have spoken with has some idea that eternity is an unending church service. We have settled on an image of the never-ending sing-along in the sky, one great hymn after another, forever and ever amen. And our heart sinks. *Forever and ever? That's it? That's the good news?* And then we sigh and feel guilty that we are not more "spiritual." We lose heart, and we turn once more to the present to find what life we can.[1]

What do *you* think heaven will be like? Ever hoped there's more than what many seem to believe—that we'll spend eternity sitting on clouds, wearing white robes? Some people believe we will turn into angels, which might be an improvement over the monotonous harp-hymn scenario—hey, at least we could fly from cloud to cloud and visit friends.

When you think of heaven in these terms, what emotions do they evoke? Boredom? Disinterest? Even dread? We need to press the delete button on our misguided, mundane notions of what eternity holds in store. To that end, let's spend some time exploring—and correcting—misconceptions about heaven and begin painting a more accurate portrait of what we can expect.

DISPELLING MYTHS

Where do some of these crazy ideas and images come from? Are they from the Bible? Surprisingly, the answer is yes. Well, sort of. While many of these impressions come from Scripture, they've been misapplied and misconstrued. Unfortunately, the resulting outlook many of us carry around is a far cry from the rich realities that await us. C. S. Lewis addressed this:

> There is no need to be worried by facetious people who try to make the Christian hope of heaven ridiculous by saying they do not want "to spend eternity playing harps." The answer to such people is that if they cannot understand books written for grown-

ups, they should not talk about them. All the scriptural imagery (harps, crowns, gold, etc.) is, of course, a merely symbolic attempt to express the inexpressible.

Musical instruments are mentioned because for many people (not all) music is the thing known in the present life which most strongly suggests ecstasy and infinity. Crowns are mentioned to suggest the fact that those who are united with God in eternity share His splendor and power and joy. Gold is mentioned to suggest the timelessness of heaven (gold does not rust) and the preciousness of it. People who take these symbols literally might as well think that when Christ told us to be like doves, He meant that we were to lay eggs.[2]

Many images we get hung up on were recorded in the Bible–mainly by John in Revelation–in *attempts* to convey what heaven is like. Human language has severe limitations, especially for describing the indescribable. I suppose we could say John and other biblical writers did the best they could with the tools at their disposal–words on paper. So when considering heaven, we can use the biblical account as a framework and let our imaginations run wild. Even then, we probably can't get close to God's everlasting wonders and delights.

Try this for starters: If you want to know what heaven *feels* like, think of your deepest longings, those insatiable soul-cravings for love, acceptance, purpose, worth, intimacy, belonging. Now imagine what it would feel like to have those longings satisfied in a more abundant fashion than you've ever dreamed. Now multiply that feeling by infinity. Suddenly, heaven starts to sound exciting and enticing.

> If you want to know what heaven *feels* like, think of your deepest longings, those insatiable soul-cravings for love, acceptance, purpose, worth, intimacy, belonging.

NO BOREDOM ALLOWED

In his book *Heaven,* Randy Alcorn helps us see eternity in new and fresh ways, unabashedly setting before us a topic that's been circumvented by most erudite contemporary thinkers. But he goes beyond why-aren't-you-talking-more-about-heaven; his greatest contribution might be portraying heaven as fun. Yes, *fun*![3]

Why we would think of heaven in any other way is beyond me. The Master Designer of all creativity and all things good would never have his most loved friends (us) in unending boredom, slogging through an eternity of navel-gazing, chanting, and yoga. Now *that* would be hell.

Heaven is for rest, riches, and reward. There will be plants, animals (perhaps even pets), music, games—everything that's good and wonderful *now* will be better *then*. There will be cities, or one major city. There will be buildings, art, culture, and music. There likely will be goods, services, major events, transportation, and communications.

What's more, there will be education. You'll continue to develop and grow. You'll have no impairments, no aversions for learning. We often associate learning with drudgery (probably from being stuck in stuffy classrooms with stern teachers), but learning and discovering will become most pleasurable.

One obstacle to learning adequately now is time. There, you'll have plenty of "time." A great frustration for me here on earth is being kept from so many books I want to read. I plan to spend part of my eternity reading every book worthy of my attention.

Let's be honest—we have a hard time grasping the concept of *forever*. We get dismayed at thinking eventually heaven's newness and excitement will wear off. What then, sitting around with nothing to do? That's our earthbound mind talking. We find it tough to fathom that God, endlessly creative and imaginative, will introduce new, amazing things for us to enjoy throughout eternity.

What Will We Do in Heaven?

Envision standing in a throng of billions, everyone's breath held with anticipation, inspiration like the wind sweeping the multitudes, and suddenly a song—stirred in our souls by God himself—begins to swell. Imagine the sound of several *billion* voices raised in worship of every style. In heaven, we will sing, but not just any song: new music written for us by the Holy Spirit himself.[4]

And if music isn't your particular source of inspiration, take heart—heaven will feature far more. Everything we *do* will be passionate, heartfelt worship, including leadership tasks and roles we'll be privileged to assume. God created us to be his heirs and inherit the earth and reign over the land—not with the power-hungry leadership prevalent here on the first earth but with the servant-leadership that so characterizes the very heart of our Lord Jesus Christ.

In heaven you'll be involved in leading. You will be a ruler. Governance there is not about being the boss of somebody else to lord it over them. No! Our ruling will be part of the *serving* plan of the entire universe over which God has ordained us to be coeternal rulers.[5] If you've wanted more responsibility, you're about to get it. Consider just a few promises:

> If we endure, we will also reign with him.[6]

> To him who overcomes and does my will to the end, I will give authority over the nations.[7]

> To him who overcomes, I will give the right to sit with me on my throne, just as I overcame and sat down with my Father on his throne.[8]

In addition to some kind of ruling responsibility, I also believe we'll enjoy something nearly all of us like to do—eating. After all, we know that Jesus—in his resurrected body—ate and drank with the disciples.[9] John creates a bountiful image: "On each side of the river stood the tree of life, bearing twelve crops of fruit, yielding its fruit every month. And the leaves of the tree are for the healing of the nations."[10]

WE'LL BE THRILLED TO GO TO WORK

Some believe there will be no work in heaven, and perhaps here the fear of boredom surfaces: What will we *do*? I believe work indeed will be part of our heavenly experience, though in a much different way than we typically think.

Want to understand what heaven will be like? Look at earth *before* the fall, before the distortion of sin. Here's what we discover: work predated evil. That's because we're made in God's image, and he is creative. In his image, we are creators. Thus we will "work."

Heavenly work will *not* be drudgery. Everything—and I mean *everything*, including work—changed after sin entered this planet. The ground, upon which an agrarian economy is based, was "cursed." Not that dirt is somehow evil—rather, to work the soil, to produce crops from it, now requires toil and strain and aching muscles. Whereas humanity once knew only a spectacular garden, now we face thorns and thistles. Work requires the "sweat of your brow."[11]

If you're thoroughly fulfilled with your vocation, then you're experiencing a little slice of heaven here and now. You already know work can be joyous and gratifying. If you find work arduous and dull, you have much to look forward to, for your work in heaven—what God has arranged for you—will be a delight!

It's inherently inadequate to envision heaven with earthly examples, but to stimulate your imagination, do two things. First, *picture what work would be like without your associated negatives.* Strip out the downsides and detriments. Never again will you have a demanding boss, crabby colleagues, relentless deadlines, mountains of paper work, income taxes, customer complaints, snarled commutes, backaches, or tedium. No more chore and bore—work is continually invigorating and inspiring. Sound like something you could enjoy for a long, long time?

Next, *think of your dream job—the absolute best description you could write for yourself.* If you're passionate about gardening, you might be in charge of designing and tending botanical gardens. If you love to cook, perhaps you'll be a chef at one of heaven's many fine restaurants. If you enjoy nothing more than being around animals, you might run a stable full of celestial creatures. Be sure, too, that there will be many fascinating roles we as yet know nothing about.

What About Those Robes and Harps?

It's both amusing and frustrating to see how harps and heaven have become so interconnected. Let's see where the whole harp idea comes from.

I saw what looked like a sea of glass mixed with fire and, standing beside the sea, those who had been victorious over the beast. . . . They held harps given them by God and sang the song of Moses the servant of God and the song of the Lamb.[12]

Another harp reference comes where John describes the four living creatures, along with the twenty-four elders, holding harps.[13]

Obviously, the harp was a familiar instrument for John. In the original language, *harp* is similar to the word that gives us *guitar*. John saw stringed and wind instruments. Since the ancient writers didn't know about guitars and pianos and many other instruments, it seems reasonable to assume that the harps and horns represent music and worship in general. We'd have a different image of heaven if the biblical text described creatures holding saxes and bongo drums. The point is that there will be music—and plenty of it—for every taste and preference.

Similarly, to these writers accustomed to traveling hot, dusty roads, robes were the clothing they would have found familiar and comfortable. That the robes they saw were white—and could *stay* white—simply made them more special than anything they'd seen or worn. Likewise, your heavenly wardrobe will be something you're used to, something you find familiar, comfortable—but with an unexpected flair that exceeds anything you've ever owned.

HUMANS ARE NOT AND WILL NOT BE ANGELS

We've seen what Hollywood has portrayed. We know what Oprah says. We've heard comforting words from well-meaning but uninformed friends at funerals. But the definitive source on this matter—the Bible—gives us the answer we can rely on, and that answer tells us people will not become angels.

To be sure, there are angels in heaven—"thousands upon thousands, and ten thousand times ten thousand."[14] In one passage, Jesus says in heaven we will be *like* the angels in that we'll have no need for marriage. Some misinterpret this to mean we will turn into angels, but this text is comparing marital status, not species. Over and over the fact is driven home that angels and humans have never been—and never will be—one and the same.

Our creation stories are different. Angels were created before humankind was given opportunity to walk the earth. Man showed up on the scene later, was created in God's image, and then was ranked a little lower than the angels.[15]

Our purposes are different. Again, angels are "ministering spirits, sent forth to minister for them who shall be heirs of salvation."[16] Humankind was created to enjoy fellowship with God, becoming his heirs and joint-heirs with Christ.

Our destinies are different. The first angel to fall into rebellion talked a third of the angelic forces into joining him. The destiny of the devil and his fallen angels is to be cast into an eternal fire prepared especially for them.[17] In contrast, when Adam and Eve rebelled and led all humankind into a state of sin, God took a much different approach, taking the punishment upon himself so that we could be redeemed and restored back into intimate fellowship with him. While he didn't take on the nature of the angels in order to rescue them, he became a man to rescue us.[18] The angels will not be given dominion in heaven; when God created man he gave him authority over the earth and one day will give him authority in heaven (the new earth).[19] Paul says in heaven we'll even receive authority to judge angels.[20]

HEAVEN'S LOCATION

We talk of heaven being "up there" or even "in the clouds." Clouds *are* mentioned in conjunction with heaven. For instance, when Jesus returns, we will see him descending on the clouds of the sky.[21] God spoke from a cloud at the transfiguration.[22] But the idea that heaven is *in* the clouds, and that we might spend eternity reclining on them, is misdirected.

We shouldn't think of heaven as a long way away; it may be much, *much* closer than we think. "In the beginning God created the heavens and the earth."[23] He looked on all he had created and said it was very good.[24] Then sin sent his handiwork spiraling toward death and decay; one day, the first heavens and earth would need to be destroyed, replaced with a heaven and earth that would be forever indestructible and perfect.

The Bible is filled with related references. God said, "Behold, I will create new heavens and a new earth."[25] Peter, comforting close friends, said despite the tough times they faced "we are looking forward to a new heaven and a new earth."[26] Jesus' dear friend John described having seen "a new heaven and a new earth, for the first heaven and the first earth had passed away."[27]

Why a new earth? Well, ours was created perfect. The heavens were perfect too. But sin entered—first through angelic rebellion and then through human disobedience—and with it came disease, pain, heartache, suffering, and death. Today, creation's breathtaking beauty is but a vestige of what it was at the start. Paradise *has* been lost. Our earth *is* broken, and it groans to be made new.

Where will the new heavens and earth be? *How* can paradise be redeemed?

Dennis Kinlaw, former president of Asbury College, is one of the most brilliant Old Testament scholars I know. One day, talking about the nature of death and the location of heaven, he said, "The Bible seems to imply that the new heaven is here—on this earth."

At the time, I was still processing my own brother's untimely death. Bewildered, I looked at Dr. Kinlaw and said, "Are you saying that they—the dead—are here? On *our* turf?"

"Oh, no," he said quickly. "I'm saying that *we* are on *their* turf."

We can't now see into that dimension, but it's possible we might be "intersecting" with heaven itself. When the new heaven and earth are made, they'll likely be right here, where the old earth currently winds down its life.

Scripture too seems to indicate there will be no need for a separate heaven and earth. They will be one and the same, meaning that if the new earth is created where the earth currently resides, the new heaven will be here also:

They will inherit *the earth*.[28]

Those the Lord blesses will inherit *the land*.[29]

Abraham . . . received the promise that he would be heir of *the world.*[30]

They will reign on *the earth.*[31]

Finally, the new heaven and new earth already are under construction. Two thousand years ago Jesus said,

> Let not your heart be troubled: ye believe in God, believe also in me.
>
> In my Father's house are many mansions: if it were not so, I would have told you. I go to prepare a place for you.
>
> And if I go and prepare a place for you, I will come again, and receive you unto myself; that where I am, there ye may be also.[32]

This means the new heaven is not "up there somewhere." It is intertwined with this earth, now, in another dimension—heaven *is* here. As Paul Marshall explains, "Our destiny is an earthly one: a new earth, an earth redeemed and transfigured. An earth united with heaven, but an earth, nevertheless."[33]

The point is heaven and earth intersect, so much so that while we can't see into heaven from where we stand today it appears heaven can see us. Every time someone becomes a new member of God's kingdom, angels in heaven rejoice.[34] When the martyrs, killed for their faith, observe happenings here, they cry out to God, "How long will you let this continue?" To which God responds, "A little longer."[35] Finally, those who have gone before us are like a "cloud of witnesses."[36] They well could be—in their own dimension—moving among us even now,[37] celebrating our victories, weeping over our persecutions, observing our struggles and our growth.

> Heaven and earth intersect, so much so that while we can't see into heaven from where we stand today it appears heaven can see us.

PRAYING TO AND TALKING TO PEOPLE IN HEAVEN

We are not to pray *to* those in heaven. God alone has power to answer our prayers. Again, he strictly forbids *seeking out* communication with the dead.

However, this is not to say they cannot contact us. If/when we sense the presence of a loved one who's now in heaven, who's to say that's not exactly what we're sensing? This isn't something to be feared—neither is it something to be pursued. My belief is that God sometimes allows this to encourage and comfort us; it's part of the rich experience of the doctrine called the "communion of the saints." This oneness, said to extend to all believers in Christ Jesus, whether on earth or in heaven, is a profound reminder that there is life after death and that those who've gone on ahead have not ceased to exist. Absent from the body, they are very much alive and enjoying the Lord's presence.

My dear friend Gerard Reed, a respected university professor, was in deep grief from the loss of his beloved wife following a battle with cancer. He expressed to me the profound comfort he felt when he sensed her clear presence. This man of Native American descent, not given to displays of emotion, said with tear-filled eyes, "I believe in the communion of the saints." He meant that even though his wife had gone on to heaven, he was still enjoying meaningful communion with her. Following scriptural directives, he was not seeking out contact with her; he simply was aware of her periodic presence.

EXTREME MAKEOVER, HEAVEN EDITION

In chapter 11, we talked about our resurrected bodies and how they will be like the resurrected body of Jesus. But what age will we be? Science tells us we tend to peak physically somewhere in our late twenties or early thirties. Scripture doesn't give us many clues, but it's worth mentioning that when God created Adam and Eve, he created them in their childbearing years. And when Jesus was raised, he was recognizable, so he was probably an age similar to that when he died, around thirty-three. Do these examples reveal anything about the age we will appear to be in heaven? Maybe, maybe not.

What about children? We can't assume that when someone dies they enter heaven at the same age and appearance with which they leave the earth. But neither can we assume heaven will be filled with thirty-somethings who never change or grow. Once more, heaven will be a perfect earth filled with, among other things, foliage and trees that bear fruit. So growth and change could apply to us as well.

And while we tend to think of heaven as timeless—after all, what better way to describe eternity—perhaps there is some concept of time. When one of the seven seals is opened, "There was silence in heaven for about half an hour."[38]

What age will we appear? And will we stay that age for eternity, or will we experience change? Some things we will have to wait to know for sure.

MARRIAGE AND SEX

When we are resurrected and living in the new heaven on earth, we will not marry.[39] This is why, during our marriage vows, we commit ourselves to our spouses "till death do us part."

I suspect some people think about the question of marriage in heaven and are relieved to envision heaven *without* their spouse. However, for most (including me), the thought of going to heaven and not being married is painful. Still, *in heaven you will know oneness with your spouse beyond what you could ever know on this earth.* You will know and live the very nature of *oneness.* You will *know* your spouse, and you will enjoy more oneness than ever before—pure, unsullied, unimaginably wonderful.

Will we keep our gender? Yes. "God created man in his own image, in the image of God he created him; male and female he created them."[40] In other words, gender distinction predated the fall; God created us that way from the beginning, and pleased with his design, he affirmed it. When Jesus was raised, he didn't stop being a man. His body was recognizable, down to the wounds in his hands and feet.

At the risk of turning you off to the idea of heaven forever, let me respond, from my earthbound perspective, to the matter of sex in heaven. The short answer is no, it won't be a feature of heaven. Biblically, sex is designed for the context of marriage, and since there's no marriage in heaven, the context for sex is missing as well.

But don't stop here. Let's take a closer look at the mysteries of marriage and sex as they relate to heaven. Sex between husband and wife is holy. It's beautiful. It pleases God. So why would anything *that* wonderful, *that* sacred, be absent in heaven? And if sexual expression is missing, what will fill the void? We are told there can be no void in heaven, no sadness or longing.[41] In reality, heaven not only will encompass the best our old earth has to offer, but these delights will be refined to levels we can't yet begin to comprehend.

Consider four wondrous benefits we receive from healthy sexual expression here on earth, and how they may be exceeded in heaven.

On earth, sex is given to us for intimacy, but *in heaven, all barriers to emotional intimacy will be removed.* We will recognize our loved ones and enjoy all the relationships we have now, except without sin's destructive influences, whether sin of our own or of others. In heaven you will experience unity and belonging beyond what you have ever known on earth.

On earth, sex is given to us for procreation, in order to keep the species alive, but *since no one will ever die in heaven, procreation won't be necessary.*

On earth, sex is given to us for joy and even ecstasy. Although this may be difficult for us to grasp and accept until we get there, *heaven itself will contain such inherent ecstasy that the delight of sex will not be missed.*

I believe the fourth benefit of earthly sexual expression holds the greatest key to the mystery of why sex will not be missed in heaven. The intimate, surrendered relationship—sexual and otherwise—between husband and wife was designed by God to represent the intimate, surrendered relationship between Jesus Christ and his bride, the church. Now, granted, human marriages are tainted and sometimes riddled with the effects of sin, meaning the worst marriages may reflect nothing of Christ's relationship with his body, while even the best marriages are a cracked and broken mirror at best. In fact, think of the happiest couples you know. Even *their* marriages—stellar by human standards—are mere shadows of the marriage to come between Jesus and his bride. *The delight of human sexual intimacy is an imperfect depiction of the perfect, all-fulfilling wonder we will experience when united with Christ.*

Human sexuality and our longing for intimacy is God's way of giving us a glimpse of what it's going to be like when Jesus is finally and fully with us in ways we cannot yet fathom. This may be part of the meaning of "You will fill me with joy in your presence, with eternal pleasures at your right hand."[42]

LONGING FOR HOME

How about you? Do you long for heaven? If your honest answer is no, I have another question: What *do* you long for? And would it surprise you to discover that the things you long for are precious to you beyond understanding because they remind you, in some fashion, of coming home? Not to the home of your childhood or even to the home you've created for yourself as an adult, but the *other* home—that elusive place of utter welcome and well-being you've always sensed was out there somewhere?

You undoubtedly have experienced moments—perhaps while watching a shaft of sunlight, hearing a moving refrain of music, watching your child lost in the pure abandon of play—when something stirred inside your soul that felt new and old all at once; something that seemed part anticipation, part distant memory, as if you were standing on the threshold of the very thing you'd been seeking your entire life. You recognize the feeling, as inconceivable as it seems. You're homesick for someplace you've never been.

What will heaven feel like?

Take your deepest longings. Think of what you crave, what fills you with delight, joy you've never experienced but yearn for just the same. Remember your longing for home, for a lover of your soul, for the contented wholeness that leads you to the place you've never been yet can't forget—the place where your every desire is satisfied more abundantly than you've ever dreamed.

Heaven is that home.

PART FOUR

Crossing Over: The Dark Descent

14

Going From
Bad to Worse

————— ✳ —————

Hades Is a "Horrible Holding Tank"
for Those Awaiting a Final, Fiery Destination

Hell isn't merely paved with good intentions, it is walled and
roofed by them.

ALDOUS HUXLEY

In the movie *Bridge to Terabithia*, ten-year-old Jesse is befriended by
Leslie, the new girl in town. Together they create an imaginary world
they call Terabithia.

At one point Jesse invites Leslie to attend church with his family,
provided she wears a dress. With the congregation, they sing "The Old
Rugged Cross," during which Leslie gazes at the light streaming through
stained glass and pretends to capture the rays in her purse. Soon the
church bells ring as people file out.

On the way home, Leslie, Jesse, and his younger sister May Belle
ride in the back of the family's pickup truck.

"I'm really glad I came," says Leslie. "That whole Jesus thing—it's really interesting, isn't it?"

"It's not interesting," May Belle responds, "it's scary. It's nailing holes through your hands. It's 'cause we're all vile sinners that God made Jesus die."

"You really think that's true?" Leslie asks somberly.

"It's in the Bible, Leslie," Jesse says.

"You have to believe it, and you hate it," she replies. "I don't have to believe it, and I think it's beautiful."

"You have to believe the Bible, Leslie," May Belle warns. "If you don't believe in the Bible, God will damn you to hell when you die."

"Wow, May Belle," Leslie says, sounding dismissive. "Where'd you hear that?"

"That's right, isn't it, Jess?" she prods. "God damns you to hell if you don't believe in the Bible."

"I think so," the boy answers.

"Well, I don't think so," Leslie proclaims. "I seriously do not think God goes around damning people to hell." She then spreads her arms wide and looks at all the scenery. "He's too busy running this."[1]

A discussion about hell—whether by children or grownups—is bound to raise questions, spark debate, and reveal conflicting perspectives. Perhaps most of all, any serious dialogue about hell is sure to make most people uncomfortable. If you believe it's a real place, you probably don't want to end up there, and you don't want anybody you love to go there either. If you don't believe in it, you may laugh it off or avoid talking about it because it's something only religious people could really ponder.

The concept of hell has been around since Old Testament times. The biblical descriptions of hell sound like a horror movie: burning lakes, dark pits, and shadowy realms filled with dragons, serpents, demons, and three-headed beasts.

These images don't fit well with today's naturalist-minded world, and some Christians even find them embarrassing. Such beliefs may come across as superstitious, ignorant, backward, or unenlightened, and people who take these passages seriously are often labeled fanatics. Many people rationalize that hell can't exist—it's an old wives' tale. Others feel a loving God couldn't possibly allow anyone to suffer eternal torment (more on this in chapters 17 and 18).

Skepticism about hell is not a unique development of the rationalistic world. Christian beliefs have been attacked and mocked for centuries by those whose faith is in human knowledge and human reason. In the West today, it isn't acceptable to openly believe in the supernatural, and many Christians either have changed or hidden certain beliefs to fit in with intellectual trends.

> Many people rationalize that hell can't exist—it's an old wives' tale. Others feel a loving God couldn't possibly allow anyone to suffer eternal torment.

But if hell is a real place, it's a supernatural one, and no afterlife discussion would be complete without asking about the evidence for its reality. A crucial information source about hell is the Bible, which is rooted in history that tells of real persons, in real places, experiencing real events. Unlike other religious texts, Scripture is not a collection of stories unrelated to historical reality, so its historicity gives it additional credibility.

The Bible says much about hell and several related places. The terms for these don't translate very well into English, and they vary in their origins and meanings:

- *sheol*—Old Testament Hebrew word; can mean a place of torment, hell, or the grave
- *hades*—New Testament Greek word; also can mean place of torment, hell, or the grave
- *gehenna*—also New Testament Greek; usually means hell

SHEOL, HADES, AND *GEHENNA*

Greek Orthodox, Roman Catholic, and Western Protestant confessions of faith (creeds) all include belief in the reality of physical and spiritual life after death. Creeds identify the core of accepted ideas held by a group of people. They define what is believed (*orthodoxy*) against what is considered incorrect (*heresy*). The most basic truth about Christ needs to be understood before believers can grow in maturity and "distinguish good from evil."[2]

One of the most popular confessions, the Apostles' Creed, is said to have been written by Jesus' disciples, but that's unlikely. This creed, officially adopted by the Roman Catholic Church several hundred years after Christ (in the eighth century), has been an almost universally foundational statement of the Christian faith.[3] It's used today by many churches in its original form:

> I believe in God the Father almighty, creator of heaven and earth;
>
> And in Jesus Christ, His only Son, our Lord, Who was conceived by the Holy Spirit, born of the Virgin Mary, suffered under Pontius Pilate, was crucified, dead and buried.
>
> He descended to hell, on the third day rose again from the dead, ascended to heaven, sits at the right hand of God the Father almighty, thence He will come to judge the living and the dead;
>
> I believe in the Holy Spirit, the holy catholic Church, the communion of saints, the forgiveness of sins, the resurrection of the body, and the life everlasting.
>
> Amen.[4]

This creed embodies the basic beliefs of the Christian faith: the crucifixion and resurrection, heaven, hell, bodily resurrection of believers, judgment, and eternal life. Perhaps the most difficult statement in this creed is that Jesus "descended to hell."

God's perfect son went to hell? Why?

The crucifixion and resurrection are commonly known. Jesus had a real physical body and suffered a true human death.[5] But Jesus also was sinless, so it seems strange he wouldn't go directly to paradise, as he promised the repentant thief hanging on the cross next to him.[6] We know that if Jesus went to hell, he didn't stay there but was "exalted to the right hand of God."[7]

Inspiration for the creedal statement about Christ's time in hell is in 1 Peter:

> Christ also died for sins once for all, the righteous for the unrighteous, that he might bring us to God, being put to death in the flesh but made alive in the spirit; *in which he went and preached to the spirits in prison, who formerly did not obey,* when God's patience waited in the days of Noah, during the building of the ark, in which a few, that is, eight persons, were saved through water. . . . They will give account to him who is ready to judge the living and the dead. For *this is why the gospel was preached even to the dead,* that though judged in the flesh like men, they might live in the spirit like God.[8]

Even Martin Luther admitted he didn't know what preaching "to the spirits in prison" meant; he called this "obscure."[9] It's sometimes interpreted to mean that during the time between his crucifixion and resurrection, Jesus traveled to where the spirits of the dead were held, awaiting judgment. In this holding place or prison—often called *sheol* (Old Testament) and *hades* (New Testament)—he preached to the captive spirits.

Whether those spirits could respond to the gospel or whether it was instead a triumphant appearance—"victory lap"—by the one who had defeated the demonic hordes, we cannot know.[10] What's important is this passage's first-century glimpse of hades. Peter later defines the spirits in prison as the "dead."[11] Hades appears to be an intermediate location for the spirits of all who died before Christ's life and ministry. Others view it as a "holding tank" for those who die without believing in him.

This is in contrast to hell, or *gehenna* (see chapter 16). Hell is a place of eternal torment created by God for the devil and his fallen angels. Tragically, it also is a permanent and final destination for unrepentant souls following judgment.[12]

Our concern here is more with hades. In the Apostles' Creed, the original Latin word for hell was *infernos*, which can be translated *underworld, nether world, sheol, grave,* or *hell.*[13] The word *hades* can mean "hell" or simply "underworld." An alternative creedal wording might be "He descended to the underworld . . ."

Sheol in the Old Testament

The concept of hell is not well developed in the Old Testament. When sheol is mentioned, it appears to have been understood as a dark, shadowy place. *Sheol* is a term for the place of the dead; it is best translated *grave.* The Psalter poetically reads,

> Truly no man can ransom himself, or give to God the price of his life, for the ransom of his life is costly, and can never suffice, that he should continue to live on for ever, and never see the Pit [the grave, or death]. Yea, he shall see that even the wise die; the fool and the stupid alike must perish and leave their wealth to others.
>
> *Their graves are their homes for ever, their dwelling places to all generations,* though they named lands their own. Man cannot abide in his pomp; he is like the beasts that perish. This is the fate of those who have foolish confidence, the end of those who are pleased with their portion. Like sheep they are appointed for Sheol; Death shall be their shepherd; straight to the grave they descend, and their form shall waste away; Sheol shall be their home.
>
> But God will ransom my soul from the power of Sheol, for he will receive me.[14]

Remarkable! This not only reflects the ancient Hebrew understanding of death, it also points to a time when God will rescue souls from sheol and from Death, the "shepherd of sheol." About a thousand years before Christ, David had a prophetic glimpse of salvation beyond sheol, although he didn't know how it would happen:

> Therefore my heart is glad, and my soul rejoices; my body also dwells secure. For thou dost not give me up to Sheol, or let thy godly one see the Pit. Thou dost show me the path of life, in thy presence there is fulness of joy, in thy right hand are pleasures for evermore.[15]

Though they didn't fully understand God's plan to take our sins so we wouldn't have to go to hell, still he was preparing the readers of this psalm for the revelations that would come centuries later.[16]

The Hebrews did not identify sheol specifically as a place of punishment, like we think of hell; sometimes it was just where the dead went. When Joseph's father, Jacob, was told the lie that his beloved son had been killed, he rejected comfort and said, "No, I shall go down to Sheol to my son, mourning."[17] Jacob believed that upon Joseph's death, his spirit went to sheol, and that he also would go there when he died.

Longsuffering Job spoke of hoping he might die and be safe from God's wrath in sheol.[18] Yet Job later acknowledged that sheol cannot hide someone from God's all-powerful vision: "The shades below tremble, the waters and their inhabitants. Sheol is naked before God, and Abaddon [destruction] has no covering."[19]

The words of Psalm 88 describe sheol as a place of darkness and forgetfulness. As the psalmist endured some kind of suffering, he imagined what it might be like:

> I am reckoned among those who go down to the Pit; I am a man who has no strength, like one forsaken among the dead, like the slain that lie in the grave, like those whom thou dost remember no more, for they are cut off from thy hand. Thou hast put me in the depths of the Pit, in the regions dark and deep.[20]

The Old Testament certainly doesn't portray sheol as a pleasant place; it never has any association with heaven or rewards or the like.

PROGRESSIVE REVELATION

Although hell isn't a well-developed Old Testament doctrine, God reveals truths to his people when they are prepared to hear them, just as Jesus held back from the disciples certain truths they weren't yet ready to grasp:

> I have yet many things to say to you, but you cannot bear them now.
>
> When the Spirit of truth comes, he will guide you into all the truth; for he will not speak on his own authority, but whatever

he hears he will speak, and he will declare to you the things that are to come.[21]

One intriguing scriptural facet is the way God takes us by the hand and shows us more truth when we can handle it. With each passing century in biblical history, God revealed more and more of his character. This gradual unveiling of truth is called "progressive revelation." The disciples had only the Old Testament and the words of Jesus they heard in his presence. First-century believers also had letters from Paul and the other great writers whose works became the New Testament. Today we have the benefit of two thousand years of hindsight as we study both Testaments.

The truth revealed by God is unchangeable; what *does* change is our human understanding, which continues to mature. On the topic of hades, we see a gradual development as information is added—we know far more about it by the end of the New Testament than we do halfway through the Old Testament.

HADES IN THE NEW TESTAMENT

> "Hades is like the county jail, where inmates await their trial date, final sentence, and transfer to the penitentiary or prison where they will serve their time."
> —MARK HITCHCOCK

The New Testament Greek word *hades* occurs ten times. Twice it simply means "grave," like *sheol*. However, usually it portrays a place where persons not destined for heaven will be held until the final judgment.[22] One writer has noted that "Hades is like the county jail, where inmates await their trial date, final sentence, and transfer to the penitentiary or prison where they will serve their time."[23] (See chapter 16 on the "permanent penitentiary," generally called hell, *gehenna,* or sometimes the "lake of fire.")

IMMEDIATELY FOLLOWING DEATH

In the previous chapters on heaven, I made the case that immediately following death, a believer is fully aware and alert, even if she hasn't passed into the permanent heaven in her glorified body. In the same way, an unbeliever is fully alert and aware after death—that's part of the message we will see in Luke 16.

There are some who believe Jesus' story of the fates of two men who died—one a believer, the other an unbeliever—shouldn't be used as evidence for this awareness. However, Jesus himself seems to use the story partly for that purpose, addressing it to the Pharisees, who placed more importance on religious rules than on following truth.

Whether literal or metaphorical, this story's message is the same: The dead men's conversation gives significant insight into the state of the spirit following death.

Lazarus, a poor man who suffered greatly during his life, lay outside the gate of a very rich man. The rich man lived luxuriously and ignored the needs of others, even those who suffered on his own street. When Lazarus died, the angels carried his spirit to a place of comfort to be with God's faithful servant Abraham. The rich man also died, but his fate was different: "in Hades, being in torment, he lifted up his eyes and saw Abraham far off and Lazarus at his side."[24]

The rich man cried out for help, but Abraham told him there was an uncrossable chasm between them. The man then asked Abraham to help save his family from hades:

> He answered, "Then I beg you, father, send Lazarus to my father's house, for I have five brothers. Let him warn them, so that they will not also come to this place of torment."
>
> Abraham replied, "They have Moses and the Prophets; let them listen to them."
>
> "No, father Abraham," he said, "but if someone from the dead goes to them, they will repent."
>
> He said to him, "If they do not listen to Moses and the Prophets, they will not be convinced even if someone rises from the dead."[25]

The rich man didn't need to go to the place of torment; he chose it by ignoring what Moses and many other people of God had taught. When God showed up in human flesh—as Jesus—the rich man (like the Pharisees) missed him.

Even before Christ's death, many people knew and served God and, like Lazarus, were spared from the darkness of hades. Others refused to heed the warnings of the Old Testament prophets and paid dearly.

God gave us free will because he wants us to *choose* him. All parents want their children to love them, not from a coerced response but out of genuine devotion. God *is* love, and he designed us with the capacity to love him back. But he won't force the issue. We have the freedom to choose him or turn away. Our choice is what determines where we will go after death. God wants us to choose heaven and eternity with him.

15

Called to Account

———— ✳ ————

The Great White Throne of Judgment—
Where Punishment Is Handed Out

When the day of judgment comes, we shall not be examined as
to what we have read but what we have done, not how well we
have spoken but how we have lived.

THOMAS À KEMPIS

I t was end of semester, and Daniel dreaded logging on to check his
chemistry grade. He'd blown his second year of pre-med, wasting
study time on video games and shooting hoops. He'd ignored warnings—
from his girlfriend, his mom, even Eli, the grad student who assisted
him on lab days. They'd all noticed he wasn't even trying. He'd just
assumed somehow it would all work out, that he was getting by, that
the TA would pass him because he was a decent guy.

Now he crossed his fingers for luck and sat down at the computer,
hoping he wouldn't have to tell his parents his academic career was

over and their hard-earned money had gone for nothing. Maybe he'd get another chance. But what came up on the screen made his heart sink: even worse than a score of 55 on the final exam was an F for the course.

Disappointment turned to anger. It wasn't his fault—*my prof is a jerk!* he thought. *Doesn't even know how to teach. Always uses grad students to fill in for him.*

Daniel knew what would happen next, though. Chloe and his mom would remind him of all those squandered hours. His dad would shake his head and sigh, weary of a son who refused to do what was necessary to reach goals. The last thing Daniel needed was to be told how lazy he'd been for neglecting to follow through. He knew the consequences were serious. It was judgment day, and that meant losing the opportunity for med school. It was over. This was it.

Failing a class is one thing—failing "life's final exam" is quite another. We humans get one chance at making decisions about our eternal future. That chance, presumably, lasts as long as we're in this life, and "after that comes judgment."[1] Unlike with reincarnation or annihilation, the Bible tells of a "great white throne judgment." What is it, and why should we care?

The Great White Throne Judgment

> Of all the biblical topics, hell and final judgment seem especially likely to turn people off.

Of all the biblical topics, hell and final judgment seem especially likely to turn people off. Few seek to study these issues or flock to hear a sermon about them. "Hellfire and brimstone" are held up for ridicule by many and rarely are taken seriously in the twenty-first century.

For Christians, the simple word *judgment* can be intimidating, even without *great white throne* before it. Few (except for trial lawyers) are enthusiastic about appearing in any kind of court for any type of judgment. What if the judge is unfair? What if the evidence is misrepresented? What if the witnesses lie?

And why is this judgment called *great*? If you stop to ponder this word's meaning, it could be anything from *wonderful* to *dreaded* or even *awful*. It could refer to the size of the throne, to the masses that will appear before the throne, or to God himself. In this context, the word inspires awe, if not outright panic.

Our trepidation is confirmed when we examine the language surrounding the biblical depiction. Found near the end of Revelation, John's words leave little room for doubt as to the seriousness of the unfolding drama:

> Then I saw a great white throne and him who was seated on it. Earth and sky fled from his presence, and there was no place for them. And I saw the dead, great and small, standing before the throne, and books were opened. Another book was opened, which is the book of life. The dead were judged according to what they had done as recorded in the books. . . . Then death and Hades were thrown into the lake of fire. . . . If anyone's name was not found written in the book of life, he was thrown into the lake of fire.[2]

In examining the event, we can pose the same questions a journalist might ask: When? Who? What? Where? and How?

When?

The chronology[3] suggests this judgment will happen on the heels of *the millennium*—a term coined for a thousand-year time of peace—and the casting of Satan, antichrist, and false prophet into the lake of fire. This is one of the final events in biblical prophecy.

Who?

As noted in chapter 12, there is much disagreement about who will appear at the great white throne. Some claim it's a judgment that includes everyone. According to this view, the final separation of the "sheep" (believers in Christ) and the "goats" (unbelievers) will take place at the great white throne.

> When the Son of Man comes in his glory . . . he will separate the people one from another as a shepherd separates the sheep from the goats. He will put the sheep on his right and the goats on his left.[4]

Some contend this separation actually refers to a different event—a third judgment—in which the nations are judged, perhaps based on their treatment of Israel. Others complicate the topic even more by naming seven judgments.[5] For our purposes we have one issue: Are there two separate judgments (the great white throne *and* the judgment seat of Christ), or are these two aspects of one event? The answer is significant— if these are two events, believers in Christ do not go before the great white throne. If there is one event, all will experience it.

A clue to "*who* appears" is that this group includes "the dead," as well as a curious reference to those dead who were "delivered up" by the sea, death, and hell.[6] It is possible Christians could be included, but the case is not closed.

So what will happen to those who appear before the throne? We are told that "books will be opened" at the judgment. John refers specifically to a "book of life" where our deeds are recorded. If he were living in today's society, he might have referred to computers being booted up and documents being opened for all to view, as God scrolls through what appears to be a record of each life. God judges individuals "according to what they had done as recorded in the books."[7] Those whose names are not found in the Book of Life are banished.

Note what's missing in this passage. Where is there any hint of rewards or of heaven? The only destination mentioned in the text—and it's mentioned twice—is the ominous-sounding lake of fire. Could that mean this judgment is an event only for those outside of Christ?

Perhaps the great white throne judgment of each person "according to what he had done" refers exclusively to the nonbeliever's deeds. That would explain the absence of any reference to heaven or rewards.

And this makes sense if the judgment seat of Christ is exclusively for believers.

On the other hand, if there is only one judgment, of Christians and unbelievers together, it might be charted as follows:

If There Is Only One Judgment

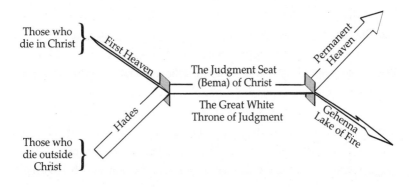

However, it appears more likely that the Bible indicates two separate judgments with separate, parallel "tracks."

Assuming There Are Two Separate Judgments

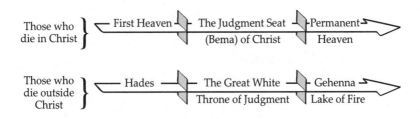

WHAT?

Assuming the great white throne judgment is only for nonbelievers, what happens to them? As we saw, books are opened, including "the book of life." We don't know the names of the other books, but we're told they contain a record of the deeds of those being judged. It isn't clear whether the Book of Life is the same as the "Lamb's book of life,"[8] but let's assume it is. This book contains names, and anyone whose name isn't recorded there is sent to the lake of fire.

Are the books figurative or literal? Will they appear as a scroll or as a thick volume? Are they a reference to the mind of God? It makes little difference. What's important is the content: the deeds of the dead and the names of the righteous.

On ABC's *Nightline*, interviewer Cynthia McFadden asked former President George W. Bush whether he believed the Bible is literally true. "Probably not," he responded. ". . . No, I am not a literalist. . . ."[9]

Perhaps a better answer would be "The Bible should be taken literally when it is clear that the writer is expressing himself literally." As literature, the Bible contains (among other things) history, poetry, symbolism, and imagery. It's relatively easy to tell which is which, and certainly all Scripture should be accepted as truth by those who believe it is God-inspired. Here's a safe rule: When uncertain, err on the side of caution and accept the literalness of inspired writing until it's clearly and convincingly proven otherwise.

> All Scripture should be accepted as truth by those who believe it is God-inspired.

Whether the "books" are codices, scrolls, or in the mind of God—what exactly is in them, and how are they filled? Is there a celestial record keeper or court reporter typing away for each person? Will video footage show everyone what we did? Will our thoughts and feelings be recorded too? The Bible says only that the books contain a record of what each person has done—his or her "deeds."

And what about our words? Your mama probably used to tell you, "If you can't say something nice, don't say anything at all." Good advice, especially in light of what Jesus says:

I tell you that men will have to give account on the day of judgment for every careless word they have spoken. For by your words you will be acquitted, and by your words you will be condemned.[10]

Suddenly, we're all recalling the times we let words fly that should've stayed in.

Think of it this way: Anytime we delete our e-mails, we assume they've disappeared forever. Phew! But most of them are still out there "somewhere." It may not be easy to retrieve them, but it's possible. Would you want all your messages recovered and read publicly? Neither would I. Yet Jesus states plainly that our words matter and are recorded on some kind of heavenly hard drive.

Moreover, the Book of Life apparently is a record of names—those of Christians. We could stretch the details a little and imagine that everyone's name is written in this book until death. Then a nonbeliever's name would be erased or blotted out.

"Blotting out" is not uncommon throughout Scripture.[11] And while most of these verses aren't pleasant to read, they give insight into the judgment books. The final reference to blotting out puts the term in a more positive light: "He who overcomes will, like them, be dressed in white. I will never blot out his name from the Book of Life, but will acknowledge his name before my Father and his angels."[12]

Not all passages using the term also refer to the book of life. What's notable, however, is the consistent pattern of something being erased. The conclusion we must draw is that what was already written can be deleted.

Did you notice what's absent? There are no references to anything being *added* to the Book of Life. Instead of a grand book with names being written down as people are coming to Jesus—a book that grows throughout history—we see a book that originally contained the name of everyone who has ever existed. If people die without choosing to believe and follow Christ, their names are erased.

The writing and the erasing must be both thrilling and heartbreaking to a loving heavenly Father. God is excited about the potential of our entrance into this life, and he's even more excited about spending eternity with us. With the grand hopes of a father before a child's birth, he notes our names in his book; then, as our lives progress, he reaches out to us. What he wants is our love and our acceptance of his Son. And our names stay in the book until our last breath. Then, if we depart without having acknowledged and accepted him as our Savior, you can imagine how his heart breaks to blot out the name of one who is his precious creation.

The "what" of the great white throne judgment is simple: The deeds of those who come will be reviewed, and their names will not be in the Book of Life. That's why they are here—at *this* judgment.

WHERE?

Though this judgment could take place on earth, more likely it's a heavenly event. God sits on the throne; his realm is in heaven. All the dead from the beginning of time will be there, and that number will be in the billions. We can't determine the location for sure, and it isn't important to know.

HOW?

Rather than ask "How did it *happen?*" let's address "how to *avoid*" the great white throne. The evidence points to an event only for the dead who died without Christ, so the key question is "How can I miss this one?" The fact is this will be the single most terrifying event *ever*. If such a scene could be adequately portrayed on the big screen, multitudes would repent with fervor—or as the evangelists of yesteryear would say, "attempt to flee the wrath to come."

If you do not believe, this chapter is written in actual hopes of "scaring the hell out of you." If you die without accepting Christ's provision for eternal life, you will stand before the most formidable judge you can imagine. And you will do so aware that he did not put you in this inescapable predicament. Like Daniel, the failed pre-med student, you will have put yourself there.

Your belief system may not embrace the great white throne judgment. That doesn't make it any less real. You may scoff at it or choose to ignore it; makes no difference. It's real, it's coming, and every person who has not placed faith in Jesus Christ will be judged and found wanting.

16

The Heat
Is On

—— ✳ ——

Hell Is an Indescribable Punishment
for Those Who Reject Salvation

What is hell? I maintain that it is the suffering of not being able
to love.

FYODOR DOSTOYEVSKY

There is plenty of disagreement about hell—whether it's a real
physical place with real flames, whether people will be fully conscious there, whether it's temporary or permanent, whether it's all a
metaphor.[1]

The previous chapters on heaven and hades showed that people
will be fully conscious and aware after death, not resting in soul sleep.
If your destination is heaven, this is a magnificent thought; if it's hell,
you should be terrified.

Let's revisit the story about the dead man who looked up from
his "agony in the fire" and saw Abraham far away, with Lazarus by

his side. He called for water to cool his tongue and asked Abraham to send word to his brothers so they wouldn't end up where he was. But Abraham couldn't cross the gulf between them and said that even if he could communicate with the brothers, they wouldn't listen.[2]

Taken as Christ's own words, this account tells us clearly what happens to those who die outside of meaningful relationship with him. They go to hades, where they're aware of their misery and conscious that they don't want their loved ones to be there.

SEPARATION ANXIETY

Paul points out that there are two parts to suffering in hell: "They will be punished with everlasting destruction and shut out from the presence of the Lord and from the majesty of his power."[3] Hell is not just a place of torment; additionally it's a place of separation from God.

> Hell is not just a place of torment; additionally it's a place of separation from God.

What's the big deal about this isolation? Some people are so overwhelmed by their sense of brokenness that the thought of being *with* God is intimidating. If they hear "In hell you'll be away from God," their reaction might be "That's how I am now—why would I care about it then?" But many people take for granted the goodness all around them. Separation from God after death means separation from everything that's right, true, and wonderful; he is the source of all that is good. Eternity without God means exposure only to what is wrong, false, and horrible.

Imagine stepping out of your house one morning only to discover that every bit of beauty is gone from this earth. All that you like, that makes you feel great, that makes life worth living has disappeared. All that's left is the hideous and the obscene.

Mortified, you realize you could have kept this from happening by making one important decision, but you didn't think it was important and/or you didn't believe the truth about it. You see now what's happened, but it's too late to change things. You're stuck—no way out.

The absence of God, of goodness and light, means being forever in the presence of evil and darkness. We weren't created for that destiny—*he made us to be with him.* As Jerry Walls wrote, "God could not make rational creatures such as ourselves in such a way that they would not need him for their fulfillment and happiness."[4]

In discussions of hell, the same question almost always comes up: If God is so loving and gracious, why would he torment people? The answer is so simple it may seem ridiculous, but it's true: *God never has sent any human to hell, and he never will.*

If you've ever hired someone to do a job, you know he expects to be paid his wages when the work is done. This life could be described as having wages—wages for living our lives as we please and wages for choosing to follow love and truth. We can choose everlasting death without Christ, or we can choose everlasting life with him.[5] Although each person makes this choice during life, the ramifications are delayed, so it's easy for some to deny that there ever will be any real results or consequences.

> Without Christ, our "goodness" isn't good enough. So he allows us to choose: eternal life or eternal death.

Hell *wasn't* made for people; God doesn't want anyone to go there. But he is utter goodness—absolute holiness—and evil cannot be in his presence. Without Christ, our "goodness" isn't good enough. So he allows us to choose: eternal life or eternal death.

THOSE WHO HAVE NEVER HEARD

Another question: What about people who die without hearing the good news? What if no one has ever told them about Jesus? This seems like a real dilemma, because if we see God as righteous—as justice itself—how could it be fair to punish someone for being born in a place and time where he or she couldn't hear the truth?

An answer is found in John's gospel, regarding "the true light that gives light to every man."[6] At some point, each is touched by aware-ness that he or she needs God and that he has made a provision. This insight may be basic, but God doesn't leave anyone in the dark. In that light-burst, that divine appointment, it becomes clear there is a personal, moral Creator—one beyond and above us, one who has made us and cares for us.

Picture a tribal hunter picking his way through heavy jungle foliage outside his village in the early morning hours. In the tangle of vines and branches, he sees an iridescent butterfly perched motionless on the edge of a leaf. Its delicate beauty takes his breath away, and in that moment he senses that *Someone made it*—Someone bigger and more powerful than anyone he's ever known. It occurs to him that this Someone has pro-vided for *everything*. He has known the difference between right and wrong since he was a child, but now he's overwhelmed by a feeling that there's something more, and that all he has to do is say *yes* to this Someone. He has received the light; it is sufficient. If he embraces it, he will receive eternal life, even though he doesn't yet know that this gift has a name: Jesus Christ.

Paul wrote about this situation also.

> What may be known about God is plain to them [those who sup-press the truth], because God has made it plain to them. For since the creation of the world God's invisible qualities—his eternal power and divine nature—have been clearly seen, being understood from what has been made, so that men are without excuse.[7]

Although it seems there will be some who enter heaven based on such an experience, God wants his people to keep telling others about him. That's one reason believers may come across as compulsive about shar-ing their faith or sending out missionaries. Coming to Christ may be as simple as seeing a beautiful butterfly on a morning hunt, but these moments will be ignored or overlooked by many.

Words for Hell

In chapter 14, we looked at the Hebrew word *sheol,* which usually refers to a holding place for the dead. A second word is the Greek *hades,* which normally denotes a place of torment, the way most people think of hell.

Though its exact meaning is ambiguous, hades appears to be a temporary location or, again, a "horrible holding tank." It's where those who die without Christ go at the moment of death. They remain there until the great white throne judgment.[8]

For those who have rejected God's offer of salvation, the worst part comes after this judgment, when what was temporary becomes permanent.

The Abyss and Tartarus

Three New Testament terms essentially mean "hell" or something related to it. There's the bottomless pit—the Greek word denotes "abyss."[9] It's not for humanity but rather a holding place for Satan and his demons.

A curious word used only once (by Peter) and translated "hell" is *tartarus*: "God did not spare angels when they sinned, but sent them to *tartarus,* putting them into gloomy dungeons to be held for judgment."[10] Jude uses a different description of this temporary place for fallen angels.[11]

Gehenna

If hades holds lost souls until the great white throne judgment, then eventually these souls must go to a permanent place. Biblically, the term used most often for what comes after hades is *gehenna,* which literally means "Valley of Hinnom." *Gehenna* surfaces thirteen times in the Old Testament, a dozen times in the New.

Jerusalem today is modern and metropolitan, but you can still see vestiges of the ancient city. It's perched on the southeast corner of a raised area, with steep drop-offs on two sides. On the southwest is a deep crevice—a ravine. For centuries the Valley of Hinnom was used as a trash depository; the bodies of animals and criminals were discarded there. This dumpsite, always smoldering, gave off a putrid smell.

But it was also more. In Old Testament times, children were sacrificed there during pagan worship of Molech. The practice, involving fire, truly is too horrific to comprehend. When writers, prophets, or priests of that time spoke about hell, they would say, "It's like *gehenna.*" Thus the lake of fire (Revelation) and *gehenna* (rest of the New Testament) are regarded as essentially the same thing.

HELL'S LOCATION

We can't pinpoint the exact location of hell—God doesn't tell us whether it's a part of our earthly realm. Paul mentions "lower, earthly regions"[12] and also those "in heaven and on earth and under the earth."[13] Although scientists believe earth's inner core is solid, perhaps with a molten outer core, popular thought among some is that hell actually is beneath our feet.

Years ago a story went around that a drilling crew had drilled down to hell. According to this tale, some had even heard the screams of the damned. Unfortunately, the story was picked up by a major Christian television network and passed along by certain preachers. That turned out to be an urban legend with no basis in fact; gullible people had turned it into something more. Regardless, what we need to know is that *there is a real place called hell, and God has made a way for us to avoid going there.*

A PLACE OF ENDLESS TORTURE

Ever burned your finger? Even a minor burn can keep you awake at night. Most anyone can relate to the agony of scorched skin, and no one likes to think of everlasting torment involving fire. Spending one day alive and conscious in a flaming jail cell would be intolerable—imagine being in that situation forever. Man has never invented such a torture—we find the very thought of it offensive, even as punishment for the most heinous criminals. Yet Scripture tells us the fiery torment prepared for the devil and his cohorts also will be peopled with unrepentant humans.

How do we handle the concept of unending torture? We have two choices:

(1) Deny the New Testament, even though it "will not allow us to wiggle out of confrontation with the fact that the wicked will pay a penalty."[14]

(2) Believe what Scripture says.

Those who claim to have "seen" hell report real fire there; Bill Wiese is one of these. In his controversial *23 Minutes in Hell,* he asserts, "I saw the pit. . . . I saw the liquid fire that falls like rain. I felt the extreme heat, and I smelled the stench of burning things. I do not believe the Scripture references are merely symbolic or allegorical."[15]

In contrast, biblical scholar Jerry Walls has said,

> The suffering of hell is the natural consequence of living a life of sin rather than arbitrary chosen punishment. In other words, the misery of hell is not so much a penalty imposed by God to make the sinner pay for his sin, as it is the necessary outcome of living a sinful life. . . . I do not think the fire of hell is literal, nor do I think hell is an ingeniously contrived place of the greatest possible pain and agony.[16]

Even Pope John Paul II, following that line of thinking, redefined hell as a post-death psychological state: "Hell is not a punishment imposed externally by God, but the condition resulting from attitudes and actions which people adopt in this life."[17]

Lest one think this view of suffering is somehow "better," Walls continues with an equally sobering assessment:

> What about physical pains of sense? Is there any good reason to think hell must also include bodily pain as many traditional theologians have insisted? I do . . . think hell includes physical distress. My reason for this involves an appeal to the traditional Christian belief that the damned as well as the blessed will be resurrected in their bodies. If the damned will have bodies in hell, it seems

only natural to suppose that there will be a bodily dimension to their suffering.[18]

LITERAL OR METAPHORICAL?

When Bill Crocket, my classmate years ago at Princeton Theological Seminary, gathered four theologians (himself included) to reflect on hell, he not surprisingly received four different views.[19] One (Zachary Hayes) was the classic Catholic take on purgatory;[20] another (Clark Pinnock) was annihilationism, wherein people will cease to exist.[21] John Walvoord expressed a third outlook: "There is sufficient evidence that the fire is literal. . . . Scripture never challenges the concept that eternal punishment is by literal fire."[22] People object to this concept, he said, out of a personal aversion, not because the biblical text doesn't support it.

Crocket represented the fourth view, which contends that the New Testament's references to hellfire are overwhelmingly figurative. For example, it speaks of hell as the "blackest darkness";[23] how could it be dark and yet be filled with fire, which is bright? Physical fire affects physical beings, not spirit beings, which is what Crocket believes entities will be in hell.

Although we don't know for sure whether the New Testament writers were referring to literal or figurative flames, we can do our best to interpret their meaning. Hermeneutics, the science of interpretation, tells us to examine context. If context indicates a literal interpretation, we should understand it that way. For example, there's an enormous difference between saying, "I put on my sweats and ran five and a half miles today" and "I probably walked a million miles today—my feet are killing me." The first statement, without further explanation, can be taken at face value; the second, given the sweeping "million miles" and "killing me," is meant to be taken figuratively.

It appears to me that the New Testament intent is metaphorical. Crockett points to an at-that-time example of such figurative speech:

> When Jesus says, "If anyone comes to me and does not hate his father and mother, his wife and children . . . he cannot be my disciple" (Luke 14:26), he does not mean we must hate our parents to

be proper disciples. That is a language vehicle used to convey . . . that loyalty to him is supreme.[24]

Such biblical admonitions as "take the plank out of your own eye" or "let the dead bury their own dead" are instances of figurative yet powerful speech.[25] Fire frequently is referenced non-literally in ancient Jewish writings.[26] Again, however, a figurative view of hell's flames needn't diminish their very real effects. One is neither less punishing nor "better" than the other.

We've noted that hell ultimately is separation from God—not only separation from all that is good but also integration with all that is evil. Hence, the punishment of hell may be less about how God designed a place for torturous suffering and more about how "the damned will inflict physical pain on one another. . . . Those whose characters have been shaped by violence may continue to feed on violence in hell."[27]

> Hell ultimately is separation from God—not only separation from all that is good but also integration with all that is evil.

WHY THE HELLISH CHOICE?

People tend to fixate on a question we addressed earlier: Why would God create a world in which we have the capacity to choose something so horrifying? If ever there was a theological obsessive-compulsive disorder, it's on this point. Answering seems akin to filling a bottomless pit, because the asking never ceases. Once again, though, it can't be overemphasized: *God did not make hell for humans, but for those who deserve it: the devil and his demons. Yet we can will it for ourselves.*

God *is* love, and God *desires* love from us—unconditional love, freely given. Genuine love requires the freedom to choose. He created humans as sentient beings with free will, able to reject him. This choice reveals something profoundly mysterious and tender: God longs for intimacy with us. Let that settle in for a moment. *God—the all-knowing, all-powerful, everywhere-present One—wants closeness with you and me!*

This desire in God is so strong that he made the issue plain in the beginning:

> I'm making this as easy as I possibly can. I'm giving you a garden and inviting you to pick any fruit you want. All you see is yours. Enjoy!
>
> I made just one rule, so you will understand what it is to obey and depend on me. There is one tree you may not touch. Just one! This is for your own good, and you must trust me.
>
> I'll even explain why I don't want you to eat from that tree. It is called the Tree of Knowledge of Good and Evil. If you were to eat from it, you would be choosing to decide for yourself what is good and what is evil. That's my role. You have yours: Care for and enjoy the rest of the garden.
>
> But do not try to be me. Don't try to decide on your own what is good and what is evil. I'll handle that.

You know the rest of the story. Adam and Eve found their way to that tree—with a little outside help—and blew it for the rest of us. They chose separation from God, who wanted intimacy with them. With capacity to choose came capacity to turn away.

Forever Is *Forever*

Must hell be eternal?[28] Some say no. Gerry Beauchemin contends that Christian teaching on hell is like

> a "crazy uncle" that the Church, with justifiable embarrassment, has kept locked in the back bedroom. Unfortunately, from time to time, he escapes his confinement, usually when there are guests in the parlor. . . . It's no wonder that the guests run away never to return. But instead of shunting the "crazy uncle" back to his asylum, and trying to cover our embarrassment . . . we need to get "our crazy uncle" healed.[29]

Beauchemin insists hell is temporary, that "though men will weep and even gnash their teeth, they will not do so forever."[30]

Randy Klassen agrees, stating succinctly, "An eternal hell serves no purpose."[31]

However, in contrast to those who reassure us that hell is "for a while," Jesus says the future promises only two prospects: "eternal punishment" for some, but for the righteous, "eternal life."[32] Later we're told again about the fate of those who reject God: "They will be tormented day and night for ever and ever."[33]

It may be popular to hand out comfort by assuring that hell is temporary, but when pop theologians deny hell and make heaven the one and only destination, they also deny our freedom to choose. This erodes the basis for authentic love: choice. If heaven can't be chosen, it becomes devoid of the one thing heaven *must* have: love.

God grants us the right to embrace or reject him. This literally is a hell of a decision. What on earth are you going to do about it, for heaven's sake?

PART FIVE

Hell-Avoidance Strategies

17

The Ultimate
Escape Hatch

—— ✳ ——

Universalism Suggests That All Will Be Saved in the End

Disbelieve hell, and you unscrew, unsettle, and unpin everything
in Scripture.

J. C. RYLE

A tax lawyer was lying on his deathbed, frantically thumbing through a little-used Bible. A friend who visited during his final hours mused, "Harvey, I didn't know you were religious." The lawyer replied, "I'm not—I'm looking for a loophole."[1]

Much of history regarding the doctrine of hell has been concerned with just that—a loophole. In my lifetime, I've only met one person who actually thought he was going to hell. Everyone else seems either to ignore the whole idea or to expect heaven.

Plato proposed that a person's soul lasts forever and ends up *somewhere*; some Supreme Good Entity figures that out. Many people since have discarded any notion of an eternal hell and hold to the idea of a cozy afterlife in some sort of heaven where everyone goes. That is, they believe heaven is *universal.* To understand how this became popular, let's look at how belief in hell has gone in and out of favor over the centuries.

A "History of Hell"

In the time of Christ, and through God's revelation in him, hell was understood as a physical destination and punishment for those who rejected him. There were alternative views of hell, but within the faith they remained on the fringes.

In the third century, Origen, a scholar and apologist from Egypt, offered a new suggestion: that hell is not a place of eternal punishment but a temporary place where sinners will be rehabilitated. All unredeemed creatures—demons and humans alike—would go through a cleansing process and be reunited with God in heaven. Even Judas, who betrayed Jesus, could be forgiven. God, a consuming fire, will consume evil, not people. Origen's theory of restoration is called by its Greek name: *apokatastasis.*

Not long thereafter, the church began to hold ecumenical councils—theological conferences to discuss concepts of orthodoxy ("right belief"). There was also a negative component: learning to refute heretical teachings. *Apokatastasis* was rejected at the fifth ecumenical council; Origen's universalist views have been considered heresy ever since.

Belief in hell as eternal punishment for the damned held firm through the Middle Ages and into the Reformation. Medieval life was harsh and uncertain; powerful (and often corrupt) clergy often used the fear of hell to control the illiterate masses. There was so much superstition in the church and such misery and oppression among the common folk that everlasting punishment for the wicked was quite acceptable. People longed for the relief that heaven offered but lived in terror of hell's torment.

In the early eighteenth century, Jonathan Edwards, a third-generation New England preacher and later president of Princeton University, delivered a hellfire-and-brimstone message titled "Sinners in the Hands of an Angry God."

The wrath of God burns against them, their damnation does not slumber; the pit is prepared, the fire is made ready, the furnace is now hot, ready to receive them; the flames do now rage and glow.[2]

Most sermons are quickly forgotten by both speaker and audience. Edwards' words, however, were so memorable that after almost two centuries a plaque was placed at the site where he preached. The sermon's influence is so significant that I traveled some distance out of my way to Enfield, Connecticut, to view the small bronze marker in commemoration of its having been given some two hundred sixty-seven years earlier. Then I traveled to Yale University's Beinecke Rare Book and Manuscript Library in New Haven, where a skilled archivist, with a heart surgeon's precision and concentration, opened the original handwritten sermon notes.

What gripped Edwards' listeners and caused "Sinners in the Hands of an Angry God" to be so revered was his graphic portrayal of hell. He emphasized the metaphors of *fire* and the *pit* so urgently that even "strong men clung to the pillars of the meetinghouse and cried aloud for mercy."[3]

Before this time, theologians were beginning to question and reject an eternal hell. A European sect called the Socinians, which later became the Unitarians, argued that hell is unjust and against God's character. Yet even these intellectual elite approved of preaching about hell to the masses, believing it kept people in line.[4]

VICTORIAN SENSIBILITIES

Most people in the late nineteenth century went to church, and overall an aura of decency and family values prevailed. Underneath all the civility, however, a theological crisis was brewing: The Bible's inspiration was suspect. God was still good, but what about hell? Typically, Victorian fathers reigned supreme over their families, yet didn't discipline too harshly, and it was difficult for people to accept God as an all-loving father who sent his wayward children to eternal damnation.

The chaplain to Queen Victoria pronounced hell a "blasphemy against the merciful God."[5] Another prominent Anglican, F. D. Maurice, arguing that eternal (spiritual) death is more consistent with God's character than eternal punishment, introduced the theology of "conditional immortality," a brand of annihilationism.[6] Lewis Carroll, author of *Alice in Wonderland*, dismissed the inspiration of Scripture and insisted that God's goodness precludes hell. In an unpublished essay titled "Eternal Punishment," Carroll said that if one believes in hell, it's illogical to believe in God.[7]

In contrast to the fiery Jonathan Edwards, Victorian preachers preferred to shelter their congregations from the distasteful, indecent concept of a literal hell. Charles Spurgeon, a British Reform Baptist, was an exception, who didn't shy away (though, unlike Edwards, he injected humor into his sermons). Spurgeon specifically challenged the notion that hellfire is metaphorical:

> . . . a metaphorical fire: who cares for that? If a man were to threaten to give me a metaphorical blow on the head, I should care very little about it; he would be welcome to give me as many as he pleased . . . [and so the wicked] do not care about metaphorical fires.[8]

MODERNIST HELL

Theologians continued to search for "acceptable alternatives" in the twentieth century. Rudolph Bultmann, a New Testament professor in Germany, had a solution: "demythologize" the Gospels. Anything that didn't fit with "scientific" understanding was discounted as myth. But mainstream theologians who still believed in authentic biblical inspiration weren't willing to accommodate; they searched for ways to explain hell without dismissing the New Testament's authority.

Meanwhile, two world wars intensified discussions of the problem of evil. Conditions in developing countries inspired liberation theology, which links "sin" to poverty and oppression. Herein salvation no longer is the saving of a soul; replacing that discarded notion was social activism addressing "social sin." Psychology claimed people couldn't be blamed for wrongs—genetics, upbringing, and environment were responsible. Rehabilitation, not punishment, was the answer to criminal behavior.

So evil was society's fault, a mindset that spawned certain theological offspring:[9]

- Anyone who speaks for God must also defend him against evil, suffering, and intolerance.
- *Love* is God's primary attribute—separate from justice, authority, constancy.
- God's justice is redefined by human standards.
- Human freedom and choice are elevated above God's holiness.

Both scholars and ordinary people were affected by these theological shifts. British New Testament scholar John Wenham agonized over the horror of hell—he saw it as worse than the horror of sin. In his quest to find a viable alternative to the doctrine of eternal punishment, he couldn't gain support for universalism and instead concluded (as had F. D. Maurice) that God created man as *inherently mortal* but grants immortality to those who choose Christ. Those who choose otherwise, then, cease to exist after death; this again is conditional immortality.[10]

Universalism—the belief that all go to heaven after death—isn't scripturally supported, but it's trendy. The Church of England jumped on the bandwagon in 1995, concluding that hell is incompatible with God's love and that the privilege of salvation should include everyone.[11]

By the turn of the century, the theological cleanup of hell had trickled down to the average person. A 1991 survey for *U.S. News & World Report* said that 60 percent of Americans believed in some kind of hell[12] but differed widely in beliefs about its nature. Almost without exception, people believed hell to be for others, not themselves.

> Universalism—the belief that all go to heaven after death—isn't scripturally supported, but it's trendy.

A God of love who doesn't judge or condemn is easier to sell. In the 1990s, Robert Brow and Clark Pinnock offered a new-millennium take on doctrine in *Unbounded Love: A Good News Theology for the 21ˢᵗ*

Century.[13] Wanting to freshen up antiquated ideas like Christ's death, sin itself, and the wrath of God,[14] Pinnock argued that the doctrine of hell needed revamping so people wouldn't dismiss it.[15] Both men supported annihilationism as kinder and gentler than eternal punishment.[16]

The world-renowned psychiatrist Karl Menninger warned against the loss of a sense of *sin* at a time when well-known preachers were abandoning the very word.[17] Norman Vincent Peale preached "the power of positive thinking," while his disciple Robert Schuler emphasized "possibility living." Some mega-church pastors have championed explosive ministry in which seeker-sensitive services avoid terms or phrases such as *salvation, born again,* and *accepting Jesus.*[18]

HELL DISAPPEARS

A prominent, dynamic pastor named Carlton Pearson also had an alternative vision. A gifted gospel singer, skilled author, and profound speaker, Pearson studied at Oral Roberts University in Tulsa, and started a church soon after; the congregation of Higher Dimensions Family quickly swelled to five thousand. He certainly had my attention—I loved his music, I listened to him speak, I read his books.

But as Pearson wrestled with the harshness of hell, he became convinced that universalism is true—that while hell is a corrective measure for some people, no one will stay there. He rejected the "classical version of hell" as "completely out of character with what we know about God,"[19] calling his variation of Origen's theory "the Gospel of Inclusion."[20] He eventually claimed that even Satan could repent. Pearson succinctly sums up his views:

> Will hell for some people last 10 minutes or 10 million years . . . ?
> We don't know. But this we do know; hell will not last for eternity; it will not be endless. . . . Don't sin. Be reunited with God now, rather than after you have put yourself (and those you love) through hell.[21]

When Pearson's council called his idea heretical, his influence began to wane, and he lost his church. Despite this, he has predicted that within five years every pastor in America will be preaching his doctrine.

UNIVERSALISM: ESCAPE HATCH FOR ALL

Universalism is based primarily on optimism and an over-simplistic view of God. The motivation is understandable: compassion for fellow humans and revulsion toward the very concept of hell. The multiple brands of universalist thinking embrace the same rationale but with different theologies and varying levels of sophistication. J. I. Packer defines three categories: secular, pluralistic, and postmortem.[22]

SECULAR UNIVERSALISM

Secular universalism doesn't involve sin, atonement (Christ's death on the cross), or salvation but instead maintains that everyone will have a pleasant eternal existence. This category includes the belief that people become angels after they die—a view upheld by Oprah Winfrey just after the tragedy of September 11, 2001. Such eschatology may entail New Age philosophy or merely wishful thinking.

PLURALISTIC UNIVERSALISM

The pluralistic approach to universalism is based on the view that there is a god of some sort and all roads lead to him. Here, all religions and belief systems have validity; the overlapping of lifestyles and practices is nothing more than a positive and enriching cultural experience; holding any worldview as superior is arrogance. All religions have equal merit and access to God, and *even Christians*, who claim salvation comes exclusively through Jesus, probably would be pardoned for this error and allowed access to the universal heaven.

Universalistic pluralism is appealing because most people would like heaven to be open to those we live, work, and play with, despite their beliefs and choices. However, it isn't compatible with Scripture.

POSTMORTEM UNIVERSALISM

Postmortem universalism, the "Christian version" (Origen's *apokatastasis*), assumes inherent human sinfulness and acknowledges our need for a savior, but it holds that God's loving patience wills to give repeated opportunities to anyone who dies without accepting Christ's atoning work. It also accounts for those who die without hearing the gospel, an issue that troubles many believers.

According to postmortem universalism, hell will be a temporary correction spot. The stop-off will last as long as necessary; rejects from purgatory can hang out there while they think things over. Eventually, though, even the most resistant atheist, the most heinous terrorist, and the most hateful mass murderer will choose salvation.

Nels Ferre, this view's most enthusiastic twentieth-century promoter, says God will tighten the screws until the recalcitrant soul relents. No one ultimately can resist his grace and goodness.

- If God *could not* save everyone, he's not all-powerful.
- If God *would not* save everyone, he's not good.
- Since God *is* all-powerful and good, everyone will be saved.[23]

This logical conclusion has flaws. For one, an omnipotent God still won't violate his own principles, which are what they are as based on his own essence. If he created human beings with the power to choose, then he cannot also make their choices for them. The annihilationist Pinnock rejects universalism for that very reason: "How can God predestine the free response of love? This is something even God cannot do."[24]

Apparently, in the postmortem scenario of hell-as-halfway-house, people can exercise free will after death. But why wouldn't some souls, having a choice, still reject God? Why *must* truly evil people choose differently, given more time?

The apostle John speaks of people who are in hell because they turned against God, and even there they curse his name and refuse to repent.[25] Pinnock agrees: "In the end he [God] will allow us to become what we have chosen."[26]

Ferre's logic also is faulty in that he defines God's goodness on his own terms. Postmortem advocates argue that God's love precludes any sort of permanent judgment or punishment because such action is unworthy of him. They insist that a God who would allow any of his creatures to go to hell is not a God of love and goodness.

But this ignores other attributes intrinsic to God's perfect character and inseparable from his love—holiness, justice, sovereignty, and, yes, anger. Any good parent knows when to show love and when to express legitimate, appropriate anger. It's the same with our heavenly Father.

———

There isn't much (if any) biblical justification for universalism. Several passages that speak of Christ's atoning work, taken out of context, can *seem* to support the idea that God will save everyone.[27] For instance, they speak of Jesus drawing all persons, God restoring everything, having mercy on them all, wanting all to be saved, not wanting anyone to perish—*all* people, the *whole* world. But careful examination shows that each statement is limited by the context of the passage and the intent of the writer.

If I say I'm "inviting everyone" to my birthday party, I'm not including everyone in the world—that's not the context of my statement. I'd be referring to everyone within a smaller group: people in my office, my church group, my neighborhood, my family, or similar group. You wouldn't know which of these I meant without learning the context.

Sometimes "all" *is* inclusive—God *does* want *all* to be saved and *everyone* to come to repentance; he offers salvation to *all*. But not everyone will accept what is offered. Some will reject it.

———

On one local freeway, the final exit ends with a sharp curve that requires slowing to about fifteen miles per hour. A mile before the curve, there's a warning sign to reduce speed. Another sign stands a little farther along, and then there's also a series of arrows that light up at night so no one will miss the curve and continue in a perilous way. But some people have ignored the signs and arrows, and they didn't brake until it was too late. Skid marks show where they've gone off the road. People can and do ignore warning signs, whether on the freeway or those given to us by God.

Remember the story Jesus told that illustrates the finality of hell, the one about the rich man and Lazarus? The rich man didn't ask Abraham to release him from his place of misery. He knew it was too late for him—he was stuck there.

The writer of Hebrews likewise confirms there won't be an opportunity to change your mind after death: "Just as man is destined to die once, and after that to face judgment, so Christ was sacrificed once to take away the sins of many people."[28] Note that Jesus takes away the sins of *many* people; forgiveness depends on our response.

> People can and do ignore warning signs, whether on the freeway or those given to us by God.

Universalist teaching is soothing to those who hate the idea of hell, but it's based on a misunderstanding of God's nature. It starts and stops on one attribute—love, which certainly is central—while ignoring justice. It ignores the clear words of Jesus and the New Testament writers not only on God's love and provision of salvation but also on those who will be forever separated from God as a result of rejecting him.[29]

When you don't like something that's clearly taught in the Bible, you have two choices: embrace it despite your dislike or try to rationalize it away. Nels Ferre has felt so strongly about his position that he claimed the disciples couldn't have understood God's love and sovereign purpose. They may even have misrepresented it, and perhaps Jesus himself misunderstood. But why does Ferre assume that *he* gets it? We can hardly uphold the Bible as testimony to God's nature and as his Word to us while assuming we understand it better than those who wrote it.

The temptation to whitewash or "air-condition"[30] hell can be strong, even among believers. But as a Christian and a pastor responsible for my congregation's welfare, I can't adopt any brand of universalism. The Bible is too explicit about hell's reality.

18

Disappearing
Acts

— ✳ —

*Annihilationism Proposes That
Those Without Faith Will Cease to Exist*

Eternity is really long, especially toward the end.

WOODY ALLEN

In C. S. Lewis's spiritual autobiography, *Surprised by Joy,* he relates an incident from his boyhood while a boarding school student in Britain. Such schools were hotbeds of humiliation and bullying, and this one was no exception. Lewis recalls being "dragged at headlong speed through a labyrinth of passages . . . beyond all usual landmarks . . . [as] one of several prisoners into a low, bare room lit by a single gas jet." He noted a row of pipes blocking the opposite wall.

> I was alarmed but not surprised when the prisoner [each boy] was forced into a bending position under the lowest pipe, in the very posture for execution. But I was very much surprised a moment later. The two gangsters gave the victim a shove; and instantly no

victim was there. He vanished; without trace, without sound. . . . Another victim was led out; again the posture for a flogging was assumed; again, instead of flogging—dissolution, atomization, annihilation![1]

Of course, young Lewis's classmates were not annihilated, much to his relief. When it was his turn to be pushed, he found himself sliding down a chute into a coal cellar, reunited with dirty classmates, a little banged up but intact.

In *conditional annihilationism*—espoused by theologians like John Wenham, John Stott, Edward Fudge, Robert Brow, David Powys, and Clark Pinnock—it's not unsuspecting schoolboys who are snuffed out but sinful humans who die without saving faith in Christ. Only those who accept salvation through Jesus will continue to exist. In this way, annihilationism contrasts with universalism, which proposes that everyone finally will be saved.

Both ideas are alternatives to the orthodox view of hell; both are based on the premise that hell as eternal punishment is contrary to God's nature. As defined here, conditional annihilation is different from the ancient Epicurean view of death as nonexistence. The Epicureans believed that upon death, a person's particles eventually would dissociate from the body and disseminate throughout the universe. Nothing more would happen—just a peaceful transition into nonbeing. No God, no soul, no afterlife for *anyone*.

Annihilation as such might make sense if there were no God. But unlike this perspective, which applies in-the-end nonexistence for everyone, we're looking at the Christian (conditional) view, which says:

- Believers are granted eternal life by God when they die.
- Unbelievers, not receiving this gift, disappear into oblivion.

This brand is also known as *conditional immortality,* and its most influential recent advocate has been John Stott. Although highly orthodox in other areas—for example, regarding the deity of Christ and the sufficiency of his atoning sacrifice—Stott wrestled emotionally with the strain of supporting hell as traditionally taught. He concluded that hell *is* a place of eternal damnation; however, to be damned means to be annihilated rather than punished.

EVANGELICALS FOR ANNIHILATIONISM

Over the last few decades a surprising number of mainstream theologians have adopted conditional immortality. After John Wenham outlined it in *The Goodness of God* (1974), an impressive number of evangelical scholars "converted." Universalism, though, is still considered unacceptable in most evangelical circles.[2]

Supporters are convinced that, for the damned, the biblical hell is not a place of eternal suffering. They base their opinions on interpretation, moral reasoning, the issue of God's character, and an appeal to emotion.[3]

The controversy over whether unrepentant sinners are annihilated or tormented is related to Scripture as well. Several New Testament Greek words, found in verses about hell, usually are translated *destruction*.[4] However, the Greek term for "destroy" has a wide range of meanings;[5] much depends on the object of destruction. For example, if I "destroy" a piece of furniture by smashing it with a sledgehammer, I can no longer use it for its intended purpose, because I now have a pile of splintered wood. But I'll still have to clean up the pieces—"destroying" the table didn't make it vanish.

Charles Hodge explains how to better understand passages used in support of annihilationism: "A soul is utterly and forever *destroyed* when it is alienated from God, rendered a fit companion only for the devil and his angels."[6]

In language that's hard for us to hear, Jesus says those alienated from God will go "into the eternal fire prepared for the

> In language that's hard for us to hear, Jesus says those alienated from God will go "into the eternal fire prepared for the devil and his angels."

devil and his angels."[7] These people will "go away to eternal punishment,"[8] which implies consciousness and existence, because you can't be punished after you've ceased to exist. Those humans who cohabit with the devil and his followers in hell will be destroyed but still will be aware of their own destruction.

Explaining the terrible fate of lost sinners, Jesus spoke to Jews who already understood from their ancient writings that there was an eternal place of suffering for the wicked. Jesus didn't refute this impression; we would expect him to, if it weren't true. The New Testament writers could have denied it as well, but they consistently describe hell as a final and everlasting state of torment for those who will not repent. We don't need further confirmation of hell's reality, and we aren't given the option of changing the Scriptures or the intents of these passages.

GOD'S JUSTICE AND PATIENCE

Despite the Bible's clear affirmation and descriptions of hell, many Christians have wrestled with the seeming contradiction between God's perfect love and the sheer awfulness of never-ending torment. Isn't God gracious and compassionate? If he can't tolerate sinful humans, why not just incinerate them? Their sins lasted a lifetime; everlasting punitive measures seem like overkill.

Only the most hardhearted or self-righteous people wouldn't struggle over these tough questions. If hell were an easier doctrine, biblical scholars wouldn't be wrangling over its meaning and searching for other explanations. How *can* we resolve the daunting issue of God's justice for wicked and unrepentant persons?

JUSTICE: FAIR IS FAIR

We all want what's "fair." The younger child gravitates toward fairness when his older sister gets the larger piece of cake. Not fair? She gets punished for not cleaning her room, while he can leave his toys strewn around the living room. Not fair. Each of us sees justice in terms of our own perceived best interests.

How can we judge what's fair or unfair in terms of sin? We can't, and that isn't our job. Furthermore, we humans will always underestimate the grievousness of sin and fail to see that the seemingly smallest act can have serious consequences. And the seriousness of the result is not always related to the intent.

Our own justice system requires payment for crimes, and God is an infinitely better judge than we are. How could annihilation pay for years of wickedness or a lifetime spent rejecting Christ? That would be a reward. Think about Adolf Hitler, a man responsible for the deaths of *millions*. In 1945, Hitler swallowed a cyanide capsule and shot himself in the head; annihilationism says that was the end for him (no consequences). Even with our limited sense of justice, *that* doesn't seem fair.

ANCIENT PERSPECTIVE ON GOD'S JUSTICE

In biblical times, people didn't spend a lot of energy debating injustice regarding the wicked. The concern of prophets like Jonah and Habakkuk was in fact just the opposite: Why does God apparently allow people to keep getting away with evil deeds? Why is he so patient? Why doesn't he punish them immediately? In that mindset, God's judgment didn't cause moral dilemmas—it solved them![9] The gods of Greek and Roman mythology, modeled after human weaknesses, were capricious and spiteful; the theistic God is perfect *and* just.

You may be familiar with Rabbi Harold Kushner's *When Bad Things Happen to Good People*, the very title of which raises many questions. We find it upsetting when calamity befalls those who don't deserve it. But equally perplexing is why *good* things happen to *bad* people. That alone might be justification for hell.

Persecuted Christians of the first century and beyond had a different take on New Testament statements about God's judgment than we do today.[10] Paul wrote to the new believers in the Macedonian city of Thessalonica, who were experiencing persecution for their faith:

> God is just: He will pay back trouble to those who trouble you and give relief to you who are troubled. . . . This will happen when the Lord Jesus is revealed from heaven in blazing fire with his powerful angels. He will punish those who do not know God

and do not obey the gospel of our Lord Jesus. They will be punished with everlasting destruction and shut out from the presence of the Lord.[11]

This sounds excessively harsh to most of us. But these people had the concern of the prophets: Why is God so patient with those who hate him? What's taking him so long? Paul's words encourage and give strength to persevere in the faith, to have confidence that God certainly will take care of evil—and evildoers.

Peter, a trusted friend of Jesus, wrote, "The Lord knows how to rescue godly men from trials and to hold the unrighteous for the day of judgment."[12] He wasn't saying God is vindictive but that God is *just*. Those who mock him and persecute his people will receive their due punishment.

EAT, DRINK, AND BE MERRY?

What if God didn't exact judgment upon sin after death? If he annihilates the wicked—vaporizes unrepentant sinners into oblivion— then it's true that "nothing is better for a man under the sun than to eat and drink and be glad."[13]

Conversely, God says to such a careless person, "You fool! This very night your life will be demanded from you."[14] Such a man's existence *won't* end with death; his soul will live on to be judged for his commitment to falsehood and repaid for his rejection of God. Jesus also says, "What good is it for a man to gain the whole world, yet forfeit his soul?"[15] If unrepentant people are annihilated after death, why *not* attempt to "gain the whole world"—there would be nothing to lose. Likewise, Hebrews refutes annihilationism in warning that "it is a dreadful thing to fall into the hands of the living God" after death.[16]

Sam Mikolaski, a Baptist minister and professor of theology, graphically sums up the rightness of God's perfect judgment: "Unless God is angry with sin, let us put a bullet in our collective brain, for the universe is mad."[17]

The annihilationist view of death and hell doesn't solve the dilemma of God's justice; rather, it redefines justice by human standards. This is compatible with our twenty-first century "tolerance" obsession and our fervent desire to explain God so as to render him tame and approachable. Nonetheless, annihilationism is inconsistent with reality.

TRYING TO GRASP ETERNITY

One of our greatest difficulties in contemplating hell is that it lasts forever. How can we comprehend a tormented, tortured existence with no end and no resolution, where time is meaningless?

My daughter Josie used to ask me a certain question frequently, late at night, in those before-I-go-to-sleep conversations. She'd say, "Dad, how long is forever? I just can't understand forever. How long is it?" I wasn't sure how to answer, except to say, "I don't know. It's just that—forever."

Human beings, caught up in time, can't truly fathom anything without beginning or end. But Jesus clearly says there is eternal existence for all: The wicked "will go away to eternal punishment, but the righteous to eternal life."[18]

Despite our inability to grasp the concept of never-ending anguish, none of us seems to have the same problem pondering never-ending joy. It's easy for universalists to postulate an all-inclusive, everlasting heaven. And it's easy for annihilationists to imagine an utter end of being for those who reject God. Hell stands for everything our culture would like to reject:

> Despite our inability to grasp the concept of never-ending anguish, none of us seems to have the same problem pondering never-ending joy.

- Human beings are sinful.
- God is holy and just.
- Sin must be paid for.
- Only Jesus paid the price for sin, and nothing else will work.

- We must accept Christ's atoning sacrifice.
- If we don't, we must pay the penalty ourselves, outside of Christ.

Several New Testament writers speak about this penalty; it *is* eternally real. Jesus himself is the chief spokesperson for the doctrine of hell. You can't reject his teaching on hell without rejecting his other words and, ultimately, his authority.

C. S. Lewis said,

> There is no doctrine which I would more willingly remove from Christianity than this [hell], if it lay in my power. But it has the full support of Scripture and specially of our Lord's own words.[19]

While we all agree with this reservation, we are compelled—if we are consistent—to accept also this conclusion.

Lewis struggled with God for many years before he "gave in and admitted that God was God, and knelt and prayed."[20] He concluded,

> There are only two kinds of people in the end: those who say to God, "Thy will be done," and those to whom God says, in the end, "Thy will be done." All that are in hell, choose it.[21]

The good news about hell is this: It wasn't intended for you, and you weren't intended for it. You don't have to go there. Choose otherwise.

19

The Celestial
Waiting Room

— ✳ —

*Is Purgatory Really a Stopover
on the Way to Heaven?*

If I have to spend time in purgatory before going to one place or the
other, I guess I'll be all right as long as there's a lending library.

STEPHEN KING

Most of us have chuckled at jokes involving someone who arrives
at the Pearly Gates and meets St. Peter. This one is updated for
our technological age.

When Sue finds herself at heaven's gates, she is surprised to find
not Peter but a lone computer terminal. On the screen are the words
"Welcome to *www.heaven.com*," with instructions to enter User ID and
Password. Sue suddenly feels panicked—she has neither. But she's comforted to see "Forgot your ID or Password? Click here." She follows
the instruction.

Then new requirements appear: "Please enter your name, date of birth, and date of death." When Sue complies, another message appears: "Sorry, no match found in database. Would you like to register with us?" Delighted that she has an option to correct this obvious error, she quickly clicks "Yes."

To her disappointment, though, an exhaustive form now appears with dozens of questions to answer. Although exasperated, she complies, meticulously handling each inquiry. At last, she finishes and clicks "Submit."

To Sue's horror, the screen reads: "Service temporarily unavailable. Please try again later."

She notices a "Back" button and with great hope, clicks on it.

But the new page says, "Welcome to *www.purgatory.com*. Please enter your User ID and Password."

That little (very little) attempt at humor aside, this chapter explores some serious questions about the in-between place most often called *purgatory:* Is there any other option besides heaven and hell? Are there second chances? Is there an opportunity, after death, to try to get it right?

Again, most people believe in the afterlife. In fact, 74 percent of Americans believe in life after death, though only 59 percent believe in hell.[1] Apparently, many people have other options in mind.

What Is Purgatory?

The short answer is: Purgatory is where one is cleansed or purged (hence the name). *Purgatory* is the noun describing a place; *purging* is the verb describing what happens there. According to this view, upon the death of someone who should not go to hell but isn't yet ready for heaven, she goes for a time to face moderate punishment in which sins are "burned away" or cleansed.

Let's look at where the idea of purgatory comes from: it starts with a brief history of Protestants and Catholics. A significant schism, Split #1, occurred within Christianity in 1054, when an East-West eruption resulted in the (Eastern) Orthodox Church and the (Western) Roman Catholic Church.

Christian Church History

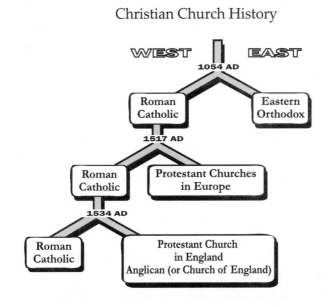

It's Split #2 that's important for our present discussion. One of Western (i.e., the Western Hemisphere) Christianity's most significant divisions occurred in 1517, with the start of the Protestant Reformation. After that, we see two distinct streams: Catholic and Protestant. Catholics trace their historical and ecclesiastical ("churchy") beginnings to Jesus and his first followers, with slow but continual developments of tradition. Protestants contend their beliefs and teachings are rooted squarely with Jesus and the New Testament accounts.[2]

On major issues—regarding such matters as Christ's divinity, death, and resurrection—the groups agree. In fact, all three (including the Eastern Orthodox) affirm many foundational aspects regarding Jesus. However, there are several key issues upon which Protestants and Catholics differ, and purgatory is one of them. To most Protestants, at death one goes to heaven or hell. To most Catholics, one might go to heaven or hell or purgatory.[3]

This gulf is demonstrated in two quotes; the first from a Catholic, the second from a Protestant:

- "We absolutely believed in Heaven and Hell, Purgatory and even Limbo. I mean, they were actually closer to us than Australia or Canada, that they were real places" (Irish author John McGahern).[4]
- "If I were a Roman Catholic, I should turn a heretic, in sheer desperation, because I would rather go to heaven than go to purgatory" (British preacher Charles Spurgeon).[5]

CAN'T WE ALL JUST GET ALONG?

Thankfully, for the sake of peace and harmony, many if not most Catholics and Protestants today have agreed to focus on their commonalities rather than their discrepancies. Despite this effort, however, there do remain a few significant differences—one involving the Bible. Protestant Bibles have sixty-six books, while the Catholic Bible includes thirteen additional books.[6]

Protestants argue that the Jewish faith (which regards the Old Testament as sacred) has never regarded the thirteen "extra" books as authentically God-inspired so as to be considered part of Scripture. Further, it was not until 1548 that Catholics officially regarded the Apocrypha (which means "hidden" or "secret") as being part of God's Word. Perhaps most important to Protestants is that the apocryphal books are never quoted in the New Testament, an indicator of their non-canonicity.

Our focus is not to resolve the validity of disputed texts (many books have been written on that subject). Simply note that Catholics and Protestants have disparate takes on this issue. This is vital for understanding the disparity in views regarding purgatory.

WHY THE MACCABEES MATTER

In the Catholic Bible are two books called 1 Maccabees and 2 Maccabees, and the latter contains a story of a Jewish hero named Judas Maccabeus, the leader of an uprising (c. 165 BC) named the Maccabean revolt in his honor. A highly acclaimed soldier, he's in the "Warrior Hall of Fame" alongside such luminaries as Joshua, Gideon, and David. On one occasion, Judas Maccabeus was in a fierce battle with a particularly high casualty rate.

> On the following day, since the task had now become urgent, Judas and his men went to gather up the bodies of the slain and bury them with their kinsmen in their ancestral tombs.
>
> But under the tunic of each of the dead they found amulets sacred to the idols of Jamnia, which the law forbids the Jews to wear. So it was clear to all that this was why these men had been slain.
>
> They all therefore praised the ways of the Lord, the just judge who brings to light the things that are hidden.
>
> Turning to supplication, they prayed that the sinful deed might be fully blotted out. The noble Judas warned the soldiers to keep themselves free from sin, for they had seen with their own eyes what had happened because of the sin of those who had fallen.
>
> He then took up a collection among all his soldiers, amounting to two thousand silver drachmas, which he sent to Jerusalem to provide for an expiatory sacrifice. In doing this he acted in a very excellent and noble way, inasmuch as he had the resurrection of the dead in view; for if he were not expecting the fallen to rise again, it would have been useless and foolish to pray for them in death.
>
> But if he did this with a view to the splendid reward that awaits those who had gone to rest in godliness, it was a holy and pious thought.
>
> Thus he made atonement for the dead that they might be freed from this sin.[7]

Why is this passage important? Because it indicates that (1) the living did something intended to impact those who were already dead, and (2) the dead were in a place where they could still be freed from their sin. This seemingly points to an impermanent place one can go after death. In other words, one can die, go somewhere other than hell, and later ascend to heaven.

Here's the crux of the matter with belief or disbelief in purgatory: This story is found in a text considered insufficiently reliable for biblical inclusion by the Jews and by the early Christians. Also, a place or stage called *purgatory* is not mentioned in the passage. Judas and his companions attempt to atone for the sins of the fallen by offering sacrifices, but there is no forthright explanation that this is to get them out of a purgatorial condition.

There's another issue too: Roman Catholics distinguish between venial (forgivable) and mortal sins. *Mortal* means "death," indicating a sin so egregious that it causes an irreparable rupture in one's relationship with God; by contrast, venial sins are burned away by purgatory. In the account involving the dead soldiers, what was their sin? Each possessed an idol. This is, by Catholic doctrine, a mortal sin, the type purgatory cannot cleanse. Standard Catholic belief underscores the seriousness of mortal sin, believing that, minus the act of penance, a person goes directly to hell. This is the only text in the Catholic Bible that might reference purgatory, yet it does not teach the doctrine of purgatory.

PROTESTANTS AND PURGATORY

A tiny Protestant minority has affirmed purgatory or its equivalent. Surely the best known pro-purgatory comments are from C. S. Lewis.

> Our souls demand Purgatory, don't they? Would it not break the heart if God said to us, "It is true, my son, that your breath smells and your rags drip with mud and slime, but we are charitable here and no one will upbraid you with these things, nor draw away from you. Enter into the joy"? Should we not reply, "With submission, sir, and if there is no objection, I'd rather be cleaned first." "It may hurt, you know"–"Even so, sir."
>
> My favorite image on this matter comes from the dentist's chair. I hope that when the tooth of life is drawn and I am "coming round," a voice will say, "Rinse your mouth out with this." This will be Purgatory. The rinsing may take longer than I can now imagine. The taste of this may be more fiery and astringent than my present sensibility could endure. But . . . it will [not] be disgusting and unhallowed.[8]

Other pro-purgatory Protestants include Jerry Walls, formerly a professor at a major evangelical theological seminary. Walls argues for a type of purgatory based in part on the reality that "Christians are imperfect lovers of God and others at the time of their death."[9]

BIBLICAL BACKING?

The primary Protestant contention is that purgatory is not in Scripture. To this, Catholics respond that neither are many accepted theological terms or concepts—say, *Trinity* or *incarnation*. Catholic theologians argue that the *concept* is present in the Scriptures, even if the *word* is not.

Pro-purgatory Christians also cite Christ's words that one's sins will be forgiven "either in this age or in the age to come,"[10] which they consider to be a clear purgatory reference. Protestants insist this actually is an affirmation that forgiveness (or the refusal of forgiveness) impacts one's life now and in eternity.

Another statement used in support of purgatory is in Paul's first letter to the believers in Corinth:

> [A man's] work will be shown for what it is, because the Day will bring it to light. It will be revealed with fire, and the fire will test the quality of each man's work. If what he has built survives, he will receive his reward. If it is burned up, he will suffer loss; he himself will be saved, but only as one escaping through the flames.[11]

Protestants insist that Paul is not talking about cleansing sins after death but about a loss of rewards that comes at the judgment seat of Christ.

So if purgatory isn't explicitly in the Bible, how did the concept become so rooted within Catholic theology?

SCRIPTURE AND TRADITION

Herein lies one key difference between Protestants and Catholics: The former affirm the Bible as the sole authoritative source of truth, while the latter affirm Scripture and "tradition." In other words, "official" church history has equal authority with the Bible.[12] If a pope or a church council affirms purgatory, then purgatory is considered to be real (unless another pope or church council changes the course).

Catholics also argue that there are examples, by way of the Jewish faith (which forms the foundation for Christianity), where praying for the dead would presume a temporary or purgatory-like place. And some early Christians in the first centuries after Jesus did indeed pray for the dead.

The concept of purgatory became more widespread and highly developed under the sixth-century leadership of Gregory the Great. Citing the "age to come" reference in Matthew, Gregory wrote:

> As for certain lesser faults, we must believe that, before the Final Judgment, there is a purifying fire. He who is truth says that who-ever utters blasphemy against the Holy Spirit will be pardoned neither in this age nor in the age to come. From this sentence we understand that certain offenses can be forgiven in this age, but certain others in the age to come.[13]

Gregory did not view purgatory as a second chance for unrepentant sinners but rather as a place for Christ-followers to get rid of the stain of sinful nature and/or for those who are guilty due to ignorance of truth. Regardless of Gregory's "greatness," though—and he was profoundly influential, well beyond this concept—most Protestants believe purgatory cannot be biblically validated.

With the passage of time, teaching about purgatory lent itself to tragic abuses. Commonly recalled is the manipulation of naïve and unschooled peasants by unethical priests, who collected fees allegedly to get people's relatives out of purgatory sooner if adequate fees were paid. The split between Protestants and Catholics historically traces to Martin Luther's reaction to a sixteenth-century monk, Johann Tetzel, who offered chances to buy, for cash, deceased relatives an earlier escape from purgatory.[14]

How Long Is the Wait?

All of us have found ourselves sitting in a crowded waiting room or standing in a serpentine line at the bank—we check our watch and think,

Wow, how long is this going to take? The same question comes to mind when we consider purgatory: How long must people stay in the "celestial waiting room"?

The answer is, "It depends." It depends on what *you* do. And it depends on what *others* do for you. And there is the rub. Notice the you-centeredness of the answer. The most correct response to "How long in purgatory?" depends on:

(1) the number of one's sins;
(2) the deliberateness with which those sins were committed;
(3) the penance performed for those sins;
(4) the actions (accelerating the "purging") of the living for the dead.[15]

> The split between Protestants and Catholics historically traces to Martin Luther's reaction to a sixteenth-century monk, Johann Tetzel, who offered chances to buy, for cash, deceased relatives an earlier escape from purgatory.

To most Protestants, this seems a tragic distraction. The concept of purgatory ultimately robs us of the sufficiency of the cross. The real response to the problem of human sin must always be that *I cannot do anything to erase it.* In all honesty, we are powerless to eradicate it. But the breathtaking answer to human sin is that Jesus *can* take care of it. And he *did*.

Posted over the cross of Christ should be a sign reading, "I did this for you, because you cannot do it for yourself. I set you free—from your sin. No stopover in purgatory needed. Embrace what I did, and go straight to heaven."

THREE GUIDING WORDS

A point made earlier bears repeating: Catholics and Protestants by and large have chosen to focus on similarities instead of differences.

I have many dear Catholic friends whom I deeply respect and whose faith I admire.[16] We simply differ on the issue of purgatory.

To me, the strongest argument against purgatory is something beyond the presence or absence of the word or concept in the Bible. It has to do with the epicenter of our faith: the death of Jesus. The most fundamental teaching of historic Christianity is the fact that Christ's death cancels out the result of sin in the hearts and lives of those who by faith embrace the Savior. Jesus took the responsibility for our sins upon himself. His death, so many years ago, was given to handle whatever purgatory supposedly is meant to purge.

> The most fundamental teaching of historic Christianity is the fact that Christ's death cancels out the result of sin in the hearts and lives of those who by faith embrace the Savior.

Let's focus on three words: *assigned, actual,* and *accomplished.* When one chooses to accept that Jesus' death truly does have relevance to one's life—now, here, today— then he has what would be called *assigned* righteousness. In other words, God in his mercy *assigns* the goodness of Christ to him. We are not righteous. However, God assigns it to us, entirely by grace, without merit. Why? Because he loves us and because we have responded to him with loving faith.

That's only the beginning. As an individual continues to grow in spiritual maturity, in her understanding of biblical truth and its application to holy living, there is more than just assignment; she begins to demonstrate *actual* righteousness. She begins to act, think, and speak more like Jesus. This is tremendously encouraging, this practical realization of personal progress.

At the same time, the holier one's life, the more she becomes attuned to God's pure holiness. With this comes awareness of one's failures, even in the midst of personal improvements. We become aware of how far we are from the perfection of Christ, the type of perfection that would merit heaven.

Here we become aware of our need for *accomplished* righteousness or purity. Only persons with complete righteousness would ever enter heaven.

In more common terminology, these phases (*assigned, actual,* and *accomplished*) are referred to as "initial salvation" (justification) ongoing "sanctification," and then, at death, "glorification." Viewed as a timeline:

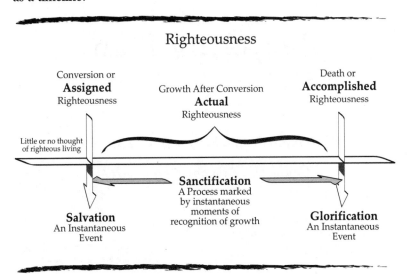

And that's what happens at death. Once again, purgatory isn't needed.

Paul says absence from the body means to be at home with the Lord.[17] Leaving this life is being immediately with Christ.[18] Not even a hint of purgatory.

His enthusiasm for an instant post-death reunion with Jesus is compelling. If one faces death having accepted the reality of Christ's accomplishment on the cross, then a spectacular reunion awaits. Not later, but sooner.

The well-known Monopoly card says "Do not pass Go. Do not collect $200." In effect, Christ's work seems to say, "Do not go to purgatory. No need." His sacrifice in effect allows you—each of us—to receive a card that says "No purgatory. Go directly to heaven."

2 0

Recycling Plan

——— ✳ ———

If Millions of People Believe in Reincarnation,
Could There Be Something to It?

Reincarnation is making a comeback.

BUMPER STICKER

Julius Caesar was one frustrated general. He was battling the fearless Celts, who were more courageous than any force he had encountered. His difficulties were rooted in the staunch Celtic belief in reincarnation—that "souls do not become extinct, but pass after death from one body to another."[1]

The soul of a soldier killed in battle would move on to inhabit another body. This assurance of an endless cycle of life presented no small problem for a military leader.

But the Celts were not alone in believing one could return to earthly life, and several religious groups today uphold reincarnation: Hindus, Buddhists, and Sikhs, for example, along with some smaller sects and an assortment of New Age groups. Differences emerge quickly: Some contend that souls were created by a "god-force," while others argue that the soul has its own intrinsic being—a preexistence.[2]

At its core, reincarnation is "the belief that a living being . . . after cessation of existence on earth, will experience a new birth and enter existence again in the form of another being." In some variations rebirth applies only to human beings. Jack London, author of *Call of the Wild* as well as a reincarnation classic called *The Star Rover*, wrote,

> I did not begin when I was born, nor when I was conceived. I have been growing, developing, through incalculable myriads of millenniums. All my previous selves have their voices, echoes, promptings in me. Oh, incalculable times again shall I be born.[3]

Reincarnation is based on two assumptions: First, time is cyclical—sometimes termed "timelessness"—therefore, whatever happens will happen again. Second, the class of a given birth depends on the deeds of the previous life.[4] This is called *karma*, viewed essentially as a law of cause and effect, echoing collectively through an ongoing series of lives, rebirths, and deaths.

Reincarnation is an ancient concept, certainly dating to before the incarnation,[5] with roots in the Hindu Vedas (scriptures). Most other reincarnation forms—for instance, Buddhist (half of all Buddhists live in China, Japan, and Thailand) and Jainist or Sikh (both mainly in India)—spring from this common source. There is some tracing of the teaching to Greek philosophy as well. Reincarnation's more Western expressions, such as Transcendental Meditation, also find their source in Hinduism.

It's not a biblical notion, but reincarnation has enjoyed increasing popularity as Eastern and New Age religions have become chic. Wide acceptance in the U.S. has been furthered by personalities like Edgar Cayce, Jeanne Dixon, and Shirley MacLaine; other well-known fans have included Henry Ford, George Patton, Salvador Dali, Mark Twain, George Harrison, John Denver, and Deepak Chopra. Consider these statistics:

- 92 percent of Americans believe in God
- 85 percent believe in heaven

- 82 percent believe in miracles
- 71 percent believe in the devil's existence (up from 63 percent in 1997)
- 34 percent believe in ghosts
- 29 percent accept astrological forecasts
- 25 percent believe in reincarnation[6]

At first glance, 25 percent may not seem like a high rate of belief, compared to the other categories. Yet in some surveys as many as 83 percent of Americans claim to be Christian.[7] Since we'll later see that the Bible denies reincarnation, it's remarkable that one in four Americans affirm it.

Why is the concept of rebirth so embraced? Its appeal lies partly in the promise of having multiple opportunities to "get it right." Renowned botanist Luther Burbank spoke glowingly in this regard:

> The theory of Reincarnation . . . is one of the most sensible and satisfying of all religions that mankind has conceived. This, like the others, comes from the best qualities of human nature, even if . . . its adherents sometimes fail to carry out the principles in their lives.[8]

EVIDENCE FOR REINCARNATION

One of America's best-known reincarnation scholars is Ian Stevenson, a psychiatrist whose long career focused on children between ages two and five who purportedly were able to recall vivid details from past lives.[9] Stevenson's extensive academic articles covered more than three thousand study cases, and many people have claimed he proved reincarnation conclusively.[10]

His research is so extensive and technical that it's helpful to read what others have said.[11] The suggested evidence for reincarnation fits into several categories:

- Memories of previous lives
- Xenoglossy, the ability to speak a language one does not know

- Presence of birthmarks or physical deformities matching a deceased person
- Personation—full identification of the living person with the deceased person's identity
- The Bible's supposed affirmation of reincarnation (we'll come back to this).[12]

Although Stevenson's work seemed to support the possibility, he was careful to refer to it as "suggestive of reincarnation."[13] Do the cases studied by such a distinguished scholar really confirm such rebirth? *Not* conclusively, he thought. He provided an alternative, one he claimed should be taken seriously: "Possession of the living by a foreign spirit."[14] This can't be overstated: *One of the world's top research scientists in the field acknowledged that a foreign spirit could occupy a living person.*

Gary Habermas,[15] a Christian scholar, is quick to caution that Stevenson is not suggesting *demonic* possession. Instead, Stevenson is explaining the phenomenon as possession by the disembodied "spirit of the actual person who had previously died."[16]

Stevenson himself acknowledges that "the distinction between reincarnation and possession becomes blurred."[17] Here is how he defines the terms:

> . . . if the previous personality seems to associate itself with the physical organism at the time of conception or during embryonic development we speak of *reincarnation*; if the association between previous personality and physical organism only comes later, we speak of *possession*.[18]

It's possible that what we think of as reincarnation is really a foreign spirit taking hold of, or possessing, a living person. This causes the person to *think* he or she was someone else in a previous life. Habermas observes:

> Researchers and theorists have not proved that these cases demand reincarnation. . . . There are several cases where either discarnate or demonic possession serves as the best explanation and seems to be accepted as such by most researchers, including Stevenson himself.[19]

Sometimes the deceased person (supposedly reincarnated) died *after* the birth of the individual who was later influenced. This sequence dispels any notion of "I died" and then "I was reborn." The timing is simply off. As Stevenson says, "No matter how you look at it, reincarnation gets the short end of the evidential stick."[20]

Xenoglossy, or speaking a previously unlearned language, can be accounted for by possession, so it doesn't constitute solid evidence for reincarnation. Neither does sharing birthmarks or a physical defect with a dead person. Stevenson cites mystics who sometimes develop stigmata, or wounds corresponding to those suffered by Jesus on the cross. Having those wounds does not make them reincarnations of Jesus. Similarity does not prove sameness.[21]

The Bible doesn't teach reincarnation; it affirms the reality of demonic influence and warns against "familiar spirits,"[22] demons who pose as someone with whom you are familiar, perhaps a deceased spouse or parent. They are *not* deceased loved ones but rather spirits under Satan's direction. Scripture says to have nothing to do with them.

> The Bible doesn't teach reincarnation; it affirms the reality of demonic influence and warns against "familiar spirits," demons who pose as someone with whom you are familiar, perhaps a deceased spouse or parent.

You may recall that in a previous chapter we stated that although one should never seek to communicate with the dead, a bereaved person might sense the presence or even witness the appearance of a deceased loved one. Does that contradict this warning regarding "familiar spirits"? No, it doesn't. Being aware of the presence of a loved one, which provides comfort and solace, is considerably different from *deliberately seeking* information from the dead. Demons do not comfort—they attempt to deceive. It is in the seeking of information that one becomes prone to error and vulnerable to deception.

Do not confuse soliciting information from spirits—which is dangerous and to be avoided—with the God-provided solace from the sensed presence of a deceased loved one.

Habermas concludes:

> Reincarnation has no real data in its favor. . . . Reincarnation simply does not offer any true or distinctive answer to the nature of life after death.
>
> It is certainly debatable if any case of reincarnation could ever be proven, due to the possibility that possession could also account for pre-birth examples of a spirit's entering another's body.
>
> . . . Even if there is no evidence for reincarnation, our discussion still produced another sort of consideration in favor of an afterlife. Since there is evidence for possession of a body by another spirit, this would appear to constitute some "back door" data in favor of a spiritual world of some sort where life after death is distinctly possible, if not likely.[23]

CAN REINCARNATION AND CHRISTIANITY COEXIST?

Advocates say reincarnation is in complete harmony with the spirit of Christianity. They claim it was taught in the days after Jesus until some began to suppress it in the sixth century. Leslie Weatherhead, pastor of London's City Temple for more than thirty years, contended that since reincarnation was the prevailing belief during the time of Jesus, and he never denied it, then he must have accepted it.[24]

Reincarnationists claim sound biblical support for their beliefs. The most commonly cited verses are:

- John 3:3, in which Jesus urges Nicodemus to be born again (interpreted as a reference to the capacities for additional lives)

- Matthew 11:13–14, in which Jesus seems to say John the Baptist was Elijah (seen as evidence of reincarnation)
- Hebrews 7:1–3, in which the writer appears to be saying Jesus had a previous life in the person of Melchizedek
- John 9:2, in which the disciples ask Jesus if a man was born blind due to sin (implying they believed in karma)

Do these Scriptures show that the Bible teaches reincarnation? In the John 3 passage, Nicodemus was bewildered by Jesus' reference to a second birth. Jesus made it clear this birth was spiritual, not physical. If Jesus believed in reincarnation, this would have been the time to teach it. Instead, he refuted it.[25]

Matthew 11:14 is equally mishandled. Reincarnationists fail to note that John himself denied he was Elijah. When asked, "Are you Elijah?" he said, "I am not." He stated flatly that he was not "the Prophet."[26]

Jesus' clear explanation that John would come "in the spirit and power of Elijah"[27] means John would be *like* him. Elijah was taken to heaven without undergoing a normal physical death,[28] which is necessary for the life-death-rebirth cycle. When he made an appearance with Moses at the Mount of Transfiguration,[29] Elijah appeared as himself, not as someone who had been reborn in another body. (Likewise, Hebrews 7:2–3 clearly says Melchizedek was *like* Jesus, not that he *was* Jesus.)

Of John 9:1–3, reincarnationists claim, "They [the disciples] were among the most knowledgeable men of Christian doctrine . . . because they got it straight from the Master; and yet these learned men asked if the man was born blind because of a previous sin."[30] However, Jesus' explanation plainly refuted any law of karma.

Is reincarnation taught in the Bible? Again, no, but let's take the question a step further. Does the Bible straightforwardly teach that reincarnation is false?

James, half brother of Jesus, certainly would have been one to know what Jesus taught. He wrote that one's life is like a mist that appears for a little while and then vanishes.[31] Had he believed in reincarnation, James might have written that life is like a persistent fog that never lifts! Hebrews says, "Man is destined to die once, and after that to face judgment,"[32] which again reinforces that death comes only once.

Can one be an authentic believer in both the Bible and in reincarnation? Since we've seen that they aren't compatible, the answer is no.

> Can one be an authentic believer in both the Bible and in reincarnation? Since we've seen that they aren't compatible, the answer is no.

THE BIG PICTURE

To comprehend the most significant difference between Christianity and reincarnation, we need to first grasp the terms *monism* and *pantheism*.

Monism holds that "all is one," that everything that exists is one. Pantheism says, "All is one, one is all, all is god." *Pantheistic monism* affirms that everything—all the created order—is god and is one with god. There is no personal God who is separate from his creation, and this is part of the reincarnationist paradigm. A pantheistic monist wouldn't say, "In the beginning God created the heavens and the earth."[33]

In sharp contrast, the *monotheistic* ("one God") faiths—Christianity, Judaism, Islam—reject pantheistic monism and affirm two distinct entities: (1) a personal Creator God, and (2) everything else, which He created.

Eastern and New Age religions are largely monist, believing in a type of all-encompassing godlike force. Reincarnation involves three cycles: first, living things die; then, based on their state of mind at death (e.g., positive or negative), they experience a deep, drugged sleep; then, they are reborn.[34] Reincarnation supposedly is impacted only by the good or bad karma of the previous life or lives.

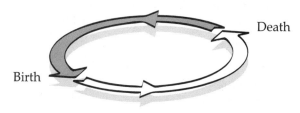

Reincarnational View of History: Cyclical

Death

Birth

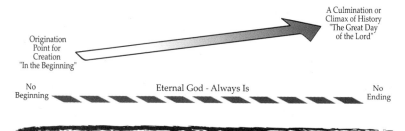

A Simplistic Biblical View of History: Linear

A Culmination or
Climax of History
"The Great Day
of the Lord"

Origination
Point for
Creation
"In the Beginning"

No
Beginning

Eternal God - Always Is

No
Ending

This cyclical portrayal is antithetical to Scripture's linear, upward historical movement toward an end-of-time crescendo: starting point ("In the beginning"); unfolding storyline (God's intervention in human affairs and his coming to earth in the person of Jesus); and end, or climax (the ultimate, final destiny of all humans).

Of course, in some ways history is bound to repeat itself. Picture the line, then, as always moving upward toward an end yet not on a two-dimensional, flat surface—more like a spiral. Think of the wire in a spiral notebook. While it comes back around to a point similar to where it was one cycle ago, it's truly not at the same place and it's closer to the top. Such is history: It may feel like "everything is the same," but it isn't. With each passing moment, we are moving closer to what Scripture calls the "great day of the Lord,"[35] the culmination of history, when time as we know it will be no more.

A Complete Biblical View of History: Spiral

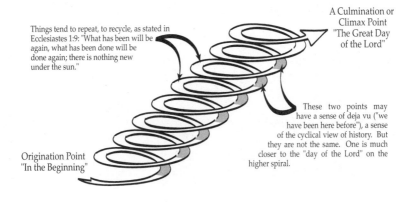

Things tend to repeat, to recycle, as stated in Ecclesiastes 1:9: "What has been will be again, what has been done will be done again; there is nothing new under the sun."

A Culmination or Climax Point "The Great Day of the Lord"

These two points may have a sense of deja vu ("we have been here before"), a sense of the cyclical view of history. But they are not the same. One is much closer to the "day of the Lord" on the higher spiral.

Origination Point "In the Beginning"

Based on the biblical view of God, an understanding of his involvement in creating the cosmos, his personal involvement in our lives, and his nudging history toward closure, we see that Christian faith and reincarnation are mutually exclusive.

Belief in reincarnation means saying "no, thanks" to a loving, tender, heavenly Father. Monism says *you* are god and god is *you*, but we humans were created to need someone bigger, greater, better, and stronger than we are. We need the one God, who loves us, cares about us, and wants us—*created* us—to belong to him.

PART SIX

Confident Before the King

21

Forever and Ever, Amen

—— ✳ ——

God Wants You to Be Comfortable With Him
in This World and the Next

Time is short. Eternity is long. It is only reasonable that this short
life be lived in the light of eternity.

CHARLES SPURGEON

Years ago the speaker at my brother's funeral said, "The older
we get, the more we realize that fewer and fewer things are truly
important."

In reality, life is like a funnel. When we're young we think every-
thing is significant. In our thirties, we discover that much less is crucial.
At fifty, the "really important things" have greatly reduced in number.
This continues in our seventies, eighties, and beyond.

If only a few things make a difference when we end this life, how
about living for those things *now*, no matter where you are in the age
continuum?

What will matter when you take your last breath? Only one thing: that you are ready to meet God. How about learning to know and enjoy him *now*, so the crossover won't be such a jolt?

When I was in high school, my pastor asked me unexpectedly, "Jim, are you ready to die?"

"I dunno," I muttered, taken aback by his abruptness.

"Because," he continued, "you aren't ready to live till you're ready to die."

At the time I thought maybe he was just posing the kind of soul-searching dilemma pastors are supposed to bring. But I've never forgotten that question, and I've realized the wisdom contained in it.

I decided I wanted to be ready to die. How about you? Are you ready?

We've explored some fascinating territory: NDEs, heaven, hell, ghosts, angels, demons, and much more. All this material could be *theoretical* or even *theological*, but nonetheless it should be highly *personal* and *practical*. Each of us one day will cross over from here to the afterlife. Becoming clear about there and then will greatly influence how we live here and now.

CHARACTERIZING THE CREATOR

There are lots of perceptions about God: powerful . . . mean . . . loving . . . preoccupied. Many see him as perpetually angry, scowling, condemning their every move. Others see him as a syrupy celestial Santa, handing out gifts and affirming everything. If what the Bible says is true, neither is accurate.

The latest Harris poll reveals that 80 percent of adult Americans believe in God, which represents no statistical change over the previous three years. However, barely a majority of adults believe *all or most* of the Old Testament (55 percent) and the New Testament (54 percent) are the Word of God. Only 37 percent (Old Testament) and 36 percent (New Testament) believe *all* of these texts are God's Word.[1] Apparently, many aren't sure they can have confidence in the Bible.

Let me pose a critical question: What's the most credible source for knowing about God? The Bible? Islam's Qur'an? Hinduism's Bhagavad

Gita? Buddhism's Buddhavacana? *Bruce Almighty*? Whatever book Oprah Winfrey endorses? *Touched by an Angel*? Deepak Chopra? How do we know about God? How are we to form our understanding of him?

Deep within, we all long to know that the one true God is knowable. In case you don't already, assume with me for now that the Bible *is* the source for knowing God.

You may ask why, in a book about life hereafter, I'm concluding with a discussion on God's nature. *The afterlife, properly understood, is all about God.* It's about his desire to be with us. It's about the great plans he has for us. It's about the close friendship he's eager to experience with us.

Therein is the question. Just how comfortable are you with God? Allow me to tell you a story—God's story. When we better understand his character and heart, we'll become clearer about his intent for our afterlife—mine and yours.

THE STORY OF GOD #1: TWO KEY WORDS

The first part of the story involves two words. One is the Old Testament Hebrew *chesed* (pronounced *KHEH*-sed, with a hard K, or guttural sound from deep in your throat). The other is the New Testament Greek *agape* (ah-GAW-pay). Both mean "love," or, as we're using them here, "the love of God," which cannot possibly be explained in a few pages. *Chesed* means "unending, unswerving loyalty"; God uses the term to try to convey his fierce loyalty to us.

In order to explain this term, I need to tell you about Joe and Georgette. Joe was consumed with Georgette's beauty. They fell in love. They married. However, when their first child was born, Joe had a sinking feeling. Observing his wife's conduct, he wondered if this really was his child. He watched as other men exchanged glances with her. A second child came. Same question. Then a third. Now there was no doubt. The babies were not Joe's. He was devastated.

Then Georgette abandoned Joe and their young children to become a prostitute. Joe was stunned and crushed. His heart broke as he tried to explain to three sobbing children why Mommy had walked away.

As best he could, he kept alive his heart's dream that someday she would return.

The passage of time was hard on Georgette. The toll taken by prostitution stole her beauty. Fewer and fewer men sought her services. She sank so low in the ranks that she was functioning virtually as a slave. After years of no contact, one day Joe caught a split-second glimpse of her on a crowded street. As his eyes met hers, he still recognized what once had been a breathtakingly beautiful girl.

He'd found her! After negotiating with her pimp, he bought her freedom.

As he led her back to the home she'd once known, he held her hand tenderly. It was the first time a man had treated her kindly since she'd left him. He cherished her as his honored wife. At first she was suspicious, waiting for his wrath. When it never came, she began to receive his affirmation and love.

I didn't make up this story. It actually happened 2,700 years ago. The man's name wasn't Joe but Hosea. The woman's wasn't Georgette but Gomer.

Chesed, used in the book of Hosea, means "love that just will not give up or let go." It's the kind of love Hosea had for Gomer. To Hosea, God says, in essence, "Just as you had love that would not give up on Gomer, even though she was unfaithful, had run away, and lost her beauty, so I will not give up on people who have been unfaithful to me, have run away from me, even if they have messed up everything in their lives." *That is God's commitment to you.*

Agape, used over and over in the New Testament, means love that's spontaneous, lavish, freely given, and undeserved or unwarranted. *That is the love God has for you.*

There's another important dimension to such love: it confers great value on you. That God—the Creator of everything—loves *you* adds enormous value to your life. That's what *agape* truly is. And this word repeatedly conveys how special you really are.

THE STORY OF GOD #2: HE CRIED

Jesus is divine; he's God. But if we're not careful we can miss out on his humanness, which is no less important than his divinity. There are perhaps few more distinctly human expressions than tears, and Jesus cried at least twice.

Lazarus was a close friend of Jesus.[2] When news of his life-threatening illness reached him, Jesus delayed coming to his aid. Martha, one of Lazarus's sisters, was thoroughly perturbed that Jesus had waited so long. *Why?* she wondered. Finally, a messenger brought word that Jesus was on the outskirts of Bethany, where Lazarus had already died—crossed over from life to the afterlife.

Martha turned to her sister Mary and said, "Do you want to go meet Jesus?"

"I can't," sobbed Mary, too heartbroken to walk across the little town.

Martha ran to meet him. Coming over the crest of the last small hill, all her other emotions were overcome by resentment. Why had Jesus not made an effort to come earlier? Gruffly, she said, "If you'd come quickly when we sent word, my brother would still be alive."

She was shocked at the abrasiveness of her own tone. Feeling a twinge of guilt, she offered a consolation statement: "But God will give you now what you ask of him." She believed that—at least she wanted to. After all, Lazarus had been dead four days.

"It will be all right. He'll rise again," Jesus responded. His declaration wasn't boastful, and something about how he said it caused her to believe him.

"Yes," she meekly responded, "everyone will rise someday."

"I'm not talking about *someday*," he told her. "I'm telling you *I am* the resurrection." He paused, looked at her eye to eye, and without flinching asked, "Do you believe that?"

She paused, not out of doubt but attempting to understand both his question and her answer. "Yes," she whispered.

Nothing more was spoken then. She ran the short distance back to the house. "Mary, come now! Come, right now! He wants you to come. *Now.*"

The grieving Mary was half-pulled by her sister to Jesus. Trailing them was a score of mourning friends and relatives.

Moments later, she was giving a hug to her good friend. Unaware of Martha's chastisement, she parroted what had been said only moments before: "If you'd been here, Lazarus would have lived." Not answering the accusation a second time, Jesus simply waited. And they awaited his response.

Then his eyes welled with tears. "Where is he?" Barely audible.

Without words, Mary motioned toward the burial cave holding her brother's body. No one spoke in the four minutes it took to get there.

Then the crowd stood still. Exactly what did they expect? Depends on which mourner you asked. But no one expected what occurred next. Jesus just stood there. He did not say a word. And then those gathered heard a sound few had ever heard before—the sound of a man crying.

> He's human.
> He feels pain.
> He feels your
> humanness,
> your hurt.
> *He cares.*

Men don't like to cry—and certainly not in public. But he cried. Audibly. The sounds were those of a man feeling the loss of a friend, a brother. Standing at a burial site containing the body, along with grieving friends, was too much. As recorded in what would become the Bible's shortest verse, "Jesus wept."[3]

He's human. He feels pain. He feels your humanness, your hurt. *He cares.* And he wants to spend a time called *forever* with you.

The second episode came as the end of Jesus' ministry was approaching. He was coming into the great capital of Jerusalem, always a challenge. A group of hypocrites tried to run the place, theologically speaking. And there was the Sanhedrin, a combination of Harvard elites and a religious supreme court—about seventy of the most nitpicky guys you could ever meet. Then there was Roman interference and oppression. Would the Jews *ever* be free from intruders?

But this trip was different: It would be Jesus' last. He knew. Most others didn't. He'd tried to explain, even to his closest friends. He was the only person who'd been born to die; his *purpose* was dying. This final foray would be "it."

Cresting the hill on the road that would take him to the Mount of Olives on the city's eastside, he tugged slightly on the reins of the small colt he rode. The crowd that had been busy singing and shouting praises noticed something was wrong. They quieted.

He didn't move. The colt, at his bidding, stood motionless. Sensing something significant, everyone froze.

And then they heard it. Barely audible. A sound was coming from Jesus.

One lone figure—or so I picture in my mind—among the crowd dared move, ever so slightly. Amani turned to his younger brother and whispered, "I've heard this before. I know it."

"What is it?" his brother asked.

Amani hesitated to speak the words, but finally they came, so quietly as to be hardly heard. "He's crying. I was there that day—when he came to Bethany. He's crying again."

And he was. Jesus cried over a city, over its people. He saw what could have been. He saw what it had become. The gap was enormous. All the dreams, the hopes . . . but Jerusalem had made its decision. The "city of peace" was just hours from rejecting the only one who could bring peace. Its destruction would come. Soon—in just four decades. The unthinkable—Jerusalem would be destroyed. And Jesus' words about no stone left on another would prove true.[4]

And he was brokenhearted. He wanted to be with them. He wanted to be close to them. The incarnation of God wanted to be with those he had created. And this same One wants to be with you.

The Story of God #3: A Plane Crash, an Adoption, and Cancer

Bob and Bill were my twin brothers, eight years my junior. They were college freshmen in Kansas City when I was a graduate student in New Jersey.

One evening as I left our house with my wife, Carol, I heard the phone ring inside. But as I turned to reenter, I realized I'd locked the door with the keys inside. I stood there helpless and exasperated, knowing I couldn't respond to the caller.

With nothing to be done at the moment, we left with our friends in their car, went to our evening engagement, and returned hours later to climb through a window. Then the phone rang again. Whatever else my father said, I do not now recall. The words I did hear were "Bob has been killed in a plane crash."

Crumpled on the floor, I heard a sound come out of me that I'd never heard before and have not heard since. It was utter, devastating shock and grief escaping my lips. My brother was suddenly dead, along with my cousin Rick and Bob's college roommate, Dave.

The funerals—plural—were excruciating. The sight of three gleaming caskets containing the remains of nineteen-years-olds was overwhelming, first at their college and then as we made our way three and a half hours to North Central Kansas, where nearly a thousand people filled the Concordia High School auditorium. Only eleven months before, Bob had graduated there.

In the days that followed, well-meaning sages waxed philosophic as to reasons for the deaths of three young men. I was well aware of the standard talking points in moments like this. I recalled the rationales I'd read for my sister's death—Janie died before I was born. Loved ones had written poems trying to help my parents through their questions and struggles; they'd only been married two years when this tragedy befell them.

One poem stands out in my mind to this day. It compared my sister to a rose that God, when seeing it, liked so much he simply picked it. Comforting to others, perhaps, but dreadful to me. What kind of God would "pick a rose" just because he liked it, with no thought for the consequences of his action?

With regard to the deaths of Bob, Rick, and Dave, the explanations were more standard fare. The defense of their deaths contained such phrasing as "Well, when you see how many youth came to know God through their funeral, you can see his hand, his plan in it all."

Plan! What kind of plan? If God wanted students to be drawn to him, he didn't need to kill three kids to do it. He could have sent Billy Graham to town! The price seemed too high. I wanted my brother back.

My struggles were not those of a rebellious juvenile. They were the heart renderings of a theology graduate student, one deeply committed to God but profoundly bothered by some of his arch-apologists.

To add insult to injury, I was told I shouldn't ask why. My response: "Why not? Why can't I ask why?"

They said, "That shows your lack of faith."

"Nonsense," I retorted. "The very fact that I'm asking *God* is proof in itself that I have confidence *in him, in God.* If I thought the devil had the power, I'd ask the devil why. But I know *God* has all power. My asking isn't evidence of insufficient faith—it shows I affirm his omnipotence. Asking why *honors* God."

I have always regarded Jesus' disciple Thomas as my hero. Many preachers say he was the doubter. I say he was the questioner. The questions Thomas asked are the exact ones I would have asked.[5]

Vigorous questions asked of God do not bother him. He's secure. He can handle it. *He understands the "Why, why, why—I wanna know why!" cries of his kids.*

In time, I had a realization. What if . . . what if God would somehow tell me the *why* of Bob's death? Would I be satisfied? No. Bob would still be dead.

I realized my key question was not "why?" but "where?" As in, "Where were you? Did you lose control? Could you not stop the plane from going down? Where were your angels that sometimes rescue people in peril?" My questions pertained more to having future confidence than trying to figure out what to do about the past death of a brother. Bottom line: Could I trust God?

About that time, a wise Kansan cowboy from Abeyville named Harv Schmucker called our home. (Harv always said Abeyville was a "poke and plum town"—if you poked your nose around the corner, you was plum out of town.)

My dad answered. Harv said, "I'll bet you wonder where God was when Bob's plane was going down that day, now don't ya?"

"Yes, that has crossed my mind," Dad responded.

"Well," Harv continued, with his distinctive twang, "God the Father was on his throne, in charge, the exact same place he was when *his* son died."

For reasons I cannot fully explain, Harv's brief down-home homily accelerated my healing, or at least moved me from one question to another. It answered the question, "Did you lose control? Could you just not stop it?"

God did not lose control. I'd not been able to answer the why to my satisfaction. And I don't understand why he didn't exercise his control. But deep in my spirit I felt I could believe that God truly *has* control of the world around me. It did not spin out of his hand.

Fast-forward several years to a different life season with different challenges. Carol and I had two adopted children, and we wanted a third. Multiple attempts ended in disappointment, but finally one seemed to be coming through. Our dreams were about to be realized.

Hearing the words "you can come now" caused us to load up our two children and drive several hundred miles to see our just-born baby girl.

Arriving the next day in a town we'd never visited, we entered the doctor's office expectantly. One glance at the nurse in the waiting room told us something was wrong. My attempt to pry information failed. Stone-faced, she escorted us to a private room. Our excitement evaporated instantly.

Finally the doctor came with the dreaded words, "There's been a problem." Cutting to the chase, the teenage birth mother who'd said "tell them to come, the baby is theirs" had changed her mind moments before we got there.

The doctor and nurses were as apologetic as possible. They seemed to fully empathize with our disappointment. We knew we would never meet "Melissa," the baby girl with a name we'd already chosen.

Then we had the long drive home. I called ahead and asked people from our church to go into our Dallas-area house, dismantle the crib, and remove all the baby items assembled in anticipation of our joyous homecoming.

That drive seemed far longer than the outbound trip. Deep into the night I drove, attempting to cover each of the miles as quickly as possible. Carol and our children had fallen asleep, their eyes stinging from crying. A light snow was falling. The roads somewhere south of Alva, Oklahoma, seemed unusually winding and hilly. Finally, at around midnight, my resolve to hold it together and be the strong one that others could lean on gave out.

I cried. I cried long and hard, trying to drive safely through both snow and tears as they fell. And in the midst of my heartache, I said, "Do you care, God? Do you really care?"

At that moment I realized I'd just taken another step in the grief journey. I had begun my questioning with "why?" regarding Bob's death, only to slowly move on to "Did you lose control?"

Now I saw that the human heart isn't adequately consoled by "No, son, I have not lost control." I needed something more . . . emotive. I wanted to know, "Do you give a rip? Does it matter? Do you see my pain? *Do you care?*"

In the Oklahoma night, on a dark, slick two-lane highway, as my family slept, I met God. Or God met me. And do you know what he said? He said, *"Jim, I care. I do care."* I learned much about him that night, and I've not been the same since. He *does* care. He wants to be with me. And he wants to be with you. He has a "forever party" planned for us. It is called the *afterlife*.

Jump ahead once again to June 20, 2007. The phone rang, and Carol was on the other end. I'd been with her all night in the emergency room, trying to find out why she felt so awful. Waiting on a doctor, she finally sent me home to get our teenagers ready for school. The 7:09 call was somber and straightforward.

"Come now," she said. Knowing she must know more, I asked, "Why?"

She responded, "A mass."

"A mass?" I mumbled. "You mean, like cancer?"

She said the one word I did not want to hear: "Yes."

It was not a mass but *many* masses. Over one hundred tumors were removed in an eight-hour surgery. Due to massive resections, a series of other problems began. The subsequent nine months would be some of the most challenging I have ever known.

I should mention that Carol's shocking call came exactly one week after I'd met with my publisher and coauthor to discuss a book about heaven and the afterlife, topics that long had intrigued me. Amazing how an "interesting" subject can become unspeakably relevant and personal with the diagnosis of a serious illness. Anyone who's heard the word *cancer* (or a similar word) come from the mouth of their doctor or the doctor of a loved one knows life instantly turns upside down. "Life as usual" is gone, replaced by endless treatments, endless research, endless concern.

The days after Carol's diagnosis were two of my darkest. Her prognosis seemed so uncertain. I was trying to hang on to her. I was grasping. I was fighting for her life.

I was about to be taken through the knothole, which involves "letting go and letting God." Alone in my home, I had to release my wife. For the first time, I faced the reality of losing her. Emotionally and spiritually, I released her to the arms of God. Through many tears, I crossed a kind of dividing line. In that process, I told God I will not, like Job's wife, "curse God and die."[6] I would love him, no matter what.

Once I crossed that boundary, I was able to fight for Carol's life again, but this time with freedom. I didn't have to walk in fear. I now walked in confidence that all would be well. And fight for her I did. Succinctly stated, she made it through the long year and did well during the many months I was working on this book. (However, on the final day of writing, we received heartbreaking news of another setback—a recurrence. So we continue on with this battle.) The key point is that I passed through "Phase 4" in understanding God. This is when you say, *"God, I will love you and serve you, no matter what."*

The previous three phases (above) are all about who God is. This phase is when you respond back to him. This one is about you. Will you trust him? I mean, *really trust him.* If you will, it prepares you for this life. And it prepares you for the life coming thereafter. Your relationship with God will move to a level in which you become amazingly comfortable being with him.

THE STORY OF GOD #4: PONDER THIS

My friend Ponder Gilliland is aptly described by his first name. He is ponderous. Brilliant but ponderous. He's a thinker. As I write these words, he's in his nineties, and his mind has been affected by age. But before Ponder's slow descent, he was a marvel of intellectual insight and incisive ideas. As a pastor, he never used notes to preach. Attorneys, recognizing his cogent debate skills and logical aptitude, would bring their cases to him so he could help craft their arguments.

What has impacted me most about him, though, isn't his mind but his view of God. One line echoes over and over in my spirit. He'd say, "My Father likes me. He likes to be with me. He wants to spend time with me."

Saying "God loves me" is not nearly as powerful as "My Father *likes* me. . . . He wants to spend time with me."

This is precisely what God wants. And that is why he offers us eternity. He wants no one in hell. He wants you with him. In heaven. Forever.

If you've spent any time in Sunday school you've probably heard—maybe even memorized—one of the Bible's most familiar verses: "For God so loved the world that he gave his one and only Son, that whoever believes in him shall not perish but have eternal life."[7] That's what this whole discussion about the afterlife boils down to: God has prepared an unimaginable place for you to spend eternity, and he wants to enjoy it with you.

> God has prepared an unimaginable place for you to spend eternity, and he wants to enjoy it with you.

God's desire? For you to become comfortable with him. Here. *Now.* It will make the next life even more wonderful.

He likes you. He wants to be with you. *Now.*

Notes

Chapter 1: The Undiscovered Country

1. This true story is factually told except for Vernon's name. Today, Dee Ring Martz is a respected psychotherapist and sought-after grief expert in Colorado Springs.
2. Alan F. Segal, *Life After Death: A History of the Afterlife in Western Religion* (New York: Doubleday, 2004), 36.
3. Jennifer Harper, "Majority in U.S. Believe in God," in *The Washington Times* (25 Dec. 2005).
4. Chen Zhiyong, "New Light on Near-Death Experience," in *China Daily* (14 Nov. 2006).
5. "Poll: One Out of Three Believes in Ghosts," in *Associated Press/AP Online* (26 Oct. 2007).
6. Norman Cousins, *The Healing Heart* (New York: Avon, 1984).
7. Raymond Moody, *Reunions: Visionary Encounters with Departed Loved Ones* (New York: Ballantine, 1993), viii.
8. Elizabeth Kübler-Ross, *On Death and Dying* (New York: Touchstone, 1969), 150.
9. John 3:16
10. 1 John 4:18

Chapter 2: There . . . and Back Again

1. Edna St. Vincent Millay, "Passer Mortuus Est," in *Second April* (New York: M. Kennerley, 1921).
2. Melvin Morse, in Raymond A. Moody, *Life After Life* (New York: HarperCollins, 1975), x.

3. Ibid., xiii.
4. Elizabeth Kübler-Ross, in Moody, *Life After Life*, xxii.
5. Emma Young, "No Medical Explanation for Near-Death Experiences," in *New Scientist* (14 Dec. 2001).
6. Hans Küng, *Eternal Life? Life After Death as a Medical, Philosophical, and Theological Problem* (New York: Doubleday, 1984), 20.
7. Moody, *Life After Life*, 164.
8. Hebrews 11:1

Chapter 3: Hints at the Hereafter

1. Robert McKee, *Story: Substance, Structure, Style, and the Principles of Screenwriting* (New York: Regan, 1997), 11–12.
2. Michael Shimanovsky, "Who Let the Grim Reaper Get His Hands on the Remote Control?" in *Journal of Evolutionary Psychology* (1 Apr. 2006).
3. Kenneth Ring and Evelyn Elsaesser Valarino, *Lessons from the Light: What We Can Learn from the Near-Death Experience* (New York: Insight, 1998), 28.
4. Moody, *Life After Life, 25th Anniversary Edition* (San Francisco: HarperCollins, 2001), 18–19.
5. Ring and Valarino, *Lessons from the Light*, 34.
6. Melvin Morse and Paul Perry, *Closer to the Light* (New York: Villard, 1990), 27.
7. 1 Corinthians 15:54–55
8. Melvin Morse and Paul Perry, *Transformed by the Light* (New York: Villard, 1992), 110.
9. Moody, *Life After Life*, 46.

10. Maurice Rawlings, *Beyond Death's Door* (Nashville: Thomas Nelson, 1978), 72.
11. Trudy Harris, *Glimpses of Heaven* (Grand Rapids: Revell, 2008), 38.
12. Ibid., 51.
13. Hebrews 13:5; Deuteronomy 31:6
14. Don Piper with Cecil Murphey, *90 Minutes in Heaven* (Grand Rapids: Revell, 2004), 31–32.
15. Morse and Perry, *Transformed by the Light*, 78.
16. Betty Eadie, *Embraced by the Light* (New York: Bantam, 2002, reprint), 51–52.
17. 1 Corinthians 13:12
18. Mark 14:36
19. John 1:4–5

Chapter 4: A Taste of Torment

1. Mark 9:48; cf., Isaiah 66:24
2. Maurice Rawlings, *Beyond Death's Door* (Nashville: Thomas Nelson, 1978), 19.
3. Ibid., 21.
4. Howard Storm, *My Descent Into Death: A Second Chance at Life* (New York: Doubleday, 2005), 23.
5. Ibid., 17.
6. Ibid., 24.
7. Ibid.
8. Angie Fenimore, *Beyond the Darkness: My Near-Death Journey to the Edge of Hell and Back* (New York: Bantam, 1995), 94.
9. Ibid., 95.
10. Ibid.
11. Ibid., 104.
12. Ronald Reagan, *To Hell and Back*, host Maurice Rawlings. TBN Films (documentary transcript).
13. See John 1:29.
14. Reagan, *To Hell and Back*.

Chapter 5: Things That Go Bump in the Night

1. Brian Righi, *Ghosts, Apparitions, and Poltergeists: An Exploration of the Supernatural Through History* (Woodbury, MN: Llewellyn, 2008), 3–4.
2. www.scarystories.ca/GhostStory/The-Wesley-Ghost-2.html
3. Matthew 14:25–26
4. Geddes MacGregor, *Images of Afterlife: Beliefs from Antiquity to Modern Times* (New York: Paragon, 1992), 11.
5. Melvin Morse, *Where God Lives* (New York: Cliff Street, 2000), 1–2.
6. Ibid., 85.
7. Righi, *Ghosts, Apparitions, and Poltergeists*, 12.
8. Adapted from ibid., 5–13.
9. M. Scott Peck, *Glimpses of the Devil* (New York: Free, 2005), 238.
10. See Mark 5:1–20.
11. Walter Martin, Jill Martin Rische, and Kurt Van Gorden, *The Kingdom of the Occult* (Nashville: Thomas Nelson, 2008), 244.
12. C. S. Lewis, "Christianity and Culture," in *Christian Reflections* (Grand Rapids: Eerdmans, 1967), 33.
13. Romans 8:38–39

Chapter 6: Grace-Filled Guests

1. Dianne Arcangel, *Afterlife Encounters: Ordinary People, Extraordinary Experiences* (Charlottesville, VA: Hampton Roads, 2005), 277–300.
2. Louis E. LaGrand, *Messages and Miracles: Extraordinary Experiences of the Bereaved* (Woodbury, MN: Llewellyn, 1999), 96.
3. Ibid., 20.
4. Ibid., 51–52.
5. Arcangel, *Encounters*, 26.
6. Ibid., 8–9.
7. LaGrand, *Messages*, 124.
8. Elizabeth Kübler-Ross, *On Grief and Grieving* (New York: Scribner, 2005), 57–58.
9. LaGrand, *Messages*, 152.
10. Joel Martin and Patricia Romanowski, *Love Beyond Life: The Healing Power of Afterdeath Communication* (New York: Harper, 1997), 12.
11. LeGrand, *Messages*, 59–60.

12. See Matthew 28:10; Mark 16:6; Luke 24:36, 38.

Chapter 7: Calling Long Distance

1. Barbara Weisberg, *Talking to the Dead: Kate and Maggie Fox and the Rise of Spiritualism* (San Francisco: Harper, 2004), 17.

2. Ibid., 19.

3. See 1 Samuel 28:3–11.

4. 1 Samuel 28:12–15

5. *http://en.wikipedia.org/wiki/Necromanteion*

6. Brian Righi, *Ghosts, Apparitions, and Poltergeists: An Explanation of the Supernatural Through History* (Woodbury, MN: Llewellyn, 2008), 44.

7. Ed Warren and Lorraine Warren, *Graveyard* (New York: Macmillan, 1993), 137–38.

8. Robert T. Carroll, "Cold Reading" (see at *www.skepdic.com/coldread.html*).

9. Gary E. Schwartz, *The Afterlife Experiments: Breakthrough Scientific Evidence of Life After Death* (New York: Pocket Books, 2002), 123–24.

10. Deuteronomy 18:10–11

11. Isaiah 8:19–20

Chapter 8: Angels Among Us

1. Doreen Virtue, *How to Hear Your Angels* (Carlsbad: Hay, 2007). Virtue has many other New Age books about angels and related topics; e.g., number sequences, oracle cards, and crystal therapy.

2. See, e.g., Matthew 4:11; 18:10; 22:29–30; 25:41; Mark 1:13; 16:1–6; Luke 2:8–15; 20:35–36.

3. See Matthew 22:28–30; Luke 20:35–36.

4. A mineral that's sometimes transparent and commonly olive-green or yellowish.

5. See Daniel 10:5–6.

6. Revelation 5:11

7. Revelation 19:10

8. Luke 16:22

9. Hebrews 1:14

10. See Psalm 148:2–5.

11. Psalm 8:5. What's more, Paul says our status will change in the future: People who are righteous through relationship with Christ will become the judges of angels (1 Corinthians 6:3).

12. C. Fred Dickason, *Angels: Elect and Evil* (Chicago: Moody, 1975), 29–32. Dickason also wrote *Names of Angels* (Chicago: Press, 1997).

Angels can learn; Peter wrote that they want to know more about God's plan of redeeming humans as told by the ancient prophets (1 Peter 1:12).

Angels feel—especially joy, since they are so close to God. In the book of Job, a poetic passage describes Creation: While God was laying earth's foundation, "the morning stars sang together and all the angels shouted for joy" (38:7). Later, Jesus told a story about a shepherd who left his flock to seek out one lone sheep that had wandered away. He rejoiced when he found it, just as the angels in heaven rejoice over one sinner who repents (Luke 15:1–7).

As far as we can tell, angels loyal to God are always doing his will; presumably they could choose one action over another at a given time while not straying from doing what God expects them to do (ibid., 33). But apparently, long ago, some angels did willfully choose to rebel. Peter says some sinned, and God sent them to hell (2 Peter 2:4), a place of "eternal fire" made for them (Matthew 25:41; hell was not intended for people). The being who is now Satan (see chapter 9), who'd been a beautiful angel, called "morning star" or "son of the dawn," asserted his own will and led the rebellion (Isaiah 14:12–14).

13. Dickason says angels, as spirits, are incorporeal (without bodies). He muses that maybe they do have a body with a structure we can't understand, or one that operates on different principles than our bodies do (ibid., 34).

14. See Daniel 10; Matthew 28:3; Revelation 15:6.

15. See Revelation 4:6–8.

16. See Ezekiel 1:4–21.

17. Angels are potent but not omnipotent: David describes them as "mighty ones who do [God's] bidding, who obey his word" (Psalm 103:20); Peter says they're stronger and more powerful than men (2 Peter 2:11). Angels can control nature: in John's apocalyptic vision, four angels hold back the winds, while another angel harnesses the sun's heat (Revelation 7:1; 16:8–9). *Nothing*—death, angels, anything—is strong enough to separate us from God's love (Romans 8:38–39).

    Angels may know more than we do, but they're not omniscient. When they know the future, it's because God commissions them to deliver messages about it. If angels knew everything, they wouldn't desire to learn (1 Peter 1:12). Jesus also indicates they don't know everything future; he will return to the earth with power and glory, and while angels will announce it, they do not know when it will happen (only the Father knows—Matthew 24:36).

18. Angels can go places in ways we cannot. The angel who rescued Peter from prison was able to go through walls and appear suddenly inside a heavily guarded cell. Leading Peter out, they passed two sets of guards and through an iron gate that opened on its own as they approached.

19. Angels have direct access to God (Matthew 18:10). They had the privilege of witnessing Christ's birth and praised God for his plan of salvation (see Luke 2; Hebrews 1:6). John witnessed many thousands of angels around God's throne, singing and praising (Revelation 5:11).

    Angels carry out judgment and punish wicked people (e.g., Genesis 19); an angel was sent to destroy Jerusalem (and then ordered to stop—2 Samuel 24:16); an angel slew 185,000 of Sennacherib's warring Assyrians (see 2 Kings 19), and struck down Herod Agrippa I (Acts 12).

    Scripturally, most often we see angels helping people (Hebrews 1:14): bringing messages, delivering from harm, guarding, guiding, and giving support and encouragement to God's servants, even assisting at death. Concerning the birth of Jesus, angels delivered messages to Daniel, Zacharias, Mary, Joseph, the shepherds, and later again to Joseph and Mary. Angels told the disciples Jesus one day would return in the same way he left (Acts 1:7–11). And when a non-Jewish man, Cornelius, explained to Peter how an angel directed him to Peter, Peter knew he had been called to deliver the good news about Jesus to Gentiles (10:1–11:18).

    Angels are our Department of Defense: "He will command his angels concerning you to guard you in all your ways; they will lift you up in their hands, so that you will not strike your foot against a stone" (Psalm 91:11–12). When facing sure shipwreck, an angel appeared to Paul in a dream and told him he and everyone else on board would be saved (Acts 27:13–25).

20. Gary Kinnaman, *Angels Dark and Light* (Ann Arbor: Servant, 1994), 82–84. For example, John Chrysostom, Origen, Basil, and Bernard of Clairvaux all supported the idea of guardian angels; John Calvin was skeptical.

21. When Jesus wanted his disciples to understand the importance of children, he said *their* angels are assigned to watch out for them—again, angels with direct access to God (Matthew 18:10).

22. Angels offer messages of encouragement, as with Paul (Acts 27:13–25) and with setting free other imprisoned apostles and giving them strength to continue their work (5:18–20). In the Old Testament, for instance, God sent an angel to comfort Hagar and Ishmael and to reveal water that sustained them both (see Genesis 16); an angel baked bread and gave water to a despondent and incognito Elijah, then gave him food for strength on his journey (1 Kings 19:3–8).

23. After Jesus' trials in the desert and

temptation by Satan, angels attended him (Matthew 4:11; Mark 1:13). Later in Gethsemane, when Jesus anguished in prayer as he faced execution, an angel came to strengthen him (Luke 22:43–44).

24. See Matthew 26:53.

25. See Colossians 1:16.

26. Ephesians 3:10

27. 1 Peter 3:22

28. See Jude 9.

29. Daniel 10:21; 12:1

30. See Jude 9; 1 Thessalonians 4:15–16.

31. Mortimer Adler claims the seraphim are the highest form of "metaphysical perfection" in God's kingdom (*The Angels and Us* [New York: Macmillan, 1982], 45), quoted in Kinnaman, *Angels Dark and Light,* 41–42.

32. Dickason: *They* are the "angelic beings of the highest order or class" (*Angels: Elect and Evil,* 61).

33. Saint Denis (pseudo-Dionysius the Areopagite), *The Celestial Hierarchy,* in Kinnaman, 18, 41.

34. On Aquinas and Augustine, see citations in Kinnaman, 42.

35. Billy Graham, *Angels: God's Secret Agents,* 2nd ed. (Dallas: Word, 1994), 55.

36. Dickason, *Angels: Elect and Evil,* 59.

37. See Isaiah 14:12–14; Ezekiel 28:12–17.

38. See 2 Peter 2:4; Jude 6; Revelation 12:7–9.

39. Frank Peretti has written about this battle with the dark side, often referred to as spiritual warfare, in his fascinating novels, including *This Present Darkness* (Crossway Books, 1986).

40. Hebrews 1:14

41. See survey results in Kinnaman, *Angels Dark and Light,* appendix 1 (213–20).

42. Ibid., 51.

43. cf. Matthew 22:30.

44. Kinnaman, 46–47, 51–52.

45. Ibid., 65–66, 220.

46. Hebrews 13:2

47. Kinnaman relates three such stories in *Angels Dark and Light:* 68–69, 94, 116–18.

48. See Billy Graham, *Angels: God's Secret Agents,* 99–100.

49. Several considerations may account for the higher proportion of angelic appearances to missionaries. First, they often work in less Westernized countries that are more open to the supernatural; some cultures don't even have such words as *super*natural or *para*normal in their language (see Kinnaman, 21–22). Second, as a foreigner in a sometimes-hostile environment, the missionary often needs help that only an angel is likely or able to give. Third, sometimes angels in human form are seen not by the (unaware) missionaries themselves but by would-be attackers.

50. Angels came to the shepherds at Jesus' birth, who then passed on the good news (Luke 2:17–18). An angel came to Philip, directing him to the Ethiopian eunuch, through whom the gospel spread to Ethiopia (Acts 8:26–39). An angel told Cornelius to fetch Peter; a Gentile received the gospel and it further spread (10:1–11:18). After an angel rescued Paul from death at sea, Paul went on to Rome to preach (27:13–25; 28:30–31). In each case, angels were messengers and guardians to God's workers. Billy Graham recalls many occasions when he had no more energy to preach before huge crowds. Just when he felt he couldn't go on, he would sense a supernatural renewing of his strength. He believes angels have ministered to him time and again (Graham, *Angels: God's Secret Agents,* xiv).

51. Kinnaman, *Angels Dark and Light,* 14–15.

52. Graham, *Angels: God's Secret Agents,* 166.

53. Ibid., 167–68.

54. Ibid., 105–06; see Luke 16:22.

55. Exodus 23:20

Chapter 9: More Than a Pitchfork and a Pointy Tail

1. "The Howling Man," *The Twilight Zone,* 1960. Written by Charles Beaumont; directed by Douglas Heyes; produced by Buck Houghton.
2. *www.quotesdaddy.com/tag/Satan*
3. *USA Today* Snapshots, "The Decline in Believers," *Harris* Interactive Poll (Jan. 21–27, 2003; Nov. 10–17, 2008).
4. As recounted in Augustine's autobiography, *Confessions.*
5. See John 1:1–13, 8:12, 9:5.
6. See Genesis 3:1–7; Mark 1:12–13; Matthew 4:1–11; Luke 4:1–3; Mark 14:10.
7. While the King James Version uses the name *Lucifer,* other versions translate the term differently.
8. Isaiah 14; Ezekiel 28; Revelation 12
9. Job 1:6–7 NKJV
10. See *www.thedivinecouncil.com/Introduction%20to%20the%20Divine%20Council%20MTIT.pdf* (writings of Michael S. Heiser); these "sons" form part of a "divine council."
11. Ezekiel 28:12–15
12. Isaiah 14:12–15 KJV
13. Ezekiel 28:16–17 RSV
14. Genesis does not explain how Lucifer indwelt a serpent or say whether animals could talk before the fall. Like many biblical narratives, Genesis often engenders so many questions in the contemporary reader's mind that he misses the entire point. Practical details were not always paramount; they were secondary to the revealed, eternal truth of God's story. The Bible is the revelation of his love for us and of his plan for our salvation. Knowing if snakes could talk doesn't compare to the greater truth that here humanity was tempted by a non-human entity and chose to disobey God rather than keep his directive.
15. Genesis 3:1 RSV
16. Matthew 10:16 RSV
17. Revelation 20:2
18. 2 Corinthians 11:3 RSV
19. Genesis 3:14–15 RSV
20. Zechariah 3:1–2 RSV
21. 1 Peter 5:8
22. Romans 8:37–39 RSV
23. Ephesians 6:12 RSV
24. *www.quotesdaddy.com/tag/Satan/5*
25. C. S. Lewis, *The Screwtape Letters* (Harper-Collins, San Francisco, 2001), ix.

Chapter 10: Demons in the Dark

1. Paul Hiebert, *Anthropological Reflections on Missiological Issues* (Grand Rapids: Baker, 1987).
2. Mark 5:1–13 RSV
3. The King James Version uses the phrase *possessed with a devil* (or *devils*) thirteen times.
4. Acts 5:16 RSV
5. Luke 6:17–18 RSV
6. New Testament examples (RSV): demoniacs (Matthew 4:24); unclean spirit (Mark 1:23; 5:2); having demons (Luke 8:27); trouble with unclean spirits (6:18); a spirit seizes (9:39); Satan entered into him (22:3; John 13:27); Satan filled him (Acts 5:3); afflicted (5:16).

   Jesus and his followers always have power over unclean spirits; demons fear the power that comes from Christ. But while those who trust in him and are filled with his Spirit have no reason to fear demonic forces, there is no reason for Christians to seek out contact with them.
7. Matthew 12:43–45 RSV
8. Luke 22:3–6 RSV
9. John 13:2–4 RSV
10. This does not invalidate contemporary writings; we shouldn't assume there are no realities and truths outside the scope of Scripture. Again, as Paul wrote, "Now we see in a mirror dimly, but then face to face. Now I know in part; then I shall understand fully, even as I have been fully understood" (1 Corinthians 13:12 RSV).
11. See Isaiah 14:13–14.

12. Mark 5:7–8
13. Matthew 12:43
14. For example, with the Inquisition, and the various witch hunts.
15. See Genesis 3:1–6.
16. 1 John 4:4 RSV
17. Mark 1:23–26 RSV
18. James 2:19 RSV
19. Luke 10:18–20

Chapter 11: A Delightful Detour

1. *Field of Dreams*, Universal Studios, 1989. Written by W. P. Kinsella (book); screenplay by Phil Robinson. Directed by Phil Robinson; produced by Lawrence Gordon and Charles Gordon.
2. John Gilmore, *Probing Heaven: Key Questions on the Hereafter* (Grand Rapids: Baker, 1989), 16, 21.
3. Ibid., 67.
4. See Genesis 1:1.
5. See 2 Corinthians 12:2.
6. Luke 23:43
7. Philippians 1:23–24
8. Luke 16:23–28
9. Randy Alcorn, *Heaven* (Wheaton, IL: Tyndale, 2004), 55–63.
10. See Genesis 5:24.
11. See Luke 9:30–32.
12. 2 Corinthians 5:1–2
13. N. T. Wright, *Surprised by Hope, Rethinking Heaven: The Resurrection and the Mission of the Church* (New York: Harper One, 2008), 147.
14. See 1 Thessalonians 4:16–17.
15. See 1 Corinthians 15:12–23.
16. 1 Corinthians 15:37, 42–44
17. See Matthew 27:50–53.
18. See Luke 24:13–32.
19. Luke 24:39–40
20. Luke 24:41

Chapter 12: A Rewarding Experience

1. A minority contends there are *three* judgments, citing Matthew 25:31–36 as a third. Here we will focus on two: rewards for those who are "in Christ"

and punishment for those who are not.
2. 2 Corinthians 5:10
3. 1 Corinthians 3:12–15
4. See also Romans 14:10.
5. 1 Corinthians 9:24–25
6. See Revelation 20.
7. For this section I am indebted to Mark Hitchcock, *55 Answers to Questions About Life After Death* (Sisters, OR: Multnomah, 2005), 146–49.
8. Daniel 12:3
9. Hebrews 6:10
10. Matthew 10:41–42
11. See Matthew 25:31–46.
12. Luke 14:12–14
13. James 1:12
14. Matthew 5:11–12
15. See, e.g., Matthew 5:44.
16. See Matthew 25:14–30.
17. Once again, Mark Hitchcock's insights (especially from pp. 150–53 of his book *55 Answers to Questions About Life After Death*) were helpful in developing this section.
18. Revelation 2:10
19. James 1:12
20. 1 Peter 5:2–4
21. 1 Thessalonians 2:19 NKJV
22. 2 Timothy 4:8
23. 1 Corinthians 9:24–25 NKJV
24. Revelation 4:10–11
25. Frederick Buechner, *Wishful Thinking: A Seeker's ABC* (San Francisco: Harper Collins, 1993), 58.
26. John 5:24

Chapter 13: Beyond Halos, Harps, and Hymns

1. John Eldredge, *The Journey of Desire* (Nashville: Thomas Nelson, 2000), 111.
2. C. S. Lewis, *Words to Live By*, Paul F. Ford, ed. (San Francisco: Harper SanFrancisco, 2007), 34–35.
3. Rather than endnote everything from Randy Alcorn's writings that has influenced my thinking, I will give

sweeping credit to this brilliant writer. Many concepts I share about what we will do in heaven are adapted from *Heaven* (Wheaton, IL: Tyndale, 2004), especially chapters 23–44 (233–435). If you want a thorough and intriguing discussion of heaven, this book is an excellent place to start.

4. See Ephesians 5:19–20; Colossians 3:16.

5. A most breathtaking view of this is portrayed in Paul Billheimer's masterful *Destined for the Throne* (Minneapolis: Bethany House, 2005).

6. 2 Timothy 2:12

7. Revelation 2:26

8. Revelation 3:21

9. See, e.g., John 21:10–14.

10. Revelation 22:2

11. See Genesis 3:17–19.

12. Revelation 15:2–3

13. See Revelation 5:7–8.

14. Revelation 5:11

15. See Psalm 8:4–5.

16. Hebrews 1:13–14 KJV

17. See Matthew 25:41.

18. See Hebrews 2:14–17.

19. See Hebrews 2:5–8; Revelation 21:7.

20. See 1 Corinthians 6:2–3.

21. See Matthew 24:30.

22. See Matthew 17:3–5.

23. Genesis 1:1

24. See Genesis 1:31.

25. Isaiah 65:17

26. 2 Peter 3:11-13

27. Revelation 21:1

28. Matthew 5:5

29. Psalm 37:22

30. Romans 4:13

31. Revelation 5:10

32. John 14:1-3 KJV

33. Paul Marshall, *Heaven Is Not My Home* (Nashville: Word, 1998), 11.

34. See Luke 15:10.

35. Revelation 6:10–11

36. Hebrews 12:1

37. See, e.g., Isaiah 8:19–22.

38. Revelation 8:1

39. See Matthew 22:30.

40. Genesis 1:27

41. See, e.g., Revelation 21:4.

42. Psalm 16:11

Chapter 14: Going From Bad to Worse

1. *Bridge to Terabithia,* Walt Disney/Walden 2007. Written by Katherine Paterson (book); screenplay by Jeff Stockwell and David Paterson. Directed by Gabor Csupo; produced by David Paterson, Lauren Levine, and Hal Lieberman.

2. See Hebrews 5:14.

3. Some churches do not use any creedal statements. They don't necessarily reject the contents of the Apostles' Creed but rather the practice of creedal rituals. The Protestant Reformation challenged the Roman Catholic Church's elaborate traditions and rejected the doctrine that holds church tradition as equal to scriptural authority. While some such churches developed their own reformed creeds, others completely rejected creeds so as to avoid the perceived Catholic error. The United Methodist Church uses the Apostles' Creed but has removed the phrase *descendit ad inferos* ("he descended to hell").

4. In John H. Leith, ed., *Creeds of the Churches: A Reader in Christian Doctrine from the Bible to the Present* (Louisville: John Knox: 1963), 25.

5. Some early contrasting Gnostic teachings: *Manichaeism:* the spiritual realm is good while the material world is evil (leading to the belief that Jesus could not have had a real body, that his appearance was an illusion); *Apollinarianism:* the Word, or *Logos,* entered into the human Jesus (so Jesus had a soul and body but not a human spirit); *Nestorianism:* the Word, or *Logos,* inhabited the body of Jesus (Jesus was a "god-bearer," and there was no union of the human and divine natures).

6. See Luke 23:43.

7. Acts 2:33

8. 1 Peter 3:18–20; 4:5–6 RSV

9. "A wonderful text is this, and a more obscure passage perhaps than any other in the New Testament, so that I do not know for a certainty just what Peter means." www.biac.org.uk/galanswer15.htm

10. Although we do not know the certain interpretation, I personally hold to the "victory lap" theory.

11. See 1 Peter 4:6.

12. See on "the sheep and the goats" in Matthew 25:31–46.

13. Leo F. Steleten, *Dictionary of Ecclesiastical Latin* (Massachusetts: Hendrickson, 1995), 131.

14. Psalm 49:7–15 RSV

15. Psalm 16:9–11 RSV

16. An example of progressive revelation: Ancient cultures were accustomed to the practice of slavery. The treatment of slaves is addressed in both Old and New Testament writings (e.g., Genesis 21:10; Colossians 4:1; Ephesians 6:5). However, Jesus taught that meekness, humility, and love are the traits of those who will inherent God's kingdom and commands all followers to "love your neighbor as yourself" (Matthew 22:39 RSV). As people began to better understand Christ's teachings, behavior changed so as to uphold his directives. Eventually Christians understood that "there is neither Jew nor Greek, there is neither slave nor free, there is neither male nor female; for you are all one in Christ Jesus" (Galatians 3:28 RSV). The revealed truth did not change; rather, the human understanding of the revelation matured.

17. Genesis 37:35 RSV

18. See Job 14:11–13 RSV.

19. Job 26:5–6 RSV

20. Psalm 88:4–6 RSV

21. John 16:12–13 RSV

22. Mark Hitchcock, *55 Answers to Questions About Life After Death* (Eugene, OR: Multnomah, 2005), 100.

23. Ibid., 100–101.

24. Luke 16:23 ESV

25. Luke 16:27–31

Chapter 15: Called to Account

1. Hebrews 9:27 RSV

2. Revelation 20:11–12, 14–15

3. See Revelation 20.

4. Matthew 25:31–33

5. These possible judgments include (1) The judgment of the cross, which includes the judgment of the believer's sins; (2) The self-judgment of the believer, whereby we avoid God's judgment for sins (1 Corinthians 11:31); (3) The judgment seat of Christ, in which the quality of a Christian's life is evaluated and rewarded (2 Corinthians 5:10); (4) The "sheep and goats" judgment (start of the millennium, determining which Gentiles will enter the kingdom); (5) Israel's judgment (beginning of the millennium; Ezekiel 20:33–44); (6) The judgment of fallen angels (Jude 6; 1 Corinthians 6:3); (7) The great white throne judgment ("last judgment") of those who don't believe in Christ.

6. Revelation 20:13

7. Revelation 20:12

8. Revelation 21:27

9. Aired December 8, 2008.

10. Matthew 12:36–37

11. See, e.g., Exodus 32:31–33; Deuteronomy 9:14; 25:19; 29:20–21; 32:26; 2 Kings 14:27; Nehemiah 13:14; Psalm 9:5; 69:28; Revelation 3:5.

12. Revelation 3:5

Chapter 16: The Heat Is On

1. See William Crockett, ed., *Four Views on Hell* (Grand Rapids: Zondervan, 1992), chapters 1–2.

2. See Luke 16:19–31.

3. 2 Thessalonians 1:9

4. Jerry L. Walls, *Hell: The Logic of Damnation* (South Bend: University of Notre Dame Press, 1992), 150.

5. See, e.g., Romans 6:23.

6. See, e.g., John 1:9.

7. Romans 1:19–20
8. See Revelation 20.
9. See Revelation 9:1–2, 11; 11:7; 17:8; 20:1–3.
10. 2 Peter 2:4
11. See Jude 6.
12. See Ephesians 4:9.
13. See Philippians 2:10.
14. Henry Blamires, *Knowing the Truth About Heaven and Hell* (Ann Arbor: Servant, 1998), 64.
15. Bill Wiese, *23 Minutes in Hell* (Lake Mary, FL: Charisma, 2006), 104.
16. Walls, *Hell*, 150–51.
17. Pope John Paul II, "General Audience" (7/28/99), Vatican News Service, in Albert Mohler Jr., ibid., 27.
18. Walls, *Hell*, 151.
19. We'll later discuss the conditional view and the purgatorial view.
20. See chapter 19.
21. See chapter 18.
22. John F. Walvoord, in Crocket, *Four Views on Hell*, 28.
23. Jude 13
24. Walvoord, in Crocket, *Four Views on Hell*, 51.
25. See Matthew 7:5; Luke 9:60.
26. Walvoord, in Crocket, 53.
27. Walls, *Hell*, 152.
28. We'll look more at this in following chapters.
29. Gerry Beauchemin, *Hope Beyond Hell: The Righteous Purpose of God's Judgment* (Olmito, TX: Malista, 2007), 4.
30. Ibid., 33.
31. Randy Klassen, *What Does the Bible Really Say About Hell?* (Telford, PA: Pandora, 2001), 87.
32. Matthew 25:46
33. Revelation 20:10

Chapter 17: The Ultimate Escape Hatch

1. See Larry Dixon, *The Other Side of the Good News* (Bridgepoint, 1992), 106–107.
2. Jonathan Edwards, "Sinners in the Hands of an Angry God," in Elizabeth Winslow, ed., *Jonathan Edwards: Basic Writings* (New York: New American Library, 1966; Meridian, 1978), 153.
3. Winslow, foreword to ibid., xx.
4. See Albert Mohler Jr., "Modern Theology: the Disappearance of Hell," in Christopher W. Morgan and Robert A. Peterson, eds., *Hell Under Fire: Modern Scholarship Reinvents Eternal Punishment* (Grand Rapids: Zondervan, 2004), 19–20.
5. Frederick Denison Maurice, "Eternal Life and Eternal Death," in *Theological Essays* (London: Macmillan, 1892), 377–407, in ibid., 23.
6. Mohler, in *Hell Under Fire*, 23.
7. Ibid., 22.
8. Charles H. Spurgeon, "The Resurrection of the Dead," quoted in Mohler, 28.
9. Discussion adapted from Mohler, 36–40.
10. John Wenham, *Facing Hell: An Autobiography 1913–1996* (London: Paternoster, 1998).
11. *The Mystery of Salvation, the Story of God's Gift: A Report by the Doctrine Commission of the General Synod of the Church of England* (London: Church House, 1995), 180, in Mohler, *Modern Theology*, 32.
12. Clark H. Pinnock, "The Conditional View," in *Four Views on Hell*, William Crocket, ed., (Grand Rapids: Zondervan, 1992), 135; he references "Hell's Sober Comeback," *U.S. News & World Report* (3/25/91).
13. Mohler, *Modern Theology*, 35; he cites Pinnock and Robert C. Brow, *Unbounded Love: A Good News Theology for the 21st Century* (Downers Grove, IL: InterVarsity, 1994).
14. Ibid.
15. Pinnock, in Crocket, ed., *Four Views on Hell*, 165–66.
16. We'll focus on eternal punishment in the next chapter.
17. Karl Menninger, *Whatever Became of Sin?* (New York: Hawthorne, 1973).

18. See, e.g., Bill Hybels, *Just Walk Across the Room: Simple Steps Pointing People to Faith* (Grand Rapids: Zondervan, 2006).

19. See *www.inclusion.ws/*

20. See *http://en.wikipedia.org/wiki/Carlton_Pearson#Early_career*

21. See *www.inclusion.ws/faq1.htm*

22. J. I. Packer, "Universalism: Will Everyone Ultimately Be Saved?" in Morgan and Peterson, *Hell Under Fire*, 179–81.

23. See Dixon, *The Other Side of the Good News,* 49.

24. Pinnock, "The Conditional View," in *Four Views on Hell,* 142.

25. See Revelation 16:9.

26. Pinnock, 151.

27. See, e.g., John 12:32; Acts 3:21; Romans 5:18; 11:32; 1 Corinthians 15:22; Philippians 2:9–11; 1 Timothy 2:3–4; 2 Peter 3:9; Titus 2:11; 1 John 2:2.

28. Hebrews 9:27–28

29. See Matthew 8:12; 25:46; John 5:28–29; Romans 2:8–10; 2 Thessalonians 1:8–10; Revelation 14:9–11; 20:10–15.

30. "Hell Air-Conditioned," in *New Oxford Review* 58 (June 1998): 4, in Mohler, 41.

Chapter 18: Disappearing Acts

1. C. S. Lewis, *Surprised by Joy* (San Diego: Harcourt Brace, 1956), 52.

2. Why do many believers admire the theology of John Stott but reject Carlton Pearson's teachings? Because Christian annihilationism can be reconciled with *most* of the faith's definitive orthodox doctrines. Biblical inspiration and authority is assumed; God is sovereign; man is sinful; the provision of salvation through Jesus' atoning death is available to all who believe. These will enjoy eternal fellowship with God, while those who choose to reject salvation from sin will *not*–this is where universalists and annihilationists part company and where the disagreement begins.

3. Dante imagined that saints in heaven would enjoy watching the damned being tortured, but I don't think most of us would agree. Augustine reasoned that the saints would rejoice to see hell's suffering because it would increase their own pleasure to know what they had avoided. One writer compares that mentality to watching a pet squirm as it's being roasted in a microwave.

4. Annihilationists cite examples such as Matthew 10:28, where Jesus cautions: "Do not be afraid of those who kill the body but cannot kill the soul. Rather, be afraid of the One who can *destroy* both soul and body in hell." Paul says of Christ's enemies, "Their destiny is *destruction*" (Philippians 3:19); Peter also speaks about the destruction of the wicked (2 Peter 2:1; 3:7). (See Pinnock, "The Conditional View," in Crocket, ed., *Four Views on Hell* [Grand Rapids: Zondervan, 1997], 146.)

5. It can mean "to perish, be ruined, die, be killed, pass away, or be lost" (*"Apollumi,"* in Warren C. Trenchard, *A Concise Dictionary of New Testament Greek* [Cambridge: University Press, 2003]). Charles Hodge suggests that "to destroy is to ruin, to make unfit for use" (quoted in Dixon, *The Other Side of the Good News* [Bridgepoint, 1992], 145).

6. In ibid.

7. Matthew 25:41

8. Matthew 25:46

9. This discussion adapted from Christopher W. Morgan, "Annihilationism: Will the Unsaved Be Punished Forever?" in *Hell Under Fire: Modern Scholarship Reinvents Eternal Punishment,* Christopher W. Morgan and Robert A. Peterson, eds. (Grand Rapids: Zondervan, 2004), 208.

10. Ibid.

11. 2 Thessalonians 1:6–9

12. 2 Peter 2:9

13. Ecclesiastes 8:15

14. Luke 12:20

15. Mark 8:36

16. Hebrews 10:31

17. Quoted in Dixon, 165.

18. Matthew 25:46
19. C. S. Lewis, *The Problem of Pain*, 106, quoted in Pinnock, "The Conditional View," in *Four Views on Hell*, William Crocket, ed. (Grand Rapids: Zondervan, 1992), 144, n. 18.
20. Lewis, *Surprised by Joy*, 228.
21. C. S. Lewis, *The Great Divorce* (New York: Macmillan, 1946), 72.

Chapter 19: The Celestial Waiting Room

1. John Jessup, Washington correspondent, *CBN News*, "Faith: What Americans Really Believe" (6/30/08); *www.cbn.com/cbnnews/397546.aspx*
2. Protestants include all non-Catholic denominations: for example, Methodist, Baptist, Episcopal, Presbyterian, Congregational, Pentecostal, Charismatic, et al.
3. For an easily understood Catholic defense of purgatory, see *www.catholiceducation.org/articles/apologetics/ap0041.html*
4. *www.brainyquote.com/words/pu/purgatory208546.html*
5. Ibid.
6. 1 and 2 Esdras, Tobit, Judith, the Rest of Esther, Wisdom of Solomon, Ecclesiasticus (the Wisdom of Jesus the Son of Sirach), Baruch, Letter of Jeremiah, Additions to Daniel, Prayer of Manasses, 1 and 2 Maccabees.
7. 2 Maccabees 12:39–45, *New American Bible*
8. C. S. Lewis, *Letters to Malcolm, Chiefly on Prayer*, cited in Jerry L. Walls, *Heaven: The Logic of Eternal Joy* (New York: Oxford University Press, 2007), 58.
9. Ibid., 59.
10. Matthew 12:32
11. 1 Corinthians 3:13–15
12. Protestants also have a sense of "tradition," as the Bible is interpreted through one's own lens of history. However, this is a subtle understanding of history's and tradition's role, as opposed to an elevating of tradition to equal status with Scripture.

13. Gregory the Great, *Dialogues* 4.39: PL 77, 396; cf. Matthew 12:31–32.
14. Johann Tetzel (1465–1519) sold indulgences with the creative promotional line "as soon as a coin in the coffer rings, the soul from purgatory springs." Raising funds for the construction of St. Peter's Basilica in Rome, the German priest's ingenuity knew no bounds, even constructing a price list for each sin. These excesses drove Martin Luther to post statements of protest; his famous "Ninety-five Theses" sparked the Protestant (from *protest*) Reformation.
15. *www.pwhs-mfi.org/read_me/remain_purgatory.htm*
16. On the day I was completing this book, I received word that the Catholic bishop of San Diego was being transferred to Oakland. This was very disappointing to me, losing the presence of a deep and abiding friend, one I respect and admire as a brother in Christ.

    The "lines of demarcation" have shifted. The opposing groups once were Catholics and Protestants, but in the last forty years there has been realignment, caused by those within both Catholicism and Protestantism throwing out scriptural authority. Now as a Bible-believing evangelical Protestant, I have much more in common with a conservative Catholic than with a non-Bible-believing Protestant. The new alignments and alliances are as follows: Bible-believing Protestants (evangelicals) and Catholics on one side, liberal Protestants and liberal Catholics joining on the other. To put it in more personal terms, I am deeply indebted to my many Catholic friends. They've stood firm for the sanctity of life and the sacredness of marriage.
17. 2 Corinthians 5:8
18. Philippians 1:23

Chapter 20: Recycling Plan

1. *www.reversespins.com/famousquotes.html*
2. F. LaGard Smith, *Out on a Broken Limb* (Eugene, OR: Harvest House, 1986), 69.

3. www.reversespins.com/famousquotes.html
4. Ravi Zacharias and Norman Geisler, gen. eds., *Who Made God? And Answers to Over 100 Other Tough Questions of Faith* (Grand Rapids: Zondervan, 2003), 171.
5. www.christiananswers.net/q-eden/edn-r009.html
6. www.foxnews.com/story/0,2933,99945,00.html
7. http://abcnews.go.com/sections/us/DailyNews/beliefnet_poll_010718.html
8. www.reversespins.com/famousquotes.html
9. www.healthsystem.virginia.edu/internet/personalitystudies/case_types.cfm#CORT
10. http://reluctant-messenger.com/reincarnation proof.htm#about
11. I am indebted to Gary R. Habermas and J.P. Moreland, *Beyond Death: Exploring the Evidence for Immortality* (Eugene, OR: Wipf & Stock, 1998), 426, citing evaluation of Stevenson's data by Paul Badham and Linda Badham, "Claimed Memories of Former Lives," in Ralph W. Clark, *Introduction to Philosophical Thinking: Readings and Commentary* (St. Paul: West, 1987), 260–69.
12. Ibid., 239–40.
13. http://en.wikipedia.org/wiki/Ian_Stevenson
14. Habermas and Moreland, in Clark, 240.
15. Although Gary Habermas and J.P. Moreland coauthored *Beyond Death,* according to page 11, Habermas wrote the chapter on reincarnation, so I refer solely to him here.
16. Habermas and Moreland, an endnote continuation from 427: "It is not immediately obvious why demonic possession should be taken any less seriously than discarnate possession. If the former is considered less 'modern,' so must the latter be, including reincarnation. Historically, all these views have old, deep roots."

17. Habermas and Moreland, citing Stevenson, 340. Also cited, Badham and Badham, 269.
18. Habermas and Moreland, 376.
19. Ibid., 243.
20. Habermas and Moreland, 244.
21. Ibid., 247.
22. Leviticus 19:31; 20:6, 27; Deuteronomy 18:9–14
23. Habermas and Moreland, 252–53.
24. Philip Kapleau, *The Wheel of Life and Death* (New York: Doubleday, 1989), 263.
25. See John 3:4–16.
26. John 1:21
27. Luke 1:17
28. See 2 Kings 2.
29. Matthew 17:2–3
30. www.reversespins.com/famousquotes.html
31. See James 4:14.
32. Hebrews 9:27
33. Genesis 1:1
34. Space does not permit us to distinguish between reincarnation, rebirth, and transmigration, which though often used interchangeably are not necessarily identical terms.
35. Zephaniah 1:14; cf. Malachi 4:5; Acts 2:20

Chapter 21: Forever and Ever, Amen

1. www.harrisinteractive.com/harris_poll/index.asp?PID=982 (10 Dec. 2008).
2. John 11:3, 5; see all of John 11 for details.
3. John 11:35
4. See Matthew 24; Mark 13.
5. See, e.g., John 20.
6. Job 2:9
7. John 3:16